SO-DMH-639

BROWN UNIVERSITY STUDIES
VOLUME XV

David Garrick

THE
Thespian Mirror

Shakespeare in the Eighteenth-Century Novel

ROBERT GALE NOYES

BROWN UNIVERSITY
PROVIDENCE, RHODE ISLAND

1953

COPYRIGHT 1953 BY
BROWN UNIVERSITY

LIBRARY OF CONGRESS CATALOG CARD NUMBER—52–14221
TYPOGRAPHY, PRINTING, AND BINDING IN THE U. S. A. BY
KINGSPORT PRESS, INC., KINGSPORT, TENNESSEE

FOR
Barbara Brayton Noyes

This therefore is the praise of Shakespeare, that his drama is the mirror of life; that he who has mazed his imagination, in following the phantoms which other writers raise up before him, may here be cured of his delirious ecstasies by reading human sentiments in human language.

Dr. Johnson

PREFACE

The present study of Shakespeare as the novelists of the age of Garrick regarded him, begun in 1941, was delayed by the war, when military service interrupted my research for three and a half years. In tentative form, however, some of the matter was published as an article, "Shakespeare in the Eighteenth-Century Novel," in *A Journal of English Literary History,* for September, 1944, to the editors of which I am indebted for permission to reprint portions. The original essay was based on a search of some two hundred fifty novels written between 1740 and 1780, a period which virtually coincides with that of Garrick's appearances on the London stage. Since then I have investigated about five hundred additional novels in American and British collections. About one hundred ten novels, mostly anonymous, of whose publication I am aware, have been impossible to locate and may be no longer extant. If statistics are desirable, it may be of interest that one novel in every seven contains some Shakespearean reference.

Since there is as yet no definitive bibliography of eighteenth-century fiction, the difficulties in discovering what novels were published and where they may be found today have been many. I should like to record indebtedness to the bibliographical work of Mr. Andrew Block and, for epistolary fiction, to Dr. Frank G. Black. The histories of the novel by Dr. Ernest Baker, Miss J. M. S. Tompkins, Dr. James R. Foster, and many special studies of individual minor novelists have been helpful throughout the course of the study.

The admirable collection of eighteenth-century fiction in the Harvard College Library has been the foundation for the present volume. Unless otherwise specified in the notes, the novels consulted may be found there. The place of publication of books throughout is London, unless otherwise noted. With regard to the text of passages quoted from the novels, common eighteenth-century spellings have been allowed to stand.

A word about the validity of the dramatic criticism of the novelists may not be amiss. In the new medium of the novel they were professed realists, whose purpose was to give an accurate reflection of the manners of the day at various social levels, ranging from the "plays, operas, routs, ridottos, masqued balls, and Pantheon subscriptions" of the titled and wealthy to the nefarious operations of highwaymen, thieves, and other denizens of the underworld, male or female. Allowing for the exaggeration and intensification to which artists and journalists are prone, particularly when they seek to stir the emotions or depict the foibles, follies, freaks, and fancies of mankind, one may accept the testimony of the novelists about the drama, the stage, and Shakespeare as not so unduly distorted as to render it nugatory. Many a professional dramatic critic has been known to strengthen his coloring for either praise or abuse of his subject. It may, I believe, be conceded that in spite of the guise of fiction, the exploitation of humor in character, and sometimes a prevailing spirit of sensibility or farce, the dramatic scene as presented in fiction is a fundamentally sound job of reporting, realistic in essence and acceptable as an imitation of life.

I hope in another volume to consider dramatists from the Restoration to Garrick's retirement, as well as conditions in the theaters as novelists viewed them.

There remains the pleasant duty of acknowledging assistance in the search, especially for minor novels. I wish particularly to express appreciation for many courtesies to the directors and staffs of the following libraries in the United States: the Harvard College Library, the Yale University Library, the Library of Congress, the Folger Shakespeare Library, the Library of the University of Pennsylvania, the Library of Brown University, the John Carter Brown Library, and the Boston Public Library. In England the vast resources of the British Museum, supplemented by those of the Bodleian, provided many novels not to be found in America, and it was a rare pleasure to work once more in those magnificent repositories, where, as always, there was no austerity in the matter of courtesy and consideration. For special assistance I wish to thank Mr. John Eliot Alden, Mr. Arthur Bauman, Mr. H. Glenn Brown, Professor Alan S. Downer, Mr. William Elton, Mr. Roger B. Francis, Professor William T. Hastings, Professor David A. Jonah, Professor Alan D. McKillop, Professor Hyder E. Rollins, Professor Philip W. Souers, and Professor Arthur Colby Sprague. In London the proprietors of Pickering and Chatto, Ltd., and McLeish and Sons kindly permitted me to investigate rare novels on their shelves, and Dr. John C. Hardy hospitably placed his handsome collection of rare minor fiction at my disposal. To my wife, Barbara Brayton Noyes, who shared the labor and the fun of poring over hundreds of forgotten volumes, I owe a world of thanks which must remain only suggested. It is her book as much as mine.

Brown University
Providence, R. I.   R. G. N.
February 1, 1952

CONTENTS

ILLUSTRATIONS

LIST OF ABBREVIATIONS

BM British Museum

BPL Boston Public Library

BU Brown University Library

ELH *ELH: A Journal of English Literary History*

HCL Harvard College Library

JEGP *Journal of English and Germanic Philology*

LC Library of Congress

MLN *Modern Language Notes*

MLQ *Modern Language Quarterly*

MP *Modern Philology*

PMLA *Publications of the Modern Language Association of America*

PQ *Philological Quarterly*

RES *Review of English Studies*

SP *Studies in Philology*

TLS *Times Literary Supplement* (London)

UP University of Pennsylvania Library

The Thespian Mirror

Shakespeare in the Eighteenth-Century Novel

The Novelists Examine Shakespeare

1. *Main Currents in the Criticism of Shakespeare, 1740–1780*

ENGLISH novels of the eighteenth century contain a body of criticism of the drama and stage which has been virtually unexplored. From the very beginning of the novel, the fascination exerted by the theater, as one of the most interesting diversions which life affords, led many writers to conduct their characters to the London pleasure-gardens and playhouses, to display in action the manners of folk there, and to criticize the plays and the actors. In the hundreds of novels published between *Pamela* in 1740 and 1780, the year after David Garrick's death, there may be unearthed criticism of repertory, acting, and audiences of a much more lively and informal nature than one discovers in the professional dramatic criticism of the Age of Johnson. Regular reviewing of current theatrical performances in the daily newspapers did not start before the series of reviews, probably by Arthur Murphy, written in 1757 for *The London Chronicle,* and even then reviewing was so sporadic that any other sources of information about the state of the stage provide valuable evidence concerning dramatic fare and public taste. Epistolary novels in particular (and half the novels of the age were epistolary) offered a natural opportunity for characters to write to their friends about their adventures at Drury Lane or Covent Garden, and in such accounts there are many delightful recreations of the scenes before and behind the footlights based on actual visits to the playhouses.

Just as the dramatists of the period criticized the contemporary novel in such plays as the elder George Colman's pleasant satirical farce, *Polly Honeycombe* (1760), or Sheridan's *Rivals* (1775)—in which Lydia Languish was obliged on the approach of Mrs. Malaprop to fling *Peregrine Pickle* "under the toilet"—, so the novelists of the day reviewed the work of writers of stage plays. Their successors have continued to do so. We find Pamela as a bride discussing in detail performances of Ambrose Philips' *Distrest Mother* and Steele's *Tender Husband*. In *Tom Jones,* as everyone knows, Partridge and Tom attend a performance of *Hamlet,* with Garrick as the melancholy hero. At Mansfield Park the Bertram children engage busily in an abortive presentation of *Lovers' Vows* by Kotzebue and Mrs. Inchbald. Wilhelm Meister reviews *Hamlet. Romeo and Juliet* is the subject of Mr. Curdle's sixty-four-page pamphlet on the character of the Nurse's deceased husband in *Nicholas Nickleby,* and Mr. Wopsle presents *Hamlet* in *Great Expectations.* The heroine of *Villette,* Lucy Snowe, attends a performance by the great Rachel, during which, for full romantic measure, the wonderful Charlotte Brontë sets the theater on fire. James Joyce includes a discussion of *Hamlet* in *Ulysses.* During that great age of English acting when nightly the visitor at the theater might behold the artistry of James Quin, David Garrick, George Anne Bellamy, Kitty Clive, Mary Ann Yates, and Hannah Pritchard, what did writers of novels think about William Shakespeare? At a time when criticism of the great dramatist was moving from the old-fashioned judicial weighing of merit and defect to the new enthusiasm for his skill in depicting human characters in "God's plenty," what contribution did creators of characters in prose fiction make to the rising tide of Shakespeare idolatry?

It is not surprising that there was little unorthodoxy in the novelists' views of Shakespeare. Actually, so far as their critical opinions are concerned, they are tributaries to the accepted streams of eighteenth-century Shakespearean criticism. Their ideas were largely determined by the conventions and the climate of opinion of the age in which they wrote. They had no revolutionary novelties to offer, nor had they need for any. Almost every opinion they held can easily be duplicated in the non-fictional criticism, academic or journalistic, of their times. But to say this is not to admit that study of their Shakespearean passages is without value, for their testimony adds to the sum total of what is already known, and their lively presentation affords much pleasure. Their manner, indeed, rather than their critical ideas, is important, for here, virtually, we have criticism in action. Their expression of opinions about Shakespeare is livelier, more dramatic, more humorous, more emotional, and hence more readable, than that of their soberer contemporaries. Much delight may be taken in the fictional projection of the novelists' attitudes through the alarums and excursions of their characters, who run the gamut of the emotions in an age of humor and sensibility, ranging from the Hogarthian and Rabelaisian to the sentimental, silly, and lachrymose. To these characters (and therefore to their creators) Shakespeare is a living issue, worth arguing and fighting over. In the great period of the English realistic novel, authors and readers alike had some of their best fun with Shakespeare.

The approaches to Shakespeare were several. Authors (or their characters) lauded his naturalness, conscious that he did not follow the rules for classical dramatic composition, but willing to grant that he was mighty despite his rapidity of writing and his lack of blotting. They pursued the time-honored tradition of comparing Shakespeare with his great rival and great friend Ben Jonson: their record of the rise of the great romantic playwright and the *pari passu* decline of the great realist, Ben, who had been, at least for critics, the most admired dramatist of the previous century, provides a sure gauge to changing taste in the theater of the ages of Cibber, Garrick, and Johnson. The development of the worship of Shakespeare is apparent in their fiction. In an era when judicial criticism was standard, there is anticipation of the impressionism of the romantic critics of the succeeding age. Indeed, it was really the eighteenth century which apotheosized Shakespeare. For many of the novelists' views one man was responsible: as meed for his rehabilitation of the plays on the stage, story-writers were enthusiastic in hailing David Garrick, whose brilliant recreations of favorite Shakespearean characters made him one of the most distinguished and most discussed figures in a society which loved distinction and discussion. He came to be esteemed as the living commentary on the Shakespearean text. Partly as a result of this common attitude towards "the English Roscius," the value of the labors of professional editors and annotators of the plays was discounted by obscurantists to whom seeing little Garrick act was like reading Shakespeare by flashes of lightning. Except for specific comments on individual plays or descriptions of performances, these were the avenues by which the novelists approached him who "was not of an age, but for all time."

2. Shakespeare and the Rules

ONE has only to skim the surface of Shakespearean criticism during the age of English classicism to perceive that, till the middle of the eighteenth century, rigid critics of the tribe of Dick Minim reproached Shakespeare incessantly for neglect to observe the mechanic "rules" of dramatic composition.[1] According to their doctrine, Shakespeare violated the unities of time, place, and action. He disregarded decorum, probability, and poetic justice. He mingled tragedy, comedy, and farce. And often he was "low." Beyond doubt the most bitter, most unimaginative, and most literal-minded attack was the notorious treatise of that "carping, verbal, and negative" critic, Thomas Rymer, whose boisterous rhetoric today moves the reader of *Tragedies of the Last Age* (1678) and *A Short View of Tragedy, Its Original, Excellency, and Corruption* (1693) to bemusement at such wrongmindedness in a man of letters. Opposition to the liberties of genius could go no further.

To perceive how far the eighteenth century progressed in attaining a reasonable attitude towards the rules, it is necessary to read only Dr. Johnson's great *Preface to Shakespeare* (1765), where "the petty cavils of petty minds" were dissipated and their objurgations contradicted. Johnson was anticipated in his arguments by George Farquhar,[2] Daniel Webb, Lord Kames, and others, but, by virtue of his prestige, in pointing the distinction between reality and the acceptance of an illusion created by an imitation of reality, he forever freed dramatists from servitude to the unities of time and place.[3] Both Rymer's and Dr. Johnson's views may be found in the work of the novelists.

About the time of Garrick's debut as a Shakespearean actor a rather adverse view of Shakespeare's mingling of serious and ludicrous characters in the same piece was taken by the author of *The Travels and*

---

[1] For Shakespeare and the rules see T. R. Lounsbury, *Shakespeare as a Dramatic Artist*, New York, 1901, pp. 1–128, "The Dramatic Unities"; D. N. Smith, ed., *Eighteenth Century Essays on Shakespeare*, Glasgow, 1903, Introduction and Preface; D. N. Smith, ed., *Shakespeare Criticism*, Oxford, 1916, Introduction; D. N. Smith, *Shakespeare in the Eighteenth Century*, Oxford, 1928; C. F. Johnson, *Shakespeare and His Critics*, Boston, 1909; L. S. Friedland, "The Dramatic Unities in England," *JEGP*, X (1911), 56–89, 280–299, 453–467 (the unities to 1700); T. M. Raysor, "The Downfall of the Unities in the Eighteenth Century," *MLN*, XLII (1927), 1–9; R. W. Babcock, *The Genesis of Shakespeare Idolatry*, Chapel Hill, 1931 (especially Part II, "Shakespeare Defended against Traditional Objections," pp. 45–110); R. W. Babcock, "The Attitude toward Shakespeare's Learning in the Late Eighteenth Century," *PQ*, IX (1930), 116–122; Herbert S. Robinson, *English Shakesperian Criticism in the Eighteenth Century*, New York, 1932; David Lovett, "Shakespeare as a Poet of Realism in the Eighteenth Century," *ELH*, II (1935), 267–289; J. W. H. Atkins, *English Literary Criticism: 17th and 18th Centuries*, 1951, chapter 7, "Shakespeare Criticism."

[2] See Farquhar's vigorous assault on Aristotle in his "Discourse upon Comedy," prefixed to *Love and Business*, 1702, ed. L. A. Strauss, Boston, 1914, pp. 3–32.

[3] For a recent study of Johnson and the "rules" see Thomas Pyles, "The Romantic Side of Dr. Johnson," *ELH*, XI (1944), 193–195.

Adventures of Mademoiselle de Richelieu, Cousin to the Present Duke of That Name, Who Made the Tour of Europe, Dressed in Men's Cloaths (1744). The heroine of this picaresque fiction arrives in England after her Continental travels and asks a French acquaintance his opinion of the English stage. He replies:

As to Tragedy, . . . if their [English] Poets could be induced to study the Language of Nature more than they do, they would excel all *Europe,* for *England* is a Country that affords a large Scene of Passions and Catastrophes, and *Shakespeare,* (one of the best Poets) has put a great Part of their History into his Tragedies; besides, the Genius of the Nation is inclined to Seriousness. The Language is bold and concise, and proper to express the Passions, and for this Reason their Tragedies excel in a great Number of fine Passages; they are not however without their Faults. The Plays as well as the Persons are a Mixture of the Comic and Serious. The most melancholy Events and the merriest Farce succeed each other alternately, which is not only ill contrived, but intirely inconsistent with the End of Tragedy. To this may be added that most of the Executions are done upon the Stage, which is sometimes covered with dead Bodies.[1]

The bright intelligence of Henry Fielding was often engaged in ridiculing commentators and critics, as any reader knows who has pored over the notes to *The Tragedy of Tragedies; or, The History of Tom Thumb the Great* (1731).[2] Without specific mention of Shakespeare, in *The History of Tom Jones, a Foundling* (1749) he anticipated Johnson's attack on the stranglehold of classical critics. He objected to a rigid interpretation of the dramatic unities:

Who ever demanded the reasons of that nice unity of time or place which is now established to be so essential to dramatic poetry? What critic hath been ever asked, why a play may not contain two days as well as one? Or why the audience . . . may not be wafted fifty miles as well as five? [3]

He challenged the impudence of men who have laid down "dogmatical rules . . . without the least foundation," and who have mistaken "mere form for substance."

Little circumstances, which were perhaps accidental in a great author, were by these critics considered to constitute his chief merit, and transmitted as essentials to be observed by all his successors. To these encroachments, time and ignorance, the two great supporters of imposture, gave authority; and thus many rules for good writing have been established which have not the least foundation in truth or nature, and which commonly serve for no other purpose than to curb and restrain genius, in the same manner as it would have restrained the dancing-master, had the many excellent

---

[1] III, 304–305. The translation of this work is attributed to a Mr. Erskine.

[2] See Richmond C. Beatty, "Criticism in Fielding's Narratives and His Estimate of Critics," *PMLA*, XLIX (1934), 1087–1100.

[3] Book V, chapter 1.

treatises on that art laid it down as an essential rule that every man must dance in chains.[1]

The liberating view of Fielding found support in the subsequent work of other novelists. For instance, William Goodall writes in *The Adventures of Captain Greenland* (1752) with typical English jingoism:

Though the Ancients have prescribed certain confined Rules for every Sort of Writing, yet those who follow them closest, to ease the Spleen of Critics, will almost be sure to give it to every body else; for Example: The *Greeks* and *Romans* have been very strict in settling the three chiefest Points to be observed in the penning of *Dramatics, viz.* Time, Place, and Action: And as a Standard for the Moderns to work by, of the latter, *Terence* seems the chiefest erected, whereby his Plays are like the Rules they are wrote by, so much confined, and the worse for being so, that they are scarce ever read but by *schoolboys*.

This Circumprescription having contracted your Prospect to so narrow a Compass, is, as one may say, a Kind of Prison to the free Soul and Pen of a more unbounded Genius; which, disdaining such a pitiful Constraint, must either burst a Passage through it, or perish in the Performance, through this paltry Confinement.

Shakespear has been the foremost to throw off this stiff and formal Yoke; and with what Success and Approbation we need not here to mention. And further, that a pure *English Genius,* without the Mixture of *foreign* and *learned Languages,* may be capable of writing in all Kinds of Eloquence, even to highly please the most *learned* Readers, as well as the unlearned, *He* stands a noble and immortal Example: Nay more, his artful Pen hath wrought such inimitable Strokes, both sublime! natural! learned! simple! and profound, that though the greatest *Geniuses* and *Scholars,* both in their own and After Times, have employed their Pens about *him* and his *Works,* they have not yet certainly discovered (or, however, settled that Point) whether he was a Man of any tolerable Learning *himself,* or not.[2]

The French rules, the only true doctrine for contemporary writers of Augustan tragedies of the *Cato* school, are treated with similar doubt in William Chaigneau's entertaining *History of Jack Connor* (1752), in a comparison between the French and English stages. The Frenchman Villeneuf, Jack's master, observes that "the Tragedies and Plays of the *English Shakespeare* gave Rise to those of *France.* His Imagination was not confin'd by the Rules of *Aristotle,* as, perhaps, he thought he had as good a Right to *Alter,* as the other had to *Make.*" He adds that such English writers as follow the new French models inspired by Voltaire may be "more regular in *Unity, Time* and *Place,*" but "I am sorry to say, their *Fire* is not so *bright,* nor will their *Heat*

[1] Book V, chapter 1.
[2] I, 79–80. LC.

last so long." Opposed to the unities, Villeneuf continues: "If twenty-four Hours Business can be shewn in so short a time [three hours], we may as well have twenty-four Years." [1]

In a comparison between Shakespeare and Corneille in his *Letters on the English Nation, by Batista Angeloni, a Jesuit* (1755), John Shebbeare similarly defends the English genius. Angeloni writes to a countess at Rome:

I frankly confess, to me it appears, that Shakespeare was the more exalted being, in all that constitutes true superiority of soul. Regularity of plan, in dramatic performances, is the work of art; conception of character, and their support thro' a whole theatric piece, the child of genius. Many men, nay all the French writers in tragedy, have reduced their productions for the stage, to the rules of the drama; yet, how few of them, or of any nation, have exalted and finished the ideas of personage in their pieces, to any degree of sublimity, and perfection. From this difference we must necessarily conclude, that the power of conceiving and preserving just characters in writing, is more rarely found, than that of planning a play; rules can teach one, which can effectuate nothing in the other; and many men may design, what not one in a million can execute. From this, must it not be concluded, that if Shakespeare exceeded the French writers in conceiving, and justly sustaining characters in tragedy, that he was of a superior genius to the greatest of the French nation? This, you, madam, who understand both languages shall decide. [2]

The Jesuit illustrates his contentions with a minute analysis of the characters of Othello and Iago in the crucial scene in the third act.

Laurence Sterne's annoyance with the stop-watch critics who were "so hung round and *befetish'd* with the bobs and trinkets of criticism," and whose heads were "stuck so full of rules and compasses . . . that a work of genius had better go to the devil at once, than stand to be prick'd and tortured to death by 'em," is amusingly dramatized in a famous passage in *Tristram Shandy*:

And how did *Garrick* speak the soliloquy last night?—Oh, against all rule, my Lord,—most ungrammatically! betwixt the substantive and the adjective, which should agree together in *number, case* and *gender,* he made a breach thus,—stopping, as if the point wanted settling;—and betwixt the nominative case, which your lordship knows should govern the verb, he suspended his voice in the epilogue a dozen times, three seconds and three fifths by a stop-watch, my Lord, each time.—Admirable grammarian! —But in suspending his voice—was the sense suspended likewise? Did no expression of attitude or countenance fill up the chasm?—Was the eye silent? Did you narrowly look?—I look'd only at the stop-watch, my Lord.—Excellent observer! . . . Grant me patience, just heaven!—Of

[1] 2nd ed., 1753, I, 204–205.
[2] II, 232–233.

all the cants which are canted in this canting world,—though the cant of hypocrites may be the worst,—the cant of criticism is the most tormenting!

I would go fifty miles on foot, for I have not a horse worth riding on, to kiss the hand of that man whose generous heart will give up the reins of his imagination into his author's hands,—be pleased he knows not why, and cares not wherefore.

Great *Apollo!* if thou art in a giving humour,—give me,—I ask no more, but one stroke of native humour, with a single spark of thy own fire along with it,—and send *Mercury,* with the *rules* and *compasses,* if he can be spared, with my compliments to—no matter.[1]

There is a long and interesting passage concerning the rules in the epistolary novel by the translator of Plutarch, John Langhorne's *Effusions of Friendship and Fancy* (1763), which anticipates Dr. Johnson's line of argument about the unities and may well have influenced him. In Letter XXX he writes:

As you are a friend to the theatres, I am surprized you never lift up your voice against those formal figures called *the three* UNITIES. They have amused the town with the words *truth* and *nature* and *probability,* till they have appointed such narrow limits to dramatic composition, that *genius* dares not give free scope to his wing, for fear he should soar beyond them. *Imagination* feels herself confined, and ventures not to exert her powers, while she beholds the finger of art limiting the sphere, and describing the circle in which she is to move. Such consequences has the reign of these petty tyrants. And what have we gained by giving up so much? A dull regularity, an insipid consistency. The bold flights of gothic genius are no more, and all is symmetry and exactness and proportion.

But it is to aid the credibility of the plot, it seems, that unity of time, place, and action is observed; and Horace said long ago, *incredulus odi.* What! then, is *incredulus odi* latin for the Three Unities? Did not the same poetical critic say, I am charmed with the Bard whose magic power *modo me Thebis, modo ponit Athenis.* What occasion for the scene to be altogether *in one apartment?* We must be sensible, if we are awake at all, that the whole representation is a fiction. And why cannot we as well follow the imagination of the poet from region to region? It is still but fiction, and, if it be *spirited* fiction, I am sure it will not be without its effect. It is the same with regard to time.

But I have yet more to say against these Unities. Far from aiding probability, they generally wound it. It is amazing to see what a hubbub of wonderful events are crowded, in every modern play, into the short space of three hours. I remember, in a late comedy, there were two or three courtships projected, begun, carried on, and finished; writings were drawn for which an attorney would have charged ten pounds, as the reward of manual labor; and the whole state and sentiments of a family were as much changed in three hours as they could have been in three years.

Nothing is more observable than that the accuracy of art has always been prejudicial to works of genius, and what they have gained in cor-

[1] III (1761), 57–61.

rectness, they have lost in spirit. It is evidently so in music: It is so with poetry in general, and with dramatic poetry in particular.[1]

In the very year of Johnson's *Preface* the artlessness of Shakespeare is described in Charles Johnstone's *Chrysal; or, The Adventures of a Guinea* (1765). The guinea reposes in the pocket of a theatrical manager who is busily rejecting the work of a poet for his ignorance of the dramatic laws:

"I am very loth to find fault, Sir!" (answered my master) "But you seem to be utterly unacquainted with all *the laws of the drama.*"

"The laws of the drama! they are but art; I write from nature. These laws have been long laid aside. *Shakespear* wrote without laws."——

"So much the worse. But he is a dangerous example to imitate. The local, temporary laws of the antient drama are laid aside, it is true; but not the immutable, general laws of propriety, and reason." [2]

The manager makes clear the decline of the rules for the drama to a second client, who insists that he has strictly adhered to them in the play he has submitted, which he believes to be "enriched with the sublimest sentiments of the antients":

"I neither dispute the original justice, nor the antiquity of them [the rules]: But I apprehend that the latter in a great measure destroys the present force of the former. The customs of mankind, the part of nature that comes within the province of the drama, are so changed since the establishment of those rules, that it would be most absurd to exact obedience to them now. Beside, may it not be said, without violation of the respect due to antiquity, that experience in a great length of time may have made many improvements in those rules. The infancy of every art is weak. . . . As for irregularity, I look upon it to be but an imaginary defect."

The shocked poet marches off, leaving the manager to say with a shrug, "I shall now have the ghosts of *Sophocles,* and *Aristotle,* and all the doughty antients raised to haunt me." [3]

Even from the French point of view the laws of the drama were relaxing, to the extent that it was possible for some to admire old English plays, as is apparent in a novel by Antoine François Prévost, *Memoirs of a Man of Quality* (1770). Prévost's Frenchman, writing of his fascination for Mrs. Oldfield, confesses that it was she who brought him to love the English stage, for which at first he had no

[1] 2nd ed., Dublin, 1770, I, 100–102. In reviewing this novel in *The Monthly Review,* XXVIII (1763), 481–483, Ralph Griffiths praised its "ingenious criticism, . . . the Author's abilities as a classical Scholar, and his good taste in polite literature."

[2] III, 213.

[3] III, 215–217.

taste. Inspired by "something so unspeakably inchanting in her voice, her air, and all her action," he perfected himself so far in English as to understand her. Attended by his companion, the Marquis, he never failed a night that she acted:

> Our method was to read the play beforehand, by which means we lost nothing of the declamation. The English are very fond of the theatre. It is true their plays are not equally good, but there are several of them which for beauty of sentiments, force of style, disposition of the plot, and justness of the characters, are no way inferior to the Greek or French stage. All their fault is want of regularity, and defect in unity of time. Their Hamlet, Don Sebastian, Orphan, and Venice Preserv'd, with many others, are incomparable Tragedies, and full of the greatest beauties. Some of their old Tragedies are disfigured by an unnatural mixture of Comedy; but this is a fault that has been long since observed and corrected by their Dramatick Writers.[1]

Not all Frenchmen, however, were so tolerant of English disregard for the rules. It was possible for the educated heroine of *Travels into France and Italy. In a Series of Letters to a Lady* (1771) to attend a performance of *Le Cid* with great pleasure, while admitting that "an English man does not insist upon being pleased according to rules, or he could not be so highly charmed by Shakespear."[2] But at Orleans, "hearing a gentleman criticise and murder Shakespear," she confesses that in tragedy the French cannot be "judges of what it is scarce possible they should understand." Not only the want of regularity, but Shakespeare's language, the variety of his characters, and his humor are "insuperable difficulties" to a nation accustomed to the easy style and the ancient characters of Racine.[3]

By 1772 the leaven of Dr. Johnson's common sense had so penetrated critical theory that the irregularities of a natural genius such as Shakespeare were no longer considered blemishes. In one of those curious, plotless, didactic, epistolary novels of the period, Shakespeare's practice is vindicated. John Preston, a teacher, purports to write his pupil Nancy Blisset edifying letters, not unmingled with affection, about Homer, Virgil, Ovid, and some English authors. The title of his book is illustrative of this type of educational fiction: *Genuine Letters from a Gentleman to a Young Lady His Pupil. Calculated to Form the Taste, Regulate the Judgment, and Improve the Morals. Written*

---

[1] II, 101. For Prévost's more formal defense of Shakespeare see George R. Havens, "The Abbé Prévost and Shakespeare," *MP*, XVII (1919), 177–198, and his *The Abbé Prévost and English Literature*, Princeton, 1921, chapter 7.

[2] I, 28. Yale.

[3] I, 117–120.

Some Years Since. Now First Revised and Published with Notes and Illustrations, By Thomas Hull, of the Theatre-Royal in Covent-Garden.[1] Preston writes to Nancy:

As for the Unities of Action, Time, and Place, which the Antients insist upon so strongly, especially that of Action, the best that can be said in their Behalf (in my Opinion) is, that it is better to have them, than be without them; for a Play, if it is not good in itself, will not become so, for the Unities being ever so religiously observed. We have many Plays extant, where they are all kept to the utmost Nicety, and yet the Pieces altogether are not worth a Perusal.

There are also Dramatic Productions, wherein the Rules are wholly set aside, which are the Admiration of every Reader of the most refined Taste. Our inimitable *Shakespeare* stands an Example of this, against all the cold Observers of Accuracy, that ever did, or ever will exist. [2]

The final word about Shakespeare and the rules during the Garrick period may be left to Richard Graves in his delightful satire on the evangelicals, *The Spiritual Quixote* (1773). The hero, Geoffry Wildgoose, meets a strolling player at a Tewkesbury inn. After admitting his admiration for Garrick, "almost the only Actor I have met with, who keeps sight of Nature in his action, and has brought her back upon the stage," Geoffry professes himself "an enemy to all Theatrical Entertainments; and even to Shakespear himself, in some respects." In protest, the player, "quite an idolater of Shakespear," inspired to his profession by "having seen Mr. Garrick play Hamlet and Othello two or three times," cries out:

"Oh! Sir, . . . I must not hear a word against our venerable Patriarch and great founder of the English Drama. I will allow every objection that you can imagine against him. I will forgive Ben Jonson his malignant wish, 'that, instead of one line, he had blotted out a thousand.' I will not pull Voltaire by the nose (though he deserves it), for calling his Tragedies *monstrous Farces.* I will grant the Frenchman, he has offended against the laws of Aristotle and Boileau, and slighted the unities of action, time, and place; that, upon some occasions, he abounds in mixt metaphors, and uses some harsh expressions, which the age he lived in might *tolerate,* and which are become venerable only by their antiquity. But read one act, or

---

[1] Thomas Hull was an actor at Covent Garden and the author of fiction and many theatrical pieces. The list of subscribers to this novel includes Garrick, George Colman, Gainsborough, John Beard, William Havard, Thomas Linley, Mrs. Mattocks, John Wilkes, Tate Wilkinson, and Josiah Wedgwood. Hull contends that the letters, which are dated 1743, are genuine. The British Museum, whose copy I examined, attributes the novel to John Preston, teacher. Since there is no available information about him, it is perhaps safer to regard the letters as fictional. *The Monthly Review,* XLVII (1772), 218–222, praises the novel for its educational purpose, pure morality, and good taste.

[2] Letter CIX, II, 217.

even one scene, in Hamlet, Othello, or Macbeth, and all these trifling criticisms disperse like mists before the orient sun."[1]

3. Shakespeare and Ben Jonson

A B O U T Shakespeare's life, character, and personality, for want of facts, novelists had little to say. After its appearance in 1709, Nicholas Rowe's life of the poet, with its exploitation of seventeenth-century traditions, remained the standard biography for over seventy-five years. Shakespeare himself, as was natural at a time when the historical novel had not been born, never appears as an important character in a novel before 1780, but his Ghost is permitted to revisit the glimpses of the moon as presenter and commentator in the anonymous and rare *Memoirs of the Shakespear's-Head in Covent-Garden. . . . By the Ghost of Shakespeare* (1755). As guardian of the Shakespear's-Head Tavern the Ghost informs the author of his early griefs, and no one should be surprised to find the deer-stealing legend, lifted from Rowe, and the chore of holding horses outside the theater particularly mentioned by the shade.

You have been informed by those who have written my Life, that in my Years of Nonage and of Folly, I was oblig'd to fly to *London,* for trespassing in a Park, not far from where I lived; and it has been lately revealed to the World, that my Distresses in *London,* consequential to my Elopement, reduc'd me to the Necessity of holding the Horses of Persons of Quality, who rode to the Play, as was then the Custom; from which Occupation my Diligence rais'd me to the Theatre; of which I have since been stil'd the Father.[2]

There is no further confession, however. Every twenty years the Ghost is allowed to confer with a human being and to narrate his woes, which have arisen from the various characters of all types who have patronized his tavern. The cast is large, and the Ghost only a device for introducing the author, who is rendered invisible, to a procession of renegades, male and female. The Ghost enjoins the author to publish these picaresque stories for the improvement of man.

Again, in 1769, the deer-stealing story is repeated in Herbert Lawrence's *Life and Adventures of Common Sense,* but Lawrence's handsome tribute to Shakespeare in this unusually interesting allegory of

[1] III, 7–11.
[2] I, 5–6. The "revelation" of the tradition of horse-holding was made by Robert Shiels in *Lives of the Poets,* 1753, I, 130. See Sir E. K. Chambers, *William Shakespeare,* Oxford, 1930, I, 60; II, 284–286. For debunking of the traditions of poaching and horse-holding see John S. Smart, *Shakespeare: Truth and Tradition,* 1928, pp. 17, 89–105.

history from ancient times to the present consists of his account of how the great poet stole his wondrous gifts from Wit, Genius, and Humour. Common Sense, son of Wit and Truth, observes:

It seems my Father, GENIUS, and HUMOUR made a Trip to *London,* where, upon their Arrival, they made an Acquaintance with a Person belonging to the Playhouse; this Man was a profligate in his Youth, and, as some say, had been a Deer-stealer, others deny it; but be that as it will, he certainly was a Thief from the Time he was first capable of distinguishing any Thing; and therefore it is immaterial what Articles he dealt in. I say, my Father and his Friends made a sudden and violent Intimacy with this Man, who, seeing that they were a negligent careless People, took the first opportunity that presented itself, to rob them of every Thing he could lay his Hands on. . . . As soon as he had got fairly rid of them, he began to examine the Fruits of his Ingenuity. Amongst my Father's Baggage, he presently cast his Eye upon a common place Book, in which was contained, an infinite variety of Modes and Forms, to express all the different Sentiments of the human Mind, together with Rules for their Combinations and Connections upon every Subject or Occasion that might Occur in Dramatic Writing. He found too in a small Cabinet, a Glass, possessed of very extraordinary Properties, belonging to GENIUS and invented by him; by the Help of this Glass he could, not only approximate the external Surface of any Object, but even penetrate into the deep Recesses of the Soul of Man—could discover all the Passions and note their various Operations in the human Heart. In a Hat-box, wherein all the Goods and Chattels of HUMOUR were deposited, he met with a Mask of curious Workmanship; it had the Power of making every Sentence that came out of the Mouth of the Wearer, appear extremely pleasant and entertaining—the jocose Expression of the Features was exceedingly natural, and it had Nothing of that shining Polish common to other Masks, which is too apt to cast disagreeable Reflections. . . . The Mask of HUMOUR was our old Acquaintance, but we agreed, tho' much against my Mother's Inclination, to take no Notice of the Robbery, for we conceived that my Father and his Friends would easily recover their Loss, and were likewise apprehensive that we could not distress this Man without depriving his Country of its greatest Ornament. With these Materials, and with good Parts of his own, he commenced Play-Writer, how he succeeded is needless to say, when I tell the Reader that his name was *Shakespear.*[1]

After Shakespeare's death perhaps the commonest attempt of critics to define his qualities as man and dramatist was to compare him with his greatest dramatic rival, Ben Jonson. There were, however, two dangers implicit in this unphilosophical kind of comparative criticism: the critics might indulge in sheer impressionism, preferring that dramatist who best suited their temperaments; or they might judge Shakespeare's plays in the light of Jonson's (and *vice versa*), a method basi-

[1] I, 145–149. The novel was reviewed by Ralph Griffiths in *The Monthly Review,* XLII (1770), 135–142.

cally unsound because the schools of art which the poets represented and their entire mental attitudes were so thoroughly incompatible. It has been recently demonstrated from a minute study of allusions that scholars may have erred historically in believing that Shakespeare was more popular in the seventeenth century than Jonson.[1] Actually, there were more allusions to Jonson as a person, more critical attention was devoted to him than to Shakespeare, and there were more references to each of Ben's four great comedies than to any play of Shakespeare's.[2] It is true that critics wrote more about Shakespeare's characters than about Jonson's—especially about Falstaff—but the conclusion has been drawn that "Jonson, and not Shakespeare, was the dramatist of the seventeenth century."[3]

Preference for Shakespeare, however, came early in the eighteenth century, as critics began to admire him in spite of his own faults and in spite of the virtues of his rivals. With changing taste, what had formerly seemed defects became virtues. Shakespeare's observance of "nature" and his untutored genius were preferred to Ben's exhibition of "art" and his heavy burden of learning. The stock of the sturdy "Spanish great galleon" met a bearish market, even though his best comedies were constantly to be seen at the patent houses. The most famous statement of the triumph of Shakespeare over Jonson appeared in Edward Young's *Conjectures on Original Composition* (1759), where his thesis was:

Shakespeare mingled no water with his wine, lower'd his genius by no vapid imitation. *Shakespeare* gave us a *Shakespeare*, nor could the first in ancient fame have given us more. *Shakespeare* is not their son, but brother; their equal; and that, in spite of all his faults. Think you this too bold? . . . *Johnson*, in the serious drama, is as much an imitator, as *Shakespeare* is an original.[4]

[1] See Gerald E. Bentley, *Shakespeare and Jonson: Their Reputations in the Seventeenth Century Compared*, Chicago, 1945; also Bentley's *The Swan of Avon and the Bricklayer of Westminster*, Princeton [1946]. See my *Ben Jonson on the English Stage, 1660–1776*, Cambridge, Mass., 1935, pp. 19–25, for the decline of Jonson's reputation and the rise of Shakespeare idolatry in the eighteenth century. Freda L. Townsend, *Apologie for Bartholmew Fayre*, New York, 1947, chapter 1, discusses the decline of Jonson's repute as Shakespeare's fame increased.

[2] Bentley, *Shakespeare and Jonson*, I, chapter 8.

[3] I, 139. For modification of Bentley's conclusions see Baldwin Maxwell's review in *PQ*, XXIV (1945), 91–93, which proposes, on the basis of a study of publishing records as well as allusions, that the critically minded of the century had a deeper admiration for Jonson, but that with the general readers, and therefore with the century as a whole, Shakespeare remained the more popular.

[4] Pages 78–80. For an admirable eighteenth-century critical comparison of Jonson and Shakespeare see Corbyn Morris, *An Essay Towards Fixing the True Standards of Wit, Humour, Raillery, Satire, and Ridicule*, 1744, pp. 29–34, a critical essay close in date to the beginning of the modern novel.

In the same fashion as the professional critics, the novelists record the glorifying of Shakespeare as "rare Ben" was transformed into "surly Ben." As early as 1744 the bluestocking sister of Henry Fielding, Sarah, who embellished her novels with literary discursions, satirizes the type of "well-informed" critic who spouts the bromidic "right things" about famous authors. In doing so, she gives by implication an insight into the orthodox attitude towards Shakespeare and Jonson at that time. In *The Adventures of David Simple,* Mr. Spatter takes the hero to a gathering of these egregious critics at a tavern. A typical exponent of the School for Triteness discusses Homer, Virgil, Milton, and Shakespeare, drawing the familiar contrast between Shakespeare's genius and Ben's studied art:

Shakespear, whose Name is immortal, had an Imagination which had the *Power of Creation,* a *Genius* which could form *new Beings,* and make a *Language* proper for them. *Ben Johnson,* who writ at the same time, had a vast deal of *true Humour* in his Comedies, and very fine Writing in his Tragedies; but then he is a *laborious* Writer, a great many of those beautiful Speeches in *Sejanus* and *Catiline* are *Translations* from the Classicks, and he can by no means be admitted into any Competition with *Shakespear.* But I think any comparison between them ridiculous: . . . to say the one or the other writes best, is like saying of a *Wilderness,* that it is not a *regular Garden;* or, of a *regular Garden,* that it does not run out into that Wilderness which raises *the Imagination,* and is to be found in Places where only the Hand of Nature is to be seen.[1]

A decade later, Miss Fielding and Jane Collier in their odd mixture of literary criticism and fiction, *The Cry: A New Dramatic Fable* (1754), provide a lengthier comparison of the two great playwrights, in which Ben's reputation is more deeply depressed. The didactic Portia discourses on envy to the ladies of "the Cry," a group opposed to Truth:

Mr. *Pope,* in his preface to *Shakespear's* works, declares it as his opinion, that *Ben Johnson's* envy first gave rise to the report of *Shakespear's* want of learning, which report hath prevailed even to this day. The surly laureat (as *Theobald,* in one of his notes, judiciously calls *Johnson*) hath left behind him a very good receipt, which gloomy malice may ever make use of, to pull down a bright contemporary genius. In the first place, *Johnson* exalted learning to a pitch beyond its value; then by making the most glaring shew of his own learning, he endeavoured to fix the highest admiration on himself; casting at the same time an imputation on *Shakespear,* for want of learning, and spared no pains in exhibiting what he thought so much his own superiority in that single point.

Whoever will take the trouble of extracting from *Johnson's* prologue to *every man in his humour,* and from various other parts of his writings, the

[1] 2nd ed., 1744, I, 162–163.

side-way reflexions which he frequently casts on *Shakespear*, need not I think seek farther for the strongest proofs of his malevolence and impudence of heart. I would not use such words, if softer terms could convey my meaning; but I cannot from complaisance, lose the use of language, and drop half the image I design to give.

Shakespear saw a rising genius in *Johnson*, and like himself, that is, like one who knew the true value of human learning, and its utmost boundaries, and whose genius was exalted by candor and good-nature, prevailed on the managers of the theatre to encourage *Johnson*, and to exhibit his first performance on the stage. After *Shakespear* had nourish'd in his breast this young and venomous snake, now grown to maturity, and warm'd by his friendly bosom, *Ben Johnson*, like himself, that is, like one who possess'd so much of genius as to make him grasp at the fame of having all, spurn'd at his generous benefactor, caught the ears of the multitude by sharp expressions against him, which he call'd humour, and I call spite, and endeavoured to throw all the obstacles he could invent in the way of *Shakespear's* race to the goal of fame. But *Shakespear* could never be provoked to return such paltry spite; he, like the strong mastiff, steadily pass'd by the whiffling cur, unheeding of his yelpings. I know the men . . . to their inmost souls; I know them by their works. *Shakespear* indeed had no cause to disguise himself; and *Johnson's* malice was too obstreperous for his management; he could not restrain it from breaking out, where gratitude should have with-held it, and with the monument he hath left to posterity of his genius, he hath join'd to it a strong picture of his unconquerable envy. . . .

I should be ashamed of myself, if I would not acknowledge the merit of *Ben Johnson* as a writer; but a capacity for writing holds so very low a place in my esteem, when weigh'd in the balance with an honest heart, that with me . . . it hath no chance of concealing one grain of malice or envy; had *Ben Johnson* known the insignificancy of genius in comparison with a benevolent heart, he had been contented with himself, had borne to have taken the second rank, had loved his friend *Shakespear,* instead of abusing him, had therefore been a happier man, whilst he lived, and left behind him postumous fame (if postumous fame could delight him) sufficient to have gratified the wishes of any reasonable man; and it might also have been untainted with that malice, which is now too visible to be concealed from observing eyes.

Altho' (as I before said) I would willingly acknowledge all *Ben's* merit as a writer; yet would I wish to set his malignant envy in full view, that the face of such envy may be known whenever it dares to make its odious appearance; nor would I willingly have mankind bully'd into becoming the paltry instruments to gratify the spleen of malignant envy, by turning their eyes averse from one of the greatest glories of the human race.

The *Cry* toss'd up their noses, and said that they should not condemn *Ben Johnson*, because *Portia* had pleased to abuse him; nor would they blindly admire *Shakespear*, because she thought proper to *puff* him off as something so very extraordinary.[1]

---

[1] I, 162–168. See the review of this novel in *The Monthly Review*, X (1754), 280–282, which explains its dramatic plan: "The sentiments are . . . just; the passions drawn from nature; and the whole performance contains more literature and good sense, than, a few only excepted, all our modern novels put together."

An admirer of Jonson's gifts in characterization (whose opinion, however, is received with some impatience) appears in *Memoirs of a Coquet; or, The History of Miss Harriot Airy* (1765). Harriot, the coquette, is invited to the country to visit an intellectual widow and her nieces Sukey and Fanny Martin. While walking, the girls meet Sybilla Jennings, a bright young woman, whose father's humor is to collect odd characters. These "very Hogarthian" fellows "push the bottle about, till they [have] just drank enough to give a free loose to their humours." Sybilla asks the others to visit her home and watch the fun:

for there will be as merry a comedy performed at our house, this afternoon, as you ever saw upon the stage: and I dare swear you will laugh very heartily at the characters you will be introduced to, and the drollery of their behaviour. Such a groupe would have been a feast to *Old Ben,* and have given him a fine opportunity to display his comic powers.—Don't you think *Ben's* a charming writer?—I doat upon him."—"*Ben,* to be sure," said Miss *Martin,* "was a very masterly writer, and had a strong idea of *humour;* he was an accurate observer of mankind, and exhibited their follies and vices in a striking light. But though I allow *Ben* a great deal of merit, *Shakespeare* is my favourite."—"Oh, well, well," said Miss *Jennings,* "with all my heart, I don't care who you like best; I haven't time to dispute about the merit of dramatic writers, I have something else to do." [1]

By 1768, according to the opinion of Edward in *The Distressed Lovers; or, The History of Edward and Eliza,* "The dramatic reputation of Shakespear and Johnson is so well established, that their grossest absurdities are tolerated." [2] Possibly he was only half right. Shakespeare's absurdities no longer mattered to an increasingly romantic age, when the Shakespeare virus was taking, and when more and more of his plays were visible on the stage in texts closer to the original than the often appalling mutilations of the Restoration and early eighteenth-century "improvers." Garrick managed to keep a couple of Ben's plays in the repertory until his retirement in 1776, after which their stage history was fitful. The outcry of the professional dramatic and literary critics that Jonson's humors were obsolete and that only Garrick's genius as Kitely or Abel Drugger could enliven them is reflected in Charles Jenner's pleasant novel, *The Placid Man; or, Memoirs of Sir Charles Beville* (1770). Sir Charles attends a performance of *The Alchemist,* historically considered to be Ben's greatest comedy, which is submitted to a long and acute act-by-act examen as the performance of Abel Drugger by Garrick proceeds. "It is a stupid play," said Lady

[1] Pages 117–121.
[2] Dublin, I, 113. UP.

Clayton; "it is so old-fashioned." And "damned low," said Sir Isaac. Despite the excellence of the satire and the diversion of the denouement, the comedy is found deficient in poetic justice and too full of obsolete learning. "Lady Clayton said, that it was called a very fine play; but it was too old for her: and Sir Isaac persisted in his opinion, that it was damned low." [1] Jonson's fortunes were eclipsed as the fame of Shakespeare increased in England, which heralded him as the greatest genius it had produced.

4. *Shakespeare Idolatry*

A S T H E decades passed, and more and more of Shakespeare's plays were restored to the stage in an era of increasingly self-conscious sensibility, there developed what has come to be known as Shakespeare idolatry.[2] Regarded increasingly as an unparalleled literary genius, Shakespeare was deified for his penetrating and understanding analysis of human nature, and even more, no doubt, for his magnificent endowment of poetry. The minor novelists continuously engage their characters in worship at his shrine. Superlatives and exclamation points abound, both before and after the notorious Shakespeare Jubilee at Stratford-on-Avon in 1769. An age which wrote treatises on the sublime found sublimity paramount in its greatest poet. Where many virtues shone in a work, it was idle to carp at a few blemishes. The ecstasy of delicate sensibilities under the spell of Shakespeare's characters will be abundantly apparent in the accounts of the separate plays. As early as 1755, John Shebbeare, in his little-known *Letters on the English Nation, by Batista Angeloni,* presents the rapture of Angeloni over the wealth of Shakespeare's characters and the sublimity of his expression:

The variety of characters to be found in Shakespeare, is no where else to be paralleled; not only almost all ranks amongst the living, from the lowest peasant to the crowned head, madmen, fools, philosophers, patriots, tyrants, wits, and men of all kinds of humour; he has past the bounds of this world, and brought back the very dead, to revisit the glimpses of the moon making night hideous; the limits of nature withheld him not in his imaginary characters of witches, Caliban, fairies, and others, combined of qualities which all that read agree ought to enter into these compositions, which he has formed without one discordant note. . . .
He had imagined all these parts from intuitive knowledge, and internal

---

[1] II, 36–43. For the brilliant stage record of *The Alchemist* in the eighteenth century see my *Ben Jonson on the English Stage, 1660–1776,* chapter 3.

[2] See Robert W. Babcock, *The Genesis of Shakespeare Idolatry, 1776–1799,* Chapel Hill, 1931, especially chapter 14, "Idolatry ad Astra."

sensation, and exprest them with truth and sublimity, by a language which he was perfectly master of.[1]

The thesis that Shakespeare was virtually beyond criticism is supported by Mr. Melville, in the anonymous *Adventures of Charles Careless* (1764). Charles is the bastard son of a wealthy young girl who has overindulged in high life below stairs with the family footman. Obliged to seek his fortune and chancing upon Mr. Melville, a man "of good sense and an excellent scholar," Charles converses with him about Shakespeare. Melville observes that "it is folly to criticise *Shakespeare* minutely, and is doing that great bard a manifest injustice."

'His sublimity of thought,' continued he, 'is astonishing; his conception of things noble; his imagination unlimited. Language faints beneath his great and glorious ideas, and is too weak to shadow his mighty excellencies; yet though there was no possibility of finding types sufficiently expressive of his vast conceptions, the language he has been forced to use, for want of a better, is the sublimest in the world. His painting is so strong, the picturesque descriptions he has every where given us, so striking, that we cannot peruse them without thinking we see the images before us. What a mind must *Shakespear* have possessed! What amazing powers! and divine illuminations!—I am astonished every time I think of him, and cannot give utterance to the big idea I have of him—the best compliment we can pay our immortal bard must be in his own words,'

> 'The poet's eye in a fine phrenzy rolling
> Doth glance from heav'n to earth, from earth to heav'n,
> And as imagination bodies forth
> The form of things unknown, the poet's pen
> Turns them to shape, and gives to airy nothing
> A local habitation and a name.'

'He was indeed a wonderful man, and certainly approached nearer to divinity, than the lower order of mankind approach to humanity.'

Careless replies that he entirely coincides in sentiment with Melville, and that he looks on *"Shakespear* as equal, if not superior to any poet that ever lived." [2]

Five years later, in the very year of the Jubilee, an interesting little novel appeared from an anonymous hand, *Private Letters from an American in England to His Friends in America.* The letters, as described in the advertisement, "are supposed to be written towards the close of the eighteenth century, by a young American, who is stimulated by curiosity to pay a visit to the country of his ancestors. The seat of government is transferred to America; and England is an al-

---

[1] II, 275–278.
[2] II, 125–126. Bodleian.

most depopulated nation; the condition of which, and the manners of
its inhabitants, he describes, as far as he is able to collect them." England is in a twilight state of universal decay. The banks of the Thames
are grown over with bushes and briars. But the visitor, doting on literary monuments, exclaims over "the almost divine Shakespear." [1]

Full realization of the worship of Shakespeare, with credit to Garrick, who was time and again acknowledged to be chiefly responsible
for rehabilitating Shakespeare by virtue of restoring and animating the
plays, is apparent in *The Correspondents* (1775). The author observes that "real genius . . . can never diminish in value. Shakespeare
is the most striking instance of this truth. How gradual his progress
from neglect to admiration, to reverence, almost to idolatry! But in
truth, (though no writer could *deserve* more) he owes most of his
fame to the singular advantage of *a practical commentator,* and must
certainly be content to divide *his* laurels with *Garrick.*" [2]

It was possible, even in this period which prided itself on delicacy
and refinement, to apologize for Shakespeare's lapses in taste and indulgence in bawdry. Although some young ladies objected to indeli-
cacies, no Bowdler was felt necessary to make the plays presentable to
heroines of sensibility at their own firesides. In his excellent fictional
essays in epistolary form, addressed to Maria and dated from Stowe in
1769, the free-thinking man-midwife, Thomas Cogan, wrote in *John
Buncle, Junior, Gentleman* (1776–1778):

> I was highly entertained sometime ago with a warm dispute between
> Charles [a friend of the author's] and a lady of very rigid notions concern-
> ing *Shakespeare's* plays. The lady said she had begun to read them, and ac-
> knowledged, that they abounded with just and beautiful sentiments; but
> she was obliged to lay the book aside, upon account of the many *bad words*
> that were intermixed.
> "As for me, says Charles, when the sentiments are good, and the tend-
> ency moral, I never stand for a few high seasoned expressions, necessary to
> support the particular character. Habitual swearing I detest; but I am not
> much terrified at a few oaths, where there is any good to be got amongst
> them."

[1] Page 12. BM.
[2] Page 116. See below, p. 67, n. 1. Garrick also shared Shakespeare's "divinity." In
Claude A. Helvetius' *The Child of Nature,* 1774, an effusive lady calls him "the
divine Garrick," "the divine man," "divine, supernatural" (II, 158–160). This
novel reappeared in the same year with the title *The Philosophy of Pleasure.* After
Garrick's death, in Charles Johnstone's *The Adventures of Anthony Varnish,* 1786,
the poet Crambo laments the passing of the old school of actors who had reformed
their art from the abuses of their predecessors: "At the head of this reformation
stood the late inimitable *Garrick,* vociferated *Crambo,* who united as many qualifications for an actor in his mind as the Almighty will perhaps admit a human
being to possess" (III, 72).

The Lady was silent, but shook her head, and lifted up her eyes and hands.

This kind of reply picqued my friend not a little, and taking his clue from the Lady's prevailing character, he answered her, "Madam I compare these exceptionable passages in *Shakespeare* to a *good turnpike road in rainy weather*. It is *dirty* in some places if you will, and I could wish it otherways; but then it is *good at bottom,* and we may travel it in safety, and with advantage: whereas the principles of some of his warmest opponents, are quite the reverse; they are like a *quagmire sprinkled over with gravel*. When we hear them cry out with a plaintive voice of patience, and acquiescence, *if it please the L—d, the L—d's will be done in all things,* we should take them for the excellent ones of the earth! But down they sink into some bog of spiritual pride, hypocrisy, or carnality, and remain so perfectly resigned in this state, that they seldom attempt to get out again!"

This, as you may suppose, did not mend the matter. The dispute grew warmer, and the Lady of consequence, proportionably more rigid in her sentiments: till at length plays, cards, songs of all sorts, but spiritual, were condemned in the strongest terms; and all those who loved or vindicated them, were anathematized without the least glimpse of mercy. Charles terminated the debate by telling her, *"you* may rest your hopes of salvation upon what you please, Madam, but *I* should as soon think of mounting up to heaven by *hanging upon the tail of a paper-kite,* as to render myself acceptable to my Maker, by the most rigid attention to such trivial circumstances as these." [1]

5. *Garrick and Shakespeare*

THE high credit due to David Garrick for his devotion to Shakespeare, the god of his idolatry, has almost always been granted. There was some disparagement, particularly in the nineteenth century, by critics who contended that his preaching was inconsistent with his practice, but his interpretations of Shakespearean characters on the stage of Drury Lane were continuously regarded in his own times as the finest comment on the meaning of the texts. At present his service to Shakespeare is held in great respect.[2] Even scholars of his day

[1] II, 246–249.

[2] For recent commentary on Garrick and Shakespeare see George W. Stone, Jr., *Garrick's Handling of Shakespeare's Plays and His Influence upon the Changed Attitude of Shakespearian Criticism during the Eighteenth Century* (Harvard doctoral dissertation), 1940; for a summary see *Harvard University Graduate School of Arts and Sciences: Summaries of Theses . . . 1940,* Cambridge, Mass., 1942, pp. 368–372; G. W. Stone, Jr., " 'The God of His Idolatry': Garrick's Theory of Acting and Dramatic Composition with Especial Reference to Shakespeare," *Joseph Quincy Adams Memorial Studies,* Washington, D. C., 1948, pp. 115–128; G. W. Stone, Jr., "David Garrick's Significance in the History of Shakespearean Criticism," *PMLA,* LXV (1950), 183–197; Arthur Colby Sprague, *Shakespeare and the Actors,* Cambridge, Mass., 1944, *passim;* Dougald MacMillan, "David Garrick, Manager: Notes on the Theatre as a Cultural Institution in England in the Eighteenth Century," *SP,* XLV (1948), 630–646; and MacMillan's Introduction to *Drury Lane Calendar, 1747–1776,* Oxford, 1938, "Drury Lane under David Garrick"; Paul S.

found solutions of editorial difficulties by watching the "great little man" perform. George Steevens wrote him in 1765:

> Often when I have taken the pen in my hand to try to illustrate a passage, I have thrown it down again with discontent when I remembered how able you were to clear that difficulty by a single look, or particular modulation of voice, which a long and laboured paraphrase was insufficient to explain half so well.[1]

The conception, however, prevalent to our own times, that Garrick was solely responsible for both the revival and the popularity of Shakespeare's plays on the mid-eighteenth-century London stage has recently been demonstrated as erroneous.[2] Yet, though actually the fashion for Shakespeare had already set in, Garrick was its most brilliant sponsor. He arrived in London in March, 1737. Increasingly available sources for stage history reveal that in the season of 1736–1737, Drury Lane offered forty-eight performances of thirteen of Shakespeare's plays, and that Covent Garden presented eight of them for twenty-five nights. The twenty-one productions included fifteen different plays. By 1741 the number of Shakespeare's plays in production had increased to twenty-five. There is some basis for the contention that Garrick "simply rode the wave of the rapidly increasing popularity of William Shakespeare."[3] But he was not content merely to exploit the current enthusiasm. He constantly endeavored to free the stage of Drury Lane from "improved" versions of the plays, and a careful scholar has recently made the significant statement that "for the thirty-five years of Garrick's connection with the stage, 1,448 performances of twenty-seven Shakespeare plays were given at his theatre alone, of which only eight can be said to have undergone serious alteration."[4] Garrick himself assumed eighteen different Shakespearean roles.

The popularity of revivals of the older dramatists, for which George Colman the Elder as well as Garrick was responsible in the fifties and

---

Conklin, *A History of Hamlet Criticism, 1601–1821,* New York, 1947, especially chapter 2 ("Histrionic Tradition to the Retirement of Garrick") and chapter 3 ("English Tradition as Presented in Formal Criticism to 1770"); Alan S. Downer, "Nature to Advantage Dressed: Eighteenth-Century Acting," *PMLA,* LVIII (1943), 1002–1037.

[1] [James Boaden, ed.], *The Private Correspondence of David Garrick,* 1831, I, 216–217.

[2] See Arthur H. Scouten, "Shakespeare's Plays in the Theatrical Repertory When Garrick Came to London," *University of Texas Studies in English* (1944), 1945, pp. 257–268.

[3] Scouten, p. 268.

[4] G. W. Stone, Jr., "David Garrick's Significance in the History of Shakespearean Criticism," p. 187. See Dougald MacMillan, ed., *Drury Lane Calendar,* for the year-by-year productions and casts.

sixties, was reflected by Oliver Goldsmith in *The Vicar of Wakefield* (1766). The beloved Doctor Primrose, having met a strolling player with his cart full of scenes and other theatrical furniture, asks the poor fellow about the condition of the stage.

"I demanded who were . . . the Drydens and Otways of the day."

"I fancy, Sir," cried the player, "few of our modern dramatists would think themselves much honoured by being compared to the writers you mention. Dryden and Rowe's manner, Sir, are quite out of fashion! Our taste has gone back a whole century; Fletcher, Ben Jonson, and all the plays of Shakespeare are the only things that go down."

"How," cried I, "is it possible the present age can be pleased with that antiquated dialect, that obsolete humour, those overcharged characters, which abound in the works you mention?"

"Sir," returned my companion, "the public think nothing about dialect, or humour, or character, for that is none of their business; they only go to be amused, and find themselves happy when they can enjoy a pantomime under the sanction of Jonson's or Shakespeare's name." [1]

Garrick's personal appearances as Richard III, Hamlet, Hamlet's Ghost, Lear, Macbeth, King John, Faulconbridge, Othello, Iago, Henry IV, Hotspur, the Chorus in *Henry V*, Benedick, Romeo, Leontes, and several other characters, excited his audiences mainly to adulation, but occasionally to abuse. And he produced, without acting in them, *The Merchant of Venice*, *As You Like It*, *Twelfth Night*, *The Merry Wives of Windsor*, *All's Well That Ends Well*, *Measure for Measure*, *Coriolanus*, *Henry VIII*, and his own versions of *A Midsummer-Night's Dream*, *The Taming of the Shrew*, and *The Tempest*. The importance of his contribution to Shakespeare has been well summarized by a recent critic:

Garrick had a care . . . for Shakespeare which was the guiding force in his whole career. It prompted him to talk and write about the dramatist from his earliest letters to the end of his life. Shakespeare dominated his theorizing and acting. Shakespeare dominated his sense of dramatic values. He was accustomed to evaluate new plays submitted to him as manager by the measure of Shakespeare's plays. Fully cognizant of the changing taste of his age he strove with remarkable consistency to mold dramatic taste more and more towards Shakespeare—authentic Shakespeare. [2]

A tribute to Garrick's infusion of life into Shakespeare's texts during his early years on the stage appears in *The History of Tom Jones, a Foundling* (1749). Fielding, whose admiration for Garrick was

---

[1] Chapter 18. The novel was written in 1762.
[2] G. W. Stone, Jr., "The God of His Idolatry," pp. 127–128.

boundless, and who in this novel praised the actor's Hamlet in the best passage about any play in any novel, calling him "in tragedy . . . the greatest genius the world hath ever produced," reflects on the need of writers for genius and knowledge of actual people rather than mere book-learning:

As we must perceive, that after the nicest strokes of a Shakespeare or a Jonson . . . some touches of nature will escape the reader, which the judicious action of a Garrick, of a Cibber, or a Clive, can convey to him; so, on the real stage, the character shows himself in a stronger and bolder light than he can be described. And if this be the case in those fine and nervous descriptions which great authors themselves have taken from life, how much more strongly will it hold when the writer himself takes his lines not from nature, but from books? Such characters are only the faint copy of a copy, and can have neither the justness nor spirit of an original.[1]

Fielding lauds Garrick for forming himself on the study of nature, not on imitation of predecessors,—a merit which has enabled him to excel all who have gone before.

By 1769, in *The Life and Adventures of Common Sense,* Herbert Lawrence ventured to hail Garrick as "that great Master of the Passions to whom every one listens with profound attention, and to whose excellent Abilities *Shakespear* is more obliged than to all the Editors, Critics, Commentators or Theatrical Performers that ever exhibited themselves or their Works to the Public." [2]

Elizabeth Bonhote's impressionistic novel, *The Rambles of Mr. Frankly, Published by His Sister* (1772–1776), a collection of "characters" and city types clearly influenced by Sterne's *Sentimental Journey,* contains an adulatory sketch of "The English Roscius":

In what various characters has that little man appeared since he walked the stage!—Yet how great—with what taste and propriety has he appeared in each!—What applause has he justly gained!—There is one part he hath particularly acted well— That is—his own. And to have performed that with propriety deserves applause in a higher degree than he, or any other hath ever received it.—He has acquired a large fortune—and he deserves it all— For Garrick was ever the known friend to merit—and many a fair blossom has he drawn from the shades of obscurity.—As a man of taste, worth, and sense, he has obtained the friendship of the world. As an actor he has shone like the sun in its meridian splendor. From his tongue, wit receives redoubled keenness—and the tale of misery sinks deep into the soul.—Grateful must be the thunder of applause, when gained by real merit.—With justice we may say, that in Garrick our Shakespeare still

[1] Book 7, chapter 1; Book 9, chapter 1.
[2] II, 30–31. Without specific Shakespearean reference Lawrence devotes a long section of his allegory (II, 149–155) to the life of "Kcirrag" and the benefits bestowed upon him by Genius and Prudence.

lives and speaks. Time has not dared to touch this favorite son of nature and the world. Still the youthful Hamlet—venerable Lear—and lively Benedict, equally lay claim to our praise and admiration.[1]

As late as 1776, Garrick's last season on the stage, "Courtney Melmoth" (Samuel J. Pratt) reiterates the theme of Garrick as the best commentator upon Shakespeare. In *The Pupil of Pleasure*, Philip Sedley, a gentleman who bases his conduct on the letters of Lord Chesterfield (which Pratt himself loathed), having stated his philosophy to a friend, concludes:

In a word, then, Thornton, what our Garrick is to Shakespeare, *I* am resolved to be to Chesterfield,—the living comment, upon the dead text.[2]

After Garrick's retirement in the spring of 1776 some novelists feared that the stage would go to the dogs. In the anonymous *'Squire Randal's Excursion Round London* (1777), the Squire, visiting the city for a week's frolic, writes home to the country about current diversions. He has been to see Sam Foote, and he approves of plays as "very rational and elevated amusements, . . . at once entertaining and useful, affording, in general, a striking moral, and some ingenious turns either of wit or sentiment." But his cousin Mr. Smart, a frequent playgoer, discerns a decline in the stage:

Our modern managers are justly chargeable with neglecting merit in favour of caprice, and will either suppress or bring on a performance, just as they happen to suit their own fantastical taste, or feed the vitiated palate of the town. Upon this principle it is, that instead of the productions of Shakespeare and old Ben Johnson, the public are amused with private satire, or mere mimical buffoonery; and now the great little Mr. Garrick is gone, it is whispered that nothing is to come before the curtain but fellows who can quaver in an opera, and women who can carry a note clean and clever out of all hearing. The deuce, a tragedy is expected all next winter, they say; and the children of catgut are to starve the heroes and heroines of blank verse, as Mr. Smart smartly says, till they are as thin and unsubstantial as the hairs of a fiddle-stick. As the man says in a poem about Mr. Garrick's Looking-glass, which stands on my cousin's table—a devilish shrewd thing, let me tell you—

" 'Tis all to sing, and nought to say."

Sheridan has taken over, and *The Duenna* has "took the nation by the ear." A singing generation has succeeded to the weeds the witches danced in, to the large truncheon, "the whole machinery, and all the trick of tragedy." The Squire concludes about the stage: "I cannot in

[1] I (1772), 50–51. I have used the copy in the collection of Dr. John C. Hardy.
[2] 2nd ed., 1777, I, 9. For other comments on Garrick as Shakespeare's best commentator see G. W. Stone, Jr., "David Garrick's Significance in the History of Shakespearean Criticism," p. 184, note 4.

justice recommend it to any of my country friends who have the least
regard for the immortal Shakespeare . . . to countenance such Italian
innovation; but I advise one and all to stay away from the British theatre, till it shall again be restored to good sense, fair morals, solid
amusement, and fine poetry. At present the drama is at a shocking low
ebb." [1]

Specific aspects of Garrick's art in presenting Shakespeare will appear in the comments of the novelists upon the plays in which he performed. There was an undoubted fascination in witnessing him in
characters high and low. The panegyrics of fictional characters can easily be duplicated in the vast testimony of actual human beings who
came under his spell in roles ranging from Macbeth and Lear to Abel
Drugger and Scrub. Sometimes it was simpler not to try to discrimi-
nate Garrick's special qualities, but to confess that the man was possessed of a strong element of *je ne sais quoi*. Witwood Borlace, to divert Tom Fool's melancholy spirits, in George Alexander Stevens'
"concealed autobiography," *The History of Tom Fool* (1760), provides an example. Borlace took his heiress bride to town and showed
her off in all public places. Although she thought society insipid, anything serious pleased her, such as Garrick's acting. Borlace comments:

> There is something in that *Garrick's* Execution excessively clever; I can,
> I believe, without Vanity, do as many droll Things, as all the choice Spirits
> put together; but I don't know how it is, I never could get at what he does;
> as to the rest of the Actors, I was at Home; but he has got a Sort of Knack
> that's past finding out, and yet he seems so easy in what he does, as if it
> was natural to him. I believe, in acting, as well as free Masonry, there's a
> Secret not to be divulged.[2]

Other novelists ventured to convey Garrick's emotional effect. Most
spectators wept; many swooned. In an early novel of manners, *Chit
Chat; or, Natural Characters and the Manners of Real Life* (1754),
we discover an example of feminine sensibility, a quality only recently
exploited in Samuel Richardson's *Clarissa*. The heroine is Charlotte
Byersley. Her mother is dead. Mr. Welford, whom she ultimately marries, has been attracted to her:

> [Welford's] favourite diversions had ever been of the theatric kind, he
> had chiefly frequented the two play-houses, and could harangue on au-
> thors and actors, with great readiness and propriety: he was silly enough

---

[1] Pages 92–95. BM. The author of the novel quotes liberally from *Garrick's
Looking-Glass; or, The Art of Rising on the Stage,* 1776, attributed to S. J. Pratt
("Courtney Melmoth").

[2] II, 183–184. LC.

to have no taste for routs, ridottos, and masquerades, and so stupid that he look'd upon gaming as a criminal amusement.

One evening, as Welford was drinking tea at Mr. Byersley's, a lady, who sometimes visited there, happened to say . . . that an affecting play of Shakespear's was to be revived on the following evening; upon which Charlotte could not suppress her inclination to see it, and as her father was easily persuaded to go with her, he engaged Mr. Welford and the lady to be of the party: they both engaged with pleasure, and a servant was order'd to secure four places in the front boxes. They went accordingly, but Welford, though he doated on the amiable Charlotte, and had placed himself close by her side, could not be inattentive to the play, while Garrick was on the stage, whose every look and gesture demanded peculiar notice. In a very tender scene, towards the end of the play, he turned round to see in what manner his mistress was affected with it, as he could not behold it himself without the greatest emotion. He turned, he saw, and he admired; for Charlotte gave him at that instant a fresh proof of the sensibility of her heart, by letting fall a shower of tears. He viewed her in a new light; but though she appeared more attractive than ever, he could not help being concerned lest the distress should be too poignant for her: he knew not how to alleviate it, but by gently pressing her hand, and looking "unutterable things."

Next morning Welford calls on her, tells her how charmed he was with her behavior, and observes:

" 'Tis, methinks, but a gloomy pleasure at best which we receive from reading a well-written, or seeing a well acted tragedy." "I am obliged to you, Sir," answer'd Charlotte, "for your kind concern about me, but the sorrow we feel at a tragedy is of too short a duration to be attended with very ill consequences; and is generally, in my opinion, much lessened, if not altogether obliterated, by our considering that the scenes we grieve at are imaginary." "I may infer from thence, madam, that your compassion would be more strongly excited, and remain much longer, by the appearance of a real object in distress." "Undoubtedly," replied she, "and I should applaud myself for being compassionate on such an occasion." [1]

An ardent lover of Garrick's Shakespearean performances rises to his defense in the rare and charming novel, *Emily; or, The History of a Natural Daughter* (1756). Emily's guardian, Mr. Hippocrene, a bookseller and a dramatic poet, converses in a coach with Mr. Smatter about his own tragic compositions. Smatter asks if they were ever acted. Hippocrene replies:

No, Sir; I told you People of Genius met with little Encouragement; but I have almost finished a *Piece,* which I design to bring upon the Stage next Winter, that will, I believe, render the Name of *Hippocrene* as well known as the immortal *Shakespear's.* Pray, Sir, said *Smatter,* which House is to be honoured with your new Production?—Lord, Sir, cried *Hippocrene,* what a Question is that—Drury-Lane, to be sure; there are no Actors at t'other

[1] I, 12–23. Yale.

House, no Actors at all. You must know, Sir, I have wrote a Part on Purpose for Mr. *Garrick*.

The role Hippocrene intends for Garrick is that of Apollo, "the God of Wit and Poesy."

You can't imagine, Sir, how I have touch'd up *Apollo's* Part, in order to shew his Representative to Advantage. . . . There is an Elegance, a Delicacy in all Mr. *Garrick's* Performances, accompanied with such Spirit and Propriety, that render him the Delight of our Stage. I have therefore prick'd him down for *Apollo,* who is every Way a fine Gentleman. Why, said *Smatter,* my Friend *Garrick* is certainly a pretty Player, a very pretty Player. What do you mean by a *very pretty Player,* cried Mrs. *Easy:* (whose Indignation rose at the affected Importance of this Coxcomb, and at his calling a Man, whom he had not Courage to speak to, with so much Familiarity, his Friend,) I have seen, Sir, Mr. *Booth,* Mr. *Wilks,* and Mr. *Cibber,* and have conversed with those who saw *Mountford* and *Betterton:* These were all eminent Actors; but I am fully persuaded that there never was so universal a Genius as Mr. *Garrick.* Was either of these Gentlemen capable of shining in a *Lear* and a *Bays,* a *Hamlet* and a *Drugger,* a *Macbeth* and a *Fribble?* Characters widely different from each other, and yet they are all supported with the greatest Spirit, and the exactest Propriety, by that Man whom you slightly call *a very pretty Player.*

To conclude the episode, Hippocrene's misfortune with Garrick is narrated by Mr. Metal, a friend of Emily's:

So what does he do but carry [the play] to the Master of *Drury-Lane* Playhouse—Mr.—— Mr.—— I can't think of his Name—but that's not material. So as I was saying— La! Mr. *Metal,* said his Lady, how strangely forgetful you are to Day— Mr. *Garrick* you know, we saw him but t'other Night in the *More of Wenus*— No, no, said *Metal,* now my dear *you* are in the wrong Box, 'twas not Mr. *Garrick,* 'twas the tall *Irishman* of *Covent-Garden.* O ay, said Mrs. *Metal,* 'twas *Barry,* so it was—but 'twas *Garrick,* Mr. *Hippocrene* carried his Play to, who told him it wou'dn't do for . . . *any Body,* and advised him to take it home and new write it; but he was obstinate and wou'dn't: So he carries it to the Master of the other House, but he refused it too; so my poor Neighbour was almost distracted, and flew into a violent Passion, and said they were all a pack of Fools, and did not know a good Play from a bad One.[1]

Again, Garrick's power to move his auditors is glanced at in George Alexander Stevens' *History of Tom Fool* (1760):

Tom Fool sat attentive to his Sister while she related her Distresses; attentive as a sensible Audience which follows Mr. *Garric* [*sic*] thro' all the Workings of *Lear, Hamlet,* &c. &c. the whole Pit seems inform'd with one Soul; smile, when he smiles; weep, when he mourns; and, like a fine In-

---

[1] I, 12–16; 186–187. The copy I have used is in the John Hay Library at Brown University. The reviewer in *The Monthly Review,* XIV (1756), 289–292, praised the superiority of this novel for natural characters and entertaining story.

strument, play'd upon by a skillful Performer, produces excellent Harmony. Thus was Mr. *Fool* agitated during his Sister's Story.[1]

So eager was the audience to show its appreciation of Garrick that spontaneous applause often ruined the effect he was trying to create, according to Mr. E—n, the hero of *A History of the Matrimonial Adventures of a Banker's Clerk with the Pretended Lady Ann Frances Caroline Boothby* (1762):

I have often observed, that there is nothing so ungovernably impetuous as excessive joy: violent grief seems to be much more tractable. I frequently remember to have heard an impatient audience, at Drury-Lane Theatre, drown the last and most important line of Shakespear's speeches, pronounced by Mr. Garrick, owing entirely to their eagerness to applaud him.[2]

And again, in *The Travels of Hildebrand Bowman, Esquire* (1778), there is reflection of the delight of the audience, as well as comment on the fortune which Garrick amassed as actor and manager. This novel is a series of imaginary travels. At Luxo-Volupto "a party was made to go next evening to one of the theatres, to see a famous actor named Garrimond in one of Avonswan's plays, which were constantly brought here and translated." To procure places "required considerable interest when that actor appeared."

When the curtain was drawn up, and Garrimond entered on the stage, there was a clapping of hands which continued for a minute or two; at last all was attention through the play, except when some sentiment or fine piece of action forced their applause. . . . I . . . must do Garrimond the justice to own, that he seemed to understand his part perfectly. . . . Garrimond appeared like a giant amongst dwarfs. If this actor has great merit, he has been also very fortunate to appear in a country where amusements are so much the fashion, and so highly valued. By what I was informed, he has made ten times more money by acting Avonswan's plays, than ever the author did by writing them; and to such a degree of frenzy has their admiration of him arose, that had he a rival of equal merit, I make no doubt but the scene of the famous pantomimes of degenerated Rome would be renewed, and the nobility would take party, wear their liveries, and follow their triumphal cars.[3]

If Garrick's genius as a Shakespearean actor commonly aroused a frenzy of admiration, he was never without envious detractors. It is only just to temper the approval of most novelists with several adverse views, which centered not so much about his abilities on the stage as about his alleged parsimony and the difficulties he placed in the way

[1] II, 219.
[2] Page 41.
[3] Pages 276–283. LC. See Philip B. Gove, *The Imaginary Voyage in Prose Fiction*, New York, 1941, pp. 369–370; *The Monthly Review*, LIX (1778), 409–410.

of hopeful young actors, or of authors who contended that they were put off from season to season while their manuscripts remained unread in the manager's desk. Many novels besides Smollett's contain passages whose vigorous, resentful tone implies that their authors had once been stage-bitten and frustrated.[1] A consideration of Garrick's critical powers and his conservatism with regard to new compositions as he aged and undertook fewer new roles belongs in another context,[2] but illustrative of the edged attitude of some novelists is a passage in the anonymous *Rosalind; or, An Apology for the History of a Theatrical Lady* (1759).[3] From infancy Rosalind was notable for great sensibility, delicacy, and strong passions controlled by reason. "She was particularly fond of the drama, even in her tender years, and would steal into privacy, with her favourite Shakespear, Addison, or Rowe, and prefer their improving and eloquent silence, to the insipid and frothy discourse of her companions." When Celadon, whom she met one evening at a performance of *Romeo and Juliet,* proved inconstant, Rosalind consoled herself by frequenting the playhouse, where she fell in love with an actor, Wou'd-be, whom, though he was vain, ostentatious, proud, and affected, she married. "Rosalind one night behind the scenes at B——, had by some means or other rubbed herself against a scene, whereon the awful figure of our Shakespear was engraved. . . . She caught the celestial spark from the bard's image, and theatric raptures filled her breast. . . . From that same moment, she determined to devote herself to the stage."[4] The couple call on Garrick in London.

Being admitted to him, "Sir your most obedient humble servant," says Wou'd-be; "I have been so bold to wait on you to know if I can serve you." "To serve thy self good"— Pray sir, may I crave your name?" "My

---

[1] See Henry Fielding, *The Adventures of Joseph Andrews,* 1742, Book 3, chapter 3; *The Lady's Drawing Room,* 1744, pp. 84–85; Tobias Smollett, *The Adventures of Roderick Random,* 1748, chapters 62, 63, for the attack on Garrick as "Marmozet"; *Great News from Hell; or, The Devil Foil'd by Bess Weatherby,* 1760, pp. 27–30; [Charles Johnstone], *Chrysal; or, The Adventures of a Guinea,* 1765, III, 204–212; *The Captives; or, The History of Charles Arlington,* 1771, II, 50–54; *The Younger Brother,* 1770–1772, II, 179–185, an attack on George Colman the Elder. Thomas Davies, in *Memoirs of the Life of David Garrick, Esq.,* 1780, I, 207–212, gives a dispassionate account of Garrick's treatment of authors, but see James Ralph, *The Case of Authors,* 1762, pp. 23–25.

[2] See Dougald MacMillan, "David Garrick as Critic," *SP,* XXXI (1934), 69–83.

[3] This novel is a disguised biography of Ann Crawford, a famous actress in tragedy and comedy, who was thrice married; her first husband was Dancer, an actor; her second, the actor Spranger Barry; her third, Crawford, an Irish barrister. The novel has reference to a scandal caused by her supposed elopement with Poicteur, a dancer. See R. W. Lowe, *A Bibliographical Account of English Theatrical Literature,* 1888, p. 77.

[4] Dublin, 1759, pp. 35–36, 66.

name is Wou'd-be sir, at your service, and if so be that my wife there, could also be admitted, 'twould give felicity." "That Lady is your wife— oh—oy, ma'am, your humble servant, what—a—a—I suppose you have a—a—a—genius for the stage." "Yes, sir, I was always fond of the drama, and should be desirous, at least, of proving my abilities. If it should be found, that it is a scene of life I am incapable of, I should decline all thoughts of it, for I could not bear to be an actress in spite of nature and my stars."—"You speak well, ma'am, but—a—a—your figure is very well; —fine complexion;—fine breasts; fine shape; and so forth; but—a—a— I'm full at present. But what characters Ma'am should you most a—a— approve of?"—"Monimia sir, is my favourite, but I should not desire to be guided by my own judgment, because it might prove erroneous, and we frequently mistake our own abilities. You, sir, wou'd be the best judge of those after a proper trial. The popular and universal esteem you have gained, convince me that you are"— "Why—ay— Ma'am as you say; but a— I don't know what to say at present. To be sure, I am one of those happy few—but—a— I am vastly full. But what parts wou'd You choose to enact sir?"—"What I sir? O sir, I'm for any thing, 'tis all as one with me; tam Marte and so forth, that's my motto sir: but the top ones where I shine most, as I may say, is Ranger, and a—King Richard the third sir, and a—Glocester in Jane Shore, and a—Castalio in the Orphan, and a— and such like parts sir."—"O then you're an universalist I find, but a— I should be glad to hear a specimen sir."—"Oh yes sir, yes sir, to be sure you shall sir; pray sir, what sort of a speech must I give you?" "Why aw— aw—suppose you was to give King Richard the third; that seems to suit your figure best." "Yes sir, that is my best part as I may say; I shine there to be sure. I'll tip ye the night scene if you choose it sir." "Ay by all means let's have that. Two of those chairs Mr. Wou'd-be will do for a couch very well."—"O yes sir, they will do very well, I've made shift with such upon a stage before now, and mayhap it pleased as much,—as much as—but now I'll give it ye sir."

Here the night scene is rehearsed.

"Well sir, howd'ye like me? don't you think I'm a pretty good hand as one may say?"—"Why—aw—aw—mr. What d'ye call 'um—a—what business might you be bred to?"—"Who I sir? I was bred sir, a silversmith, but I soon left that."—"Why then sir—a—a—the best advice I can give you is, to mind—a—your forge, and a—your shop, for you may do better there than—a—upon the stage."—"But I would engage for a small salary sir; what you think proper sir; I wou'd not stand out upon occasion as one may say." "No sir, no sir, I want nobody at present; I'm too full already." —"I'm sorry I can't serve you sir; I should be glad if I could; but mayhap another time as occasion shall serve sir." "I can say nothing to that mr. a— a— Wou'd-be, upon my soul you stop me in my career of business at pres- ent, I have my lady what's her name, the countess of what d'ye call her, and the duke of Thing'ummy to wait on. A—a— Ma'am I should have been glad—but a—a—a, as things are—you'll excuse me ma'am; I must wait on my Lord Duke immediately." [1]

[1] Pages 67–70. Garrick's halting speech is similarly imitated in an interview between Kitty F[ishe]r, who aspires to the stage, and Garrick, in the disreputable novel, *The Juvenile Adventures of Miss Kitty F[ishe]r*, 1759, II, 47–49, a work

In her novel *The Excursion* (1777), published after Garrick's retirement, Mrs. Frances Brooke avenged herself for Garrick's rejection of her tragedy *Virginia* (1754), as well as of a later tragedy, by lampooning him for his reputed unwillingness to encourage new dramatists.[1] Her heroine, Maria Villiers, has composed a tragedy with an interesting and pathetic fable, strongly marked characters, and mellifluous language. A literary friend, Mr. Hammond, presents the script to Garrick, who, when pressed later for his decision, criticizes the play's defects without having read it. With that Jinglelike stammer which seems to have marked his oral discourse, he rejects the play. Hammond reports the interview to Maria:

I went accordingly at eleven, the hour which I supposed would be most convenient to him. As he loves to keep on good terms with all authors of reputation who have the complaisance not to write for the theatre, . . . I was admitted the moment I sent up my name. I found him surrounded by a train of anxious expectants, for some of whom I felt the strongest compassion. . . . The train which composed this great man's levee all retired on my entrance, when the following conversation took place; a conversation which will convince you I over-rated my little interest, in supposing I could secure your tragedy a candid reading.

"My good sir, I am happy any thing procures me the pleasure of seeing you— I was talking of you only last week"—

"I am much obliged to you, sir, but the business on which I attend you"—

"Why—a—um—true—this play of your friend's— You look amazingly well, my dear sir— In short—this play— I should be charmed to oblige you—but we are so terribly overstocked"—. . . .

"You have read the play, I take for granted"—

---

listed in the Catholic Index. I have used the copy in the Bodleian. Tate Wilkinson, in *Memoirs of His Own Life,* York, 1790, I, 26, describes Samuel Foote's imitation of Garrick at one of his "morning's diversions" in 1748: "He was also very severe on GARRICK, who was apt to hesitate, (in his dying scenes in particular) as in the character of Lothario—

> adorns my fall, and
> chea-chea-chea-chea-chea-chears my heart
> in dy-dy-dying."

Wilkinson reproduces Garrick's hesitant speech during an actual interview and offers an explanation: "His hesitation and never giving a direct answer, arose from two causes—affectation, and a fear of being led into promises which he never meant to perform; and therefore 'By—nay—why—now if you will not—why I cannot say but I may settle that matter. . . . But Mrs. Garrick is waiting—and you now— I say now—hey—now Tuesday' " (I, 236).

[1] See *Virginia*, 1756, Preface, p. viii; John Nichols, *Literary Anecdotes of the Eighteenth Century,* II (1812), 347; *Biographia Dramatica*, 1812, III, 383.

"Why—a—um—no—not absolutely read it— Such a multiplicity of affairs— Just skimmed the surface— I—a— Will you take any chocolate, my dear friend?"

"I have only this moment breakfasted, sir— But to our play."

"True—this play—the writing seems not bad—something tender—something like sentiment—but not an atom of the *vis comica*."

"In a tragedy, my good sir?"

"I beg pardon: I protest I had forgot— I was thinking of Mr. What-d'ye-call-um's comedy, which he left with me last Tuesday. But why tragedy? why not write comedy? There are real sorrows enough in life without going to seek them at the theatre— Tragedy does not please as it used to do, I assure you, sir. You see I scarce ever play tragedy now? The public taste is quite changed within these three or four years. . . . But as I was saying, sir—your friend's play—there are good lines— But—the fable— the manners—the conduct—people imagine—if authors would be directed —but they are an incorrigible race— Ah! Mr. Hammond! we have no writers now—there was a time—your Shakespeares and old Bens— If your friend would call on me, I could propose a piece for him to *alter*, which perhaps"—

"My commission, Sir, does not extend beyond the tragedy in question; therefore we will, if you please, return to that."

"Be so good, my dear sir, as to reach me the gentleman's play: it lies under the right-hand pillow of the sopha."

He took the play which was still in the cover in which I had sent it, and it was easy to see had never been opened. He turned over the leaves with an air of the most stoical inattention, and proceeded:

"There is a kind of a—sort of a—smattering of genius in this production, which convinces me the writer, with proper advice, might come to something in time. But these authors—and after all, what do they do? They bring the meat indeed, but who instructs them how to cook it? Who points out the proper seasoning for the dramatic ragoût? Who furnishes the savoury ingredients to make the dish palatable?—Who brings the Attic salt?—The Cayenne pepper?—the—the—a— 'Tis amazing the pains I am forced to take with these people, in order to give relish to their insipid productions"—

"I have no doubt of all this, sir; but the morning is wearing away. You have many avocations, and I would not take up your time; I have only one word to add to what I have said: I know we are too late for the present season; but you will oblige me infinitely if you will make room for this piece in the course of the next."

"The next season, my dear sir!—why—a—it is absolutely impossible— I have now six-and-twenty new tragedies on my promise-list—besides, I have not read it?—That is—if—if—a—your friend will send it me in July—if I approve it in July, I will endeavour—let me see—what year is this?—O, I remember—'tis seventy-five— Yes—if I think it will do, I will endeavour to bring it out in the winter of—the winter of—eighty-two". . . .

I wished him a good morning, madam; and have brought back your tragedy.[1]

Hammond advises Maria to keep the piece "till more liberal maxims of government . . . take place in the important empire of the theatre."

"That a man of excellent understanding, of the most distinguished talents, the idol of the public; with as much fame as his most ardent wishes can aspire to, and more riches than he knows how to enjoy; should descend to such contemptible arts, with no nobler a view than that of robbing the Dramatic Muse, to whom he owes that fame and those riches, of her little share of the reward, is a truth almost too improbable to be believed."[2]

But he cannot refuse a compliment to Garrick's acting:

"[He] deserves, in his profession, all the praise we can bestow: he has thrown new lights on the science of action, and has, perhaps, reached the summit of theatrical perfection. . . . It is possible he may be excelled, though that he may be equalled is rather to be wished than expected, whenever (if that time ever comes) his retiring shall leave the field open to that emulation which both his merit and his management have contributed to extinguish. I repeat, that, as an actor, the publick have scarce more to wish than to see him equalled."[3]

Mrs. Brooke herself, without recanting opinions about the discouragement of new talent, praised Garrick's acting and expressed a wish that "the dramatic Muse may again raise her head; and new Shakespeares, new Sophocleses, new Garricks, arise, under the auspices of a manager who has sufficient genius to be above envy, and sufficient liberality of mind to be incapable of avarice."[4]

[1] I, 39; II, 21–28.
[2] II, 32–33.
[3] II, 34–35.
[4] II, 36, footnote. Garrick was charged with avarice in the anonymous novel, *The Devil Upon Crutches in England; or, Night Scenes in London,* 4th ed., 1759, pp. 42–46. The devil Asmodeus exhibits the vices of London to Eugenio, an Oxford student. At Drury Lane Eugenio is impressed with the brilliant audience: "But certainly Mr. *Garrick* must appear in one of his best Characters, To-night, to draw such a Company together. *Hamlet, Lear,* or *Mackbeth,* I would venture a Wager. Then you would certainly lose, answered his Companion. To-night is to be performed the most barefaced baudry Farce . . . that ever disgraced the Stage; in which the Manager, who has caused it to be revived, is to perform the principal Part. The Play, Sir, is called *The Chances,* written by the witty and wicked Duke of *Buckingham.* . . . What can we think of the Manager? said *Eugenio,* surely he must have played his *Lears* and *Hamlets* to empty Houses, and is obliged to have resource to these extraordinary Proceedings, to pay his Expences. . . . *Asmodeus* smiling answered, . . . In one Word, Friend, let the Resolutions of Men be as good and as strong as they will, it is an Hundred to one, but the *sacred* Lust

The task of reviewing this disagreeable passage in *The Monthly Review* was assigned, as we know now, by the editor, Ralph Griffiths, to no less a person than its victim—Garrick himself.[1] Under the cloak of anonymity the retired actor and manager could refute Mrs. Brooke's charges, and the entire review provides a fascinating insight into Garrick's self-esteem and the resentment accumulated from many similar attacks throughout his career. The book, he declares, is "an heterogeneous mass, compounded of novel and libel":

The aspersions . . . unjustly cast on our old friend ROSCIUS, demand our particular attention. The public owe him too many obligations, and we owe too much to the public, not to endeavour to remove the obloquy with which this lady has loaded him, in his late capacity of manager. . . . It is not because Mr. Garrick is the best actor in the world, but because we think him a worthy man too, that we take the pains to inquire into the grounds of the charge brought against him. . . . The manager is vilified, and his character blackened. . . . [The author retails] the dull and hackneyed jest of the awful monarch of the theatre giving haughty audience to a levee of hungry poets—a jest which has been imitated from *Smollet* [*sic*], which, by the way, he was afterward very sorry for.

In answer to the author's attack, Garrick records the gratitude of authors whose plays have reached production as "the strongest and most unanimous testimony to his zeal and integrity as a man, and to his almost unerring abilities as a manager. To his conduct they, in a great measure, ascribe the success of their pieces." Quoting from a number of laudatory prefaces, which were beyond doubt immediately at hand on the shelves of his admirable library at Hampton, he cites chapter and verse in his praise.

We cannot avoid one more remark on this subject, which is, that the reflection on Mr. Garrick's character is as malignant with respect to the time, as injurious with regard to the circumstance. Nothing can be more ungenerous than to attack a man, after he has quitted the field, and has retired, not only crowned with the laurel of genius, as Mrs. Brooke herself allows, but with the palm of virtue also, and what is infinitely precious to an heart of sensibility, with the good wishes, and warm esteem of an admiring public.

In worse taste, because it shows no regard for the dictum *de mortuis nil nisi bonum,* a rancorous attack appeared after Garrick's death, in a

---

of Gold will break through and destroy them—though the Ways to the Temple of *Plutus* are thorny and rugged, yet how many disregard Danger and Difficulty, and boldly pierce to its inmost Recesses.—But are not these Adventurers, said the Student, sometimes obliged to leave their Conscience and Honour behind them?—And a good Riddance too, replied the Infernal, for Men who are resolved to be rich, cannot have greater Clogs upon them."

[1] LVII (1777), 141–145. See B. C. Nangle, *The Monthly Review, First Series, 1749–1789,* Oxford, 1934, p. 67, no. 533.

section entitled "Garrick's Farewell," in the Sternean popular novel, *The Adventures of a Hackney Coach* (1781). The coach as narrator summarizes the ambiguous attitude towards the old man at the close of his brilliant career.

An uncommon demand for coaches this evening, by the enthusiastic admirers of dramatic excellence, who were hurrying to Drury-lane theatre, to see that great luminary of theatric genius, Mr. Garrick, take his farewel of an admiring and polished audience, who for thirty years shewed him the highest mark of their favor, drew me to the house of a distinguished gentleman in the republic of letters; he was accompanied by his wife and daughter.

A taciturnity, the companion of men of severe study, deprived me of this gentleman's observations on the occasion while he was going, but he made me ample amends on his return.

"Well, my dear," says his wife, "what do you think about the little man's departure?" "I am sorry for his departure, as an actor, but must confess myself highly pleased at his leaving the literary chair, in which he reviewed dramatic composition so disingenuously.—I would not be the primary cause of as many heart-achs as he has occasioned, to purchase the universe.—He was a wonderful actor! the mirror of our immortal Shakespeare—in whom we saw the life and soul of his matchless muse: divest him of this—what is he? Is he an honest man?—yes—simply so.—Where are his good actions? do they consist in cruel oppression, and sordid avarice? fie on them! they are rank weeds!—do they consist in patronizing flatterers, the weathercocks of indigence?

"Call me the children of affliction, from the cave of obscurity: see what a croud lay their sufferings at his door! Observe that pensive genius, wrapt in the gloom of pining anguish:—the years of captivity crowded on him so fast, that his abilities perished almost unnoticed, in the wreck of oppression before this mock monarch quit his mimick kingdom. What is his name? L——; see his Ranger, Benedict, Iago, Pierre, Wolsey, and Richard: —where lies the superiority?—criticism is puzzled to find it out. Did he use him cruelly? So tyrannically, that when he found him treading close on his heels in the public favor, he engaged him at a great salary for a number of years at his theatre, and exhibited him in the cyphers of the stage; such as the Prince in Romeo and Juliet, when himself played Romeo. In this manner did he exercise his monarchical tyranny, till he reduced him in public estimation to the applause of a scene shifter.— Hundreds can authenticate my assertion; it is not built upon the base of retaliation, for I know him not—thank Heaven.

"Is this the object of universal admiration!—Observe that literary being with the manuscript—what says he? That he gave him a comedy, highly approved by his ingenious friends, which he kept till the opening of the ensuing season, and then returned it, with a compliment to the author on his abilities, and his judicious advice to amend and correct it: at the same time he stript it of its most brilliant thoughts, and tortured the poor man's ears, next season, with the plagiary in a piece from his own manufactory at Hampton.

"What says Mossop to him? That the best critics of the age could get him to say only— *The man had some genius.*—Then where lies this man's

munificence, his honesty, and loud-boasted virtues.—Shame on the world!
—He is a gay convivial companion—that gives a varnish to his crimes:—
full master of the superficial etiquette of polished life; a member of the
first literary societies in London; and *quietly inurns* the children of his
fertile imagination, now and then, at Bath-Easton.

Tell me, ye puffing tribe, is this his liberality? ye who partook of his
bounty such a number of years, disclose the popular secret?—what, all
mute! is Lear, then, abated of all his train? His office of bribery is closed,
and the pen of dissimulation is employed for a new master. He made the
ingenious Cunningham a present of two guineas for the dedication of his
poems to him!—Excellent patron! how I envy thy liberality of soul!—the
public did not reward thee so, for thy flowers from the foot of Parnassus
—they were lavish in their praises of them—a century will show which
blooms longest"[1]

6. *Garrick's Vagary: The Shakespeare Jubilee*

MEANWHILE, during the years of Garrick's triumphs at Drury
Lane, the "Shakespeare industry" was on the rise. It became fashionable to make pious pilgrimages to Stratford-on-Avon and to sit under
Shakespeare's mulberry tree at New Place. According to tradition,
Shakespeare planted with his own hands this tree, which thrived enor-
mously until 1758, when the impious Francis Gastrell, of surly temper, peevish at disputes over assessment, retaliated by chopping down
the sacred wood.[2] There is an allusion to the tree in Richard Graves'
fine "comic romance," *The Spiritual Quixote* (1773). Geoffry Wild-
goose, the hero, having imbibed the Methodist doctrine, sets out with
his Sancho Panza, Jerry Tugwell, to convert the Midlands. At one
point their conversation turns to Stratford-on-Avon:

"Oh!" says Jerry, "I know Stratford upon Avon well enough: it's the place
where Shakespeare, the *great Jester,* was born.—Grandfather's father lived

---

[1] 3rd ed., 1781, pp. 91–96. "L——" was the actor John Lee, who died in
1781. It is possible that the author of the novel was one of his acquaintances. Lee
was vain and somewhat of a coxcomb, with a good person and voice. His Iago
was respectable, according to William Cooke, who states that Lee "wanted to be
placed in the chair of Garrick, and in attempting to reach this, he often deranged
his natural abilities" (*Memoirs of Charles Macklin,* 1804, pp. 167–168). Hugh
Kelly, in *Thespis,* 1766, speaks highly of him. All of the roles mentioned by the
novelist were played by Lee (see Genest, *Some Account of the English Stage,* Bath,
1832, VI, 167–168). Tate Wilkinson notes that Garrick was obliged to put the
law in force against Lee for breach of his articles in 1750. Having gone over to
Covent Garden, Lee was compelled by Garrick to return to Drury Lane, "where
Garrick from that day held a rod of iron over him" (*Memoirs of His Own Life,*
IV, 160).

[2] For the Shakespeare industry see Ivor Brown and George Fearon, *Amazing
Monument: A Short History of the Shakespeare Industry,* 1939. For the history of
the mulberry tree see Sir Sidney Lee, *A Life of William Shakespeare,* New York,
1927, pp. 288, 513–514; *Biographia Dramatica,* 1782, I, 404; *The Gentleman's
Magazine,* LXI (1791), 601–602.

a servant with the Jester himself; and there is a mulberry-tree growing there now, which he helped Mr. William Shakespeare to plant, when he was a boy."

"Well, Master Tugwell," (says Dr. Greville) "you may go and visit the mulberry-tree which your great grandfather helped to plant; and meet us to-morrow morning about eleven o'clock at the White-Lion; and then we will proceed together." [1]

From the wood of the ill-fated tree a local craftsman, Thomas Sharp, began to manufacture a prodigious number of mementos: goblets, boxes, standishes, and toys. When the Corporation of Stratford elected Garrick an honorary burgess in 1768, hoping to receive from him a statue of Shakespeare for their town hall, they forwarded the document in an elegant chest of mulberry wood, engraved with images of Shakespeare and the actor in the character of Lear in the storm scene. From this episode the Shakespeare Jubilee of 1769 developed. There is no need to review those three September days of torrential rains, platitudinous verse, Mr. Angelo's sodden fireworks, and James Boswell's posturings in Corsican costume.[2]

During the ceremonies Garrick recited an ode of his own composition.[3] The mulberry tree was poetically noticed in *The Jubilee*, the elaborate entertainment and pageant of characters from nineteen of Shakespeare's plays which Garrick produced at Drury Lane in October.[4] The quality of the verse may be judged from the refrain of the ode to the mulberry tree:

All shall yield to the mulberry-tree,
Bend to thee,

[1] III, 282.
[2] See Brown and Fearon, pp. 74–94; Margaret Barton, *David Garrick*, 1948, pp. 214–226; "The Jubilee in Honour of Shakespeare," *TLS*, April 18, 1929; *The London Magazine*, XXXVIII (1769), 407; *The Gentleman's Magazine*, XXXIX (1769), 446; *The Oxford Magazine*, III (1769), 103–108; "*A Letter from* James Boswell, *Esq.; on* Shakespeare's *Jubilee* at Stratford-upon-Avon," *The London Magazine*, XXXVIII, 451–454; Robert E. Hunter, *Shakespeare and Stratford-upon-Avon*, 1864, pp. 73–79.
[3] *An Ode upon Dedicating a Building and Erecting a Statue to Shakespeare at Stratford upon Avon*. By D. G., 1769. The ode was printed and reviewed in *The Gentleman's Magazine*, XXXIX, 446–447; *The Oxford Magazine*, III, 104–107; *The London Magazine*, XXXVIII, 481–484.
[4] Elizabeth P. Stein, ed., *Three Plays by David Garrick*, New York, 1926, pp. 59–111. For analysis see her *David Garrick, Dramatist*, New York, 1938, pp. 126–142, and for the production, Genest, V, 252–257. The lyrics were printed as *Songs, Chorusses, &c. Which Are Introduced in the New Entertainment of the Jubilee at the Theatre Royal in Drury-Lane*, 1769; they were reprinted by Arthur Murphy in *The Life of David Garrick, Esq.*, 1801, II, 315–325, and in excerpt by Percy Fitzgerald, *The Life of David Garrick*, 1899, p. 332.

The procession of Shakespeare's characters at the jubilee at Stratford upon Avon, 1769

> Blest mulberry;
> Matchless was he
> Who planted thee,
> And thou, like him, immortal be.

James Boswell declared the poem "very fine," but no modern is likely to concur. Garrick himself was able to regard the Jubilee with humor, for he incorporated into the text of the Drury Lane entertainment a poetical paraphrase of Sam Foote's witty definition of a jubilee:

A jubilee, as it has lately appeared, is a public invitation, urged by puffing, to go post without horses, to an obscure borough without representatives, governed by a mayor and aldermen who are no magistrates, to celebrate a great poet whose own works have made him immortal, by an ode without poetry, music without harmony, dinners without victuals, and lodgings without beds; a masquerade where half the people appeared barefaced, a horse-race up to the knees in water, fireworks extinguished as soon as they were lighted, and a gingerbread amphitheatre, which, like a house of cards, tumbled to pieces as soon as it was finished.[1]

That Garrick was somewhat suspicious about the multitude of articles which purported to be of the true mulberry is apparent in the comments of a skeptical Irishman who plays a part in *The Jubilee*.

Enter Fellow [with a box of wooden ware etc.]: Tooth pick cases, needle cases, punch ladles, Tobacco Stoppers, Ink-stands, nutmeg Graters, and all sorts of boxes, made out of the famous Mulberry tree.

Irishman: Here you Mulberry tree,—let me have some of the true Dandy, to carry back to my wife and Relations in Ireland. [*looks at the ware*]

Enter 2nd Man [with ware]: Don't buy of that fellow your honour, he never had an Inch of the Mulberry tree in his life, his Goods are made out of old Chairs and Stools and colour'd to cheat Gentlefolks with— It was I your honour bought all the true Mulberry tree, here's my Affidavit of it.

1st Man: Yes, you villain, but you sold it all two years ago, and you have purchas'd since more Mulberry trees than would serve to hang your whole Generation upon. . . .

Irishman: I'll tell you what you Mulberry Scoundrels you, if you don't clear the Yard of yourselves this minute, and let me see you out of my sight, you Thieves of the world, my Oak plant shall be about your Trinkets, and make the Mulberry Juice run down your rogue-Pates— Get away you Spalpeens you. [*beats 'em off*] [2]

The Jubilee itself was celebrated in fragmentary verses, not greatly inferior to Garrick's, in *The Correspondents* (1775):

---

[1] *The Town and Country Magazine,* I (1769), 477. There is a *jeu d'esprit* about the mulberry tree in the same issue, pp. 342–344.

[2] Pages 80–81.

Daughters of *Britannia's* isle,
    Of ev'ry age and each degree,
Leave your native plains a while,
    And haste to *Shakespeare's* Jubilee.

O gather ev'ry beauteous flow'r,
    And roses fair with laurels twine,
And rob each fragrant myrtle bow'r,
    To deck your poet's hallow'd shrine.

And let no gentle voice be mute
    In the full chorus of his praise,
And let the sweetly sounding lute
    Your soft harmonious concert raise.

But first, arrang'd in decent throng,
    Repose on *Avon's* verdant side,
(How oft to hear the poet's song
    Has *Avon* stopp'd his crystal tide!)

Repose, and listen to my lays;
    Trembling, I seize the vocal shell,
And in *peculiar* strains of praise
    Your *Shakespeare's* merits aim to tell.

Let heroes sing his warlike pow'rs,
    Let kings his regal talents own,
Let poets, patriots, lovers _____

_____

Far diff'rent theme _____
    I sing the man, of taste refin'd,
Whom wise unerring nature made
    The judge, the friend of *woman-kind.*

O master of the female heart,
    To whom its ev'ry spring was known,
What rapt'rous joy did'st thou impart
    To those who once possess'd thine own.

How blest her lot, how envied now!
    Who clasp'd in thee a darling heir,
Or shar'd thy tender plighted vow,
    Or claim'd thy fond paternal care.

Ye virgins, pluck the freshest bays,
    Ye matrons, deck his honour'd bier,
Ye mothers, teach your sons his praise,
    Ye widows, drop the silent tear.

Now spread th' immortal volumes wide,
    And mark _____

_____

_____

No female guilt deforms the scene,
  No female plots of terror rise,
See where he shews the murth'rous Queen
  Stain'd with ambition's *manly* vice.

E'en while he acts *th' historian's* part
  He smooths unnat'ral Regan's brow,
And softens Cleopatra's art,
  And faithless Cressid's broken vow.

Nor partial fact _____

_____

_____

  Behold the lovely train appear.

With innocence, Miranda charms;
  With virgin honour, Isabel;
The filial heart Cordelia warms,
  And Portia's praise let *wisdom* tell.

Bright shines the hymenæal flame
  When Imogen's distress is past,
And vindicated Hero's fame,
  And Helen's patience crown'd at last.

Thus diff'rent states are mov'd by turns;
  E'en aged hearts for Cath'rine glow;
And when distracted Constance mourns,
  Maternal bosoms throb with woe.

But where, O Muse, can strains be found
  T' express each virtue, charm, and grace
With which benignant *Shakespeare* crown'd
  The female mind, the female face?

Let me restrain my grateful tongue,
  And the exhaustless subject quit;
Let Celia's truth remain unsung,
  And Rosalinda's sprightly wit.

More tragic scenes I now relate,
  And tears of soft compassion crave;
O pity Desdemona's fate!
  O weep on poor Ophelia's grave!

And check not yet the tender tear,
  Nor *yet* the rising grief restrain;
O'er hapless Juliet's early bier,
  Still let it flow, nor flow in vain.

When virtuous sorrow prompts the sigh,
  And swells the gen'rous feeling heart,

She adds to ev'ry glist'ning eye,
A charm beyond the reach of art.

Cetera desunt.[1]

The Jubilee is said to have cost Garrick, whom Boswell called at the time "the colourist of Shakespeare's soul," the sum of two thousand pounds, for which he was no doubt amply recompensed from the proceeds of ninety performances of *The Jubilee* at his theater during the season of 1769–1770.[2] Though the gibes at what was thought his vanity were endless, the celebration was a datum point in his Shakespearean career, outdone only by the farewell performances of 1776.

7. *Editors and Annotators*

T H E eighteenth-century editors of Shakespeare, together with literary vandals who sought to regularize or rewrite his plays, met with little of the approval awarded to David Garrick. It is perhaps curious that novelists should consider them at all. But it was an age when pure fiction was not completely divorced from the essay, and the most diverse materials were grist for the novelist's mill. So far as the editing of Shakespearean texts was concerned, Herbert Lawrence's comment in *The Life and Adventures of Common Sense* (1769) is typical:

Every One knows how strangely the Commentators upon *Shakespear* and others have blotted out Beauties, introduc'd Deformities, and restor'd the true Reading (as they call it) which the Authors never wrote, nor probably never thought of.[3]

Although in this novel Wit, the father of Common Sense, introduces Dr. Johnson himself to his family, there is little praise for the learned undertakings of the great scholar:

'This Man, says my Father, stands in the foremost Rank of all my modern Pupils for Knowledge and Learning. But I question much whether the World will do him Justice, or give him Credit for half his Deserts; for tho' he is very Candid and honest in his Declarations and Opinions, he

---

[1] Pages 175–180. The poem, significant for presenting a view of Shakespeare's female characters resembling the one now universally held, is discussed by T. R. Lounsbury, *Shakespeare as a Dramatic Artist*, New York, 1901, pp. 373–374. *The Gentleman's Magazine*, XLV (1775), 371–372, in a review of the novel, stated that the poem places Shakespeare "in a new point of view." The poem was reprinted on pp. 394–395.

[2] George Colman the Elder capitalized on the Jubilee at Covent Garden. See his amusing comedy, *Man and Wife; or, The Shakespeare Jubilee*, 1770, presented on October 7, 1769 (*The Dramatick Works of George Colman*, 1777, II, 223–294).

[3] II, 26–27.

advances them in so Cinical a Manner, and shews such Contempt of the Person whose Work he is criticising, that it carries along with it the Appearance of Envy, which must create him many Enemies'. . . . His Thoughts and Sentiments are clear and animated, and his Language is *always* Nervous and Gigantic like himself; but for this Reason I think he has not succeeded so well on familiar Subjects. . . . Of his *Shakespear,* much has been said by others, and perhaps a good deal more than is significant. I will only add, that in my Opinion, it was an unnecessary Undertaking, the original Text of that Author having been sufficiently explained away by former Editors.[1]

A similar obscurantist view at a time of active Shakespearean scholarship is professed by Madame de Forge, the well-educated heroine of thirty, in Mrs. M. Austin's excessively rare novel, *The Noble Family. In a Series of Letters* (1771). Brought up in a nunnery, she writes to Father Bouthillia de Rance. Since her letter, though shamelessly pilfered from Dryden's *Essay of Dramatic Poesy* (1668), contains not only reflections upon editors, but mirrors as well the current idolatry of Shakespeare, praise of Garrick, and the Shakespeare Jubilee, she summarizes compactly the general attitude of the novelists towards Shakespeare.

I have lately read, dear father, a new edition of the works of Shakespeare; the obsolete language is certainly modernized, and the stile is more smooth and agreeable; yet I must acknowledge I receive more pleasure from reading them in their native dress, than from all the commentators and selectors of beauties that ever corrected, endeavored to improve, or explain the production of this great man. Shakespeare was an author, who, of all modern (and, perhaps, ancient) poets, had the largest and most comprehensive soul: all the images of nature were still present to him; and he drew them happily. When he describes any thing, one more than sees it—for one feels it too. His want of a more extensive learning was no disadvantage to him, he was learned (if one may be allowed the expression) by nature, whose volumes he perused with a careful attention. Abroad he examined her works; he looked inwards, and bracing the feelings of the heart, he still found her there. The words of a good writer thus pathetically descriptive and lively, will make a deeper impression than all that an actor can insinuate—I cannot say Shakespeare is every where alike, were he so, he must indeed have been superior to the greatest of mankind.—But I will observe, that even his contemporaries, who had the advantages of him in point of learning; though their language was more correct sometimes, yet never did they give such proofs of a lively and a striking genius, never could they draw characters with such a masterly fire and boldness; his language is noble, though natural, and generally full and significant. Every alteration, (in short, in my opinion,) robs his plays of their beauties, and is only dressing them in tinsel ornaments, when their native charms are infinitely more engaging.

[1] II, 187–188.

You have doubtless read the French edition of Shakespear, though the translator has done the poet all possible justice, yet it is very far from being equal to the English.

One of the best actors on the English stage has gained great reputation, by performing some of Shakespeare's principal characters, and by the indulgence and munificence of the public, has acquired a large fortune; prompted by gratitude to his favorite poet, he was determined to celebrate his birth: an ode was composed, and several of the principal vocal and instrumental performers were engaged, a hall was erected, and the Roscius endeavored to do justice to the poet— A multitude of people were drawn together: the town was small, the weather bad, and the whole scene ended in riot and confusion.[1]

[1] I, 119–123. UP. I am not able to determine what "new edition of the works of Shakespeare," with modernized text, the lady refers to. The text was progressively modernized by the eighteenth-century editors. See R. B. McKerrow, "The Treatment of Shakespeare's Text by His Earlier Editors, 1709–1768," *Proceedings of the British Academy,* 1933, pp. 89–122. The edition could have been Edward Capell's of 1768. The French translation available to the priest was that by Antoine de La Place, *Le Théâtre Anglois,* Paris, 1746, which included translations of eleven of Shakespeare's plays. For the praise of Shakespeare in the first paragraph above, compare Dryden's *Essay of Dramatic Poesy,* 1668, ed. W. P. Ker, *Essays of John Dryden,* Oxford, 1900, I, 79–80. It is interesting to read in Henry Mackenzie's *Man of Feeling,* 1771, that Tom, a youth of poetic bent, "pawned his great-coat for an edition of Shakespeare" (chapter 33); and in *The Modern Fine Gentleman,* 1774, Miss Melmoth writes to Miss Pembroke that she is giving her a present of "the variorum edition of Shakespeare, published by Stevens [*sic*] and Johnson" (I, 38), which appeared in 1773.

CHAPTER TWO

The Plays: The Comedies

THE fortunes of Shakespeare's plays in the theaters or "on the road," the social scene in the playhouses at Drury Lane, Covent Garden, or in the provinces, when audiences assembled to see the Shakespearean roles of Garrick, James Quin, Henry Woodward, Ned Shuter, Mrs. Hannah Pritchard, Mrs. Cibber, George Anne Bellamy, Kitty Clive, Peg Woffington, Mrs. Yates, or the veriest strolling hams, were happier and more proper subjects for fictional treatment than abstract criticism of dramatic values. Most of the novelists, both the known and the almost as numerous anonymous writers, were devotees of realism. In theatrical society of all kinds, whether they were fond of picaresque adventure, burlesque humors, or the manners of folk at every level in a world that was hard-living at one extreme and supersentimental at the other, they found excellent hunting for the prototypes of their characters and for the germs of their episodes. Their tone varies, and the pictures of actors and audience that emerge from inspired and pedestrian pens range from the sublime to the lowest farce, horseplay, and hurly-burly. Not only because the human mind appears to be naturally more impressed by dramatic imitations of tragic life, but also because Shakespeare's tragedies were presented much more frequently in the eighteenth century than the comedies, the novelists reflect the tragic repertory more often than the comic. Their greatest contribution to Shakespearean criticism, indeed, lies here. Their main concern was with the great tragedies.

A revival of taste for Shakespearean comedy arose slowly during the course of the eighteenth century. As is well known, the comedies were not held in high regard during the Restoration, nor were they fully restored to favor until almost the middle of the next century. A significant aspect of the age's curious criticisms of Shakespeare was the conviction that nothing much could be said for his comedies of love. Considerable responsibility for their renewed popularity rests, perhaps, with "Shakespeare's Ladies," the Ladies of the Shakespeare Club, in the late thirties, who persuaded Rich (or Fleetwood) to present two Shakespearean performances a week.[1] The romantic movement was well on its course before audiences welcomed the delicate comedies. A brief survey of the stage histories of the comedies reveals the reasons for the paucity of comment by the novelists on this group.

The Comedy of Errors was never popular. From 1741 to the nineteenth century it was sometimes presented in altered versions. It might be seen at Covent Garden, but Garrick never revived it. *The Taming of the Shrew* was subjected to various alterations, the most notable being Garrick's three-act version, *Catharine and Petruchio,* first acted in 1754,[2] a long-lived piece, in which, however, Garrick himself did not act. With Mrs. Clive as Catharine and Harry Woodward as Petruchio, the condensation, popular as an afterpiece well into the next century, was adroit in perserving much of Shakespeare. Smollett objected to it: "We do not remember to have seen a more flagrant imposition of the kind, than the exhibition of this performance. . . . He must have great taste and infinite veneration for *Shakespear,* who thus fritters his plays into farces."[3] Shakespeare's *Taming of the Shrew* waited longer than any other of his plays for restoration to the stage; it remained unacted until the revival by Benjamin Webster in 1844.

The Two Gentlemen of Verona was virtually unknown. No post-Restoration record of production has survived before Garrick's presentation of Benjamin Victor's adaptation in 1762, which was shelved after six performances. The first recorded performance of the original play is for Covent Garden in 1784. For *Love's Labour's Lost,* there is no record until 1839.

[1] See Arthur Murphy, *The Life of David Garrick, Esq.,* 1801, II, 158–159; G. C. D. Odell, *Shakespeare from Betterton to Irving,* New York, 1920, I, 260; Allardyce Nicoll, *A History of Early Eighteenth Century Drama, 1700–1750,* Cambridge, 1925, pp. 68–69. Odell is invaluable, as are the stage histories for the separate comedies by Harold Child in the New Cambridge Shakespeare. Odell attributes to Macklin the favorable attitude towards the romantic comedies in the third and fourth decades of the eighteenth century. Emmett L. Avery believes that it was Fleetwood of Drury Lane who responded to the ladies' appeal; see his "Cibber, *King John,* and the Students of the Law," *MLN,* LIII (1938), 272–275.

[2] *Catharine and Petruchio. A Comedy,* 1756; reprinted in *The Dramatic Works of David Garrick, Esq.,* 1768, II, 165–202.

[3] *The Critical Review,* I (1756), 145–146. See also G. M. Kahrl, "The Influence of Shakespeare on Smollett," *The Parrott Presentation Volume,* ed. Hardin Craig, Princeton, 1935, pp. 399–420.

A Midsummer-Night's Dream was subjected to ruthless operatic treatments during the eighteenth century. Apparently its combination of realism, classical mythology, and fairy lore was displeasing. At any rate, its stage history is spotty. In 1755 Garrick plundered the comedy for his spectacular *The Fairies,* ten performances of which brought the house over fifteen hundred pounds. The music was by John Christopher Smith. Then in 1763 the Garrick-Colman version [1] was presented once and failed "about as completely as any play ever did on the eighteenth-century stage." [2] The only mention of the comedy in fiction appears in Thomas Amory's *Memoirs of Several Ladies of Great Britain* (1755), in which an unnamed man narrates in two letters to Mr. Hugolin Jewks the story of Marinda Bruce, later Mrs. Benlow, whom he met in the hills of Northumberland in 1739:

She had a volume of *Shakespear* in her hand, as I came softly towards her, having left my horse at a distance with my servant, and her attention was so much engaged with the extremely poetical and fine lines which *Titania* speaks in the third act of the Midsummer night's dream, that she did not see me until I was quite near her.

> Be kind and courteous to this gentleman,
> Hop in his walks, and gambol in his eyes,
> Feed him with apricocks, and dewberrys,
> With purple grapes, green figs, and mulberrys;
> The honey bags steal from the humble bees;
> And for night-tapers crop their waxen thighs,
> And light them at the fiery glow-worms eyes;
> To have my love to bed, and to arise,
> And pluck the wings from painted butterflies,
> To fan the moon-beams from his sleeping eyes.
> Nod to him elves, and do him courtesies.[3]

As the beautys of thought are joynd with those of expression, in these lines, one would think it impossible that any thing that has but the lest humanity, should be dull enough not to relish, not to be moved, nay charmed with this passage. Yet *Rymer* is the man. *Apt, clear, natural, splendid,* and *numerous* as the lines are, this *hypercritic,* in his short view

---

[1] *A Midsummer-Night's Dream. Written by Shakespeare: with Alterations and Additions, and Several New Songs. As it is Performed at the Theatre-Royal in Drury Lane,* 1763.

[2] G. W. Stone, Jr., "*A Midsummer-Night's Dream* in the Hands of Garrick and Colman," *PMLA,* LIV (1939), 467–482. Dr. Stone has studied the extant text for the 1763 version in the Folger Library. He concludes that a comparison of the Folger copy with the play as printed anonymously in 1763 "proves beyond a doubt that the printed version, the one for which Garrick has been criticised, should be fathered upon George Colman" (p. 473). Colman reworked the text and produced the play while Garrick was abroad. For the prompter's note about the reception see Dougald MacMillan, ed., *Drury Lane Calendar,* p. 100.

[3] *A Midsummer-Night's Dream,* III. i. 167–177.

of tragedy, blasphemes their visible excellence, as he does many other noble flights and matchless beautys in the incomparable *Shakespear*. In this respect, to be sure, *Rymer* deserves the highest contempt.[1]

The Merchant of Venice was known for forty years after 1701 in George Granville's adaptation, *The Jew of Venice,* with Shylock played as a low comic role. An important datum point in its history was Charles Macklin's famous revival of Shakespeare's play in 1741, with Shylock a cunning and ferocious villain.[2] Since then revivals have been pretty constant. Garrick staged it but did not act in it. In his revival of 1747, one of the earliest efforts to produce a play of Shakespeare's as it was written, Macklin was Shylock, and Mrs. Clive was Portia. It is surprising that there is no mention by the novelists of Macklin's famed interpretation of "the Jew that Shakespeare drew," for his malevolence in the role made his reputation. He played it frequently for half a century. Highly favored at both theaters, the comedy attracted King and Henderson as Shylock, as well as a succession of excellent Portias: Peg Woffington, Mrs. Pritchard, Mrs. Abington, and Sarah Kemble (later Mrs. Siddons). The only reference to Shylock in fiction, apparently, occurs in the excessively rare autobiographical *Alwyn; or, The Gentleman Comedian* (1780), by Thomas Holcroft. This lively novel, inscribed to R. B. Sheridan, was characterized by *The Monthly Review* as "a vulgar narrative of uninteresting incidents in the peregrinations of a strolling player."[3] The story, in fact, gives a valuable picture of the life of the strollers. A jealous old actor, T. Stentor, describes the infelicities of "our booby of a manager," all of which are Shakespearean:

I can never mention this last fool without recollecting some of his absurdities. He wants to have Shylock, the Jew, in the Merchant of Venice, spoken in the dialect of Duke's-place, and swears *Shakspur* intended it so. He is seldom perfect enough in his part to be able to repeat two lines together, without the assistance of the prompter; and, when he blunders, always lays the blame upon others. You know what a happy knack he has at mutilating. The other night, instead of *angels,* he wanted *anglers* to visit his *Cordelia's* dreams. He told the duke in Othello, a messenger was arrived from the *gallows,* instead of the *gallies*. Again, instead of saying to Posthumus, in Cymbeline, "Thou basest thing avoid; hence from my sight"

[1] Pages 3–4. Actually, there is no analysis of these lines in Rymer's *Short View of Tragedy.*

[2] Odell, *Shakespeare from Betterton to Irving,* II, 25–27, discusses the text in Bell's *Shakespeare,* 2nd ed., 1774, II, 153–229, on the basis that it may be Macklin's edition and concludes that it well represents the eighteenth-century *Merchant of Venice.* See also F. T. Wood, "*The Merchant of Venice* in the Eighteenth Century," *English Studies,* XV (1933), 209–218.

[3] LXIII (1780), 233.

— He came spluttering on, and bawled out, *"Thou bass string, hence in a fright."* He seemed in an excellent mood in this play, for discovering his talent; for, when he should have said to Cloten, "Attend you here, the door of our stern daughter?" he asked, *"Attend you here, our daughter's stern door?"*—But this to you, who are so well acquainted with the booby, is superfluous.[1]

Much Ado about Nothing, after Davenant's mutilation, *The Law Against Lovers* (1662), was abandoned, was staged at Lincoln's Inn Fields by John Rich in 1721, but the revival did not restore the comedy to the stage. James Miller's rewriting, *The Universal Passion,* was produced at Drury Lane in 1737. The original play was presented at Covent Garden in 1737, and again in 1746, with Mrs. Pritchard as Beatrice, Lacy Ryan as Benedick, and the competent low comedian John Hippisley as Dogberry. Garrick's revival two years later at Drury Lane re-established the play, which was acted sixteen times that season and might be seen at least once each season (except 1764–1765) until Garrick retired in 1776.[2] Until 1756 Mrs. Pritchard acted Beatrice to his Benedick, which became one of his finest roles, and surely one of his favorites, for at the great Shakespeare pageant at Drury Lane which followed the Jubilee of 1769 he personally contributed Benedick. During his farewell to the stage he acted the part for the last time on May 9, 1776. His other notable Beatrices were Miss Macklin and Miss Jane Pope. Among his Dogberrys were Mr. Taswell, Richard Yates, and William Parsons. Covent Garden offered no competition in this comedy, for it was not revived there until 1774. After Garrick's retirement the Beatrices were more famous than the Benedicks.

There is an oblique glance at the comedy in "Sir" John Hill's *Letters from the Inspector to a Lady, with Genuine Answers* (1752). The writer has seen the lady at breakfast at Ranelagh. Charmed with her, he asks to be received, but she has no notion of deserting her present benefactor. Upon his importuning her, she begs that if he see her at the play, he will not speak to her. He replies:

[1] II, 70–71. Bodleian. For an analysis of *Alwyn* see E. A. Baker, *The History of the English Novel,* V (1934), 240; Virgil R. Stallbaumer, "Thomas Holcroft as a Novelist," *ELH,* XV (1948), 196–201; Elbridge Colby, ed., *The Life of Thomas Holcroft, Written by Himself, Continued . . . by William Hazlitt,* 1925, I, 219–227. Colby observes, in "A Supplement on Strollers," *PMLA,* XXXIX (1924), 647, that strolling actors acquired so many different parts that it was easy for them to get mixed up in their lines: "Small wonder that occasionally the members of the craft inserted into their common conversation a strange jargon of quotation."

[2] The text, described by Odell, II, 27, as "admirable acting copy" and "a reverent treatment," is in Bell's *Shakespeare,* 2nd ed., 1774, II, 231–300.

Heaven and earth! Where did you learn this art of charming? Learn it? but the expression is a contradiction. What you have and no other ever had, must be innate: would it could be communicated!

Did not you see how all the people in the box next to us, gave up the play to attend to you; they were in the right. Shakespear and Garrick were below regard in the comparison; and the spirit of Benedict and humour of Beatrice combined, came short of your pleasantry. This was conversation, and only you are formed for it; this is the pleasure of rational creatures: and shall I refuse it to myself?—in honest truth I can't.[1]

Another allusion occurs in George Alexander Stevens' *History of Tom Fool* (1760). At Bath, Batilda, daughter of a rich scrivener, as eager for a husband as Beatrice was uneager, observes: "About a Month ago, I was with Lady *Beltre,* in the Stage Box, at *Garrick's,* to see him do *Benedict;*—I *doat* upon his *Benedict.*"[2] Beatrice's sharp tongue induced Arthur Young to imitate her wit combats with Benedick in *Julia Benson; or, The Sufferings of Innocence. In a Series of Letters* (1775). As the result of her father's effort to marry her to Mr. Slingsby, Julia, a paragon of beauty and learning, has come to detest men. Three other men, however, fall in love with her, among them Lord William W——, to whom Sir Philip Egerton describes her behavior at a masquerade at Almack's.

Tuesday night, in a lounging humour, I went to a masquerade which our club gave at Almack's. . . . I was only in a domino, that I might have the better opportunity of observing the folly of others, and be the less bespattered by it myself. After a few turns, I remarked a masque prettily fancied, that assumed the character of Beatrice, she attracted not my notice alone, for I observed a croud of Benedicks in pursuit of her. There was something in her air, manner, and carriage, that were remarkably striking; more grace and elegance could not be displayed under an assumed character. Her appearance, at a small distance, made me sollicitous to know if she attracted her attendants merely by the fineness of her figure, or whether her wit could keep up a character, which seemed to have put Shakespear's to the stretch. I approached within hearing, and while she was in full play upon three or four of her followers. I do not remember a scene, that ever pleased me more. Nothing could exceed the sprightliness of her wit. A masque in the character of Benedick, thought it incumbent on him to attack every Beatrice in the room; and, being a likely little fellow, he had made his part good with two or three of them; when, espying this stranger, he opened his trenches, but they were levelled in a moment. The figure of one was ridiculous; the dulness of another; the mistakes of a third; the ignorance of a fourth; and with so superior a strain of humour, and such flashes of wit, that none could be found that would have stood the encounter for a moment, had the shame been visible in their countenance.

"Beatrice, (said I) you over-act your part, you forget that Benedick

[1] Page 12. BM. The title-page of the British Museum copy contains a manuscript note that the "Lady" was a "courtezan known by the name of Diamond."
[2] I, 213. BM.

THE PLAYS: THE COMEDIES

alone is not only to appear—but Benedick the married man, and where's the he that will be Benedick of such a termagant!"

"Oh, your sex is so full of wit, that Benedicks will rise up like mushrooms."

"True; and exist as long; you cut them off with such keen wit, you toss them up with such high flavoured sauce that they—"

"I find them most unpalatable morsels, but I suppose you, Signior—"

"Aye, to be sure!—you have a mind to see what a ragoo you can make of my brains; but stop that merciless tongue;—the arbour scene is past; you mar your character, if you turn not out a most kind nymph."

"And you are the sighing simpleton that wants to experience my kindness.—"

"Beatrice must at last give with one hand a kind jest, and with the other a still kinder heart."

"Benedicks that deserve a jest are easily found, but where's he that merits the heart of Beatrice?"

"Keep it yourself, Beatrice, but remember it is a perishable commodity."

"Should I lay it by in Lavender to be brought out like a faded ribbon, and worn as a favour at the marriage of the antiquated Benedick! Truly it would then be good enough for him."

"I will have nothing to say to hearts, that are manufactured like a face. But here is a dance, Beatrice, if you have as much grace in your motion, as wit in your conversation, I protest you shall be my Beatrice."

"I accept the challenge, but shall never claim the reward."

She danced like an angel.[1]

As You Like It was the first of the romantic comedies to be staged after the Restoration, when Charles Johnson's rewriting, an insipid mélange called *Love in a Forest,* was presented at Drury Lane in 1723. A version closer to Shakespeare's was produced there in 1740,[2] with Quin as Jaques, Mrs. Pritchard as Rosalind, Mrs. Clive as Celia, Thomas Chapman as Touchstone, and William Milward as Orlando. Performances thereafter were common during the rest of the century. Under Garrick's management, although he never acted in it, the comedy missed only six seasons at Drury Lane. From 1741 to 1750 the rival Rosalinds were Mrs. Pritchard and Peg Woffington, the latter of whom played the part until 1757. After her, all the leading actresses tried Rosalind: Miss Macklin, Mrs. Dancer, Miss Younge, Mrs. Barry, Mrs. Yates, and Mrs. Robinson. Of the Celias, Mrs. Clive's was the best: she acted it until 1763. Spranger Barry, Luke Sparks, James Aickin, and John Henderson were well known as Jaques. Of the

[1] Dublin, 1784, I, 92–94. After such a pleasant passage one regrets that the plotting of a villainess leads to the destruction of Julia and her husband, Lord William W——. For a discussion of the novel see J. R. Foster, *History of the Pre-Romantic Novel in England,* New York, 1949, pp. 157–158.

[2] The text is in Bell's *Shakespeare,* 2nd ed., 1774, I, 133–207. Odell, II, 21–23, describes it as "undoubtedly about the version that was employed throughout the Garrick period, and is the only form in which we can find that version."

Touchstones, the finest was Thomas King, with Harry Woodward, Ned Shuter, Richard Yates, John Quick, and John Palmer also appearing in that philosophical motley.

Jaques' meditation on the seven ages of man has been so frequently quoted and alluded to in literature that it is not surprising to find a novelist making use of a passage of such universal appeal. During the course of William Toldervy's rare *History of Two Orphans* (1756), the orphans, Tom Heartley and George Richmond, view a strolling performance of *Cato,* during which a shameless mountebank's indulgence in an indecent exhibition arouses the spectators to riot. To calm them, the actor Duroy throws himself into a proper attitude and recites, "with infinite humour" and to great applause, the "All the world's a stage" speech.[1] Pleased with this reception, Duroy attempts to recite a passage from *Julius Caesar.*

'No, no, my good Sir, cried one of the plebeians, none of your *Julys* or *Seasons,* but give us the speech that you spoke e'er while: for I am sure you can't make a better for the heart of you.' [2]

Duroy willingly complies.

Writers in an era devoted to burlesque, travesty, parody, and mock-heroics, did not refrain from parodying well-known Shakespearean passages, as occasional parodies of Hamlet's "To be or not to be" soliloquy testify.[3] In 1773 Richard Graves included a parody of "All the world's a stage" in *The Spiritual Quixote.* The hero, Geoffry Wild-goose, meets Mr. Rouvell, who is about to apply to the bishop for orders in the church. Rouvell shows Geoffry a "ludicrous composition" given him by a friend when he first talked of taking the gown. Geoffry disapproves of this buffoonery, "but, as he would hear all the objections Rouvell had to the profession he was now engaging in, Rouvell read the following parody on Shakespear's celebrated description of the seven stages of human life."

"As this parody is put into the mouth of a fop," (says Rouvell) "it is rather a compliment to the Clergy, than any reflection upon them.

—Sir Plume,
—Religion's all a farce;
And Parsons are but men, like you or me.
They have their foibles, and their fopperies:

[1] II, 161. Bodleian.
[2] II, 166.
[3] See *The Scots Magazine,* VI (1744), 176; *The General Advertiser,* September 24, 1747; Richmond P. Bond, *English Burlesque Poetry, 1700–1750,* Cambridge, Mass., 1932, pp. 421, 439.

And one sees amongst them sundry characters.
To mention only seven.—And first,—the Curate,
Humming and *hawing* to his drowsy herd.—
And then the Pedagogue, with formal wig,
His night-gown and his cane; ruling, like Turk,
All in his dusty school.—Then the smart Priest,
Writing extempore (forsooth!) a sonnet
Quaint, to his Mistress' shoe-string.—Then the Vicar,
Full of fees custom'ry, with his burying gloves;
Jealous of his rights, and apt to quarrel;
Claiming his paltry penny-farthing tithes,
E'en at the Lawyer's price.—Then the Rector,
In sleek surcingle with good tithe-pig stuff'd;
With eyes up-swoln, and shining double-chin;
Full of wise nods and orthodox distinctions:
And so he gains respect.—Proceed we next
Unto the old Incumbent at his gate,
With silken scull-cap tied beneath his chin;
His banyan, with silver clasp, wrapt round
His shrinking paunch; and his fam'd, thund'ring voice,
Now whistling like the wind, his audience sleeps
And snores to th' lulling sound.—Best scene of all,
With which I close this reverend description,
Is your Welsh Parson, with his *noble living,*
Sans shoes, *sans* hose, *sans* breeches, *sans* every thing."

Geoffry hopes that Rouvell will henceforth refuse to indulge in such levities, which are more "characteristic of the Clergy of the last age." [1]

The comedy received pleasanter consideration from the author of *The Correspondents* (1775), in a letter on the theatrical taste of one of his (?her) characters, whose admiration for Shakespeare arises from the sound reflection of human life to be found in his works. The character, who is nameless, writes:

My theatrical taste . . . has undergone several revolutions. When I was about half my present age, I admired nothing but pantomime, and the agile tricks of Harlequin, though, at the same time, prompted by childish vanity, I affected to despise them. Soon after that period, my taste really altered. *Romeo* and *Alexander* became my heroes. I was pleased with alternate sighing and storming; and the most extravagant scenes of the most extravagant tragedies appeared to me the noblest and most delightful. Weaned from this folly, I took a strong fancy to *musical* pieces, on account of performing them on my own instruments; then ascending, as I thought, a full scale in the climax of refinement, nothing would please me but the *Italian* opera: this, however, was a short-liv'd passion; and was succeeded by a fondness of the historical drama, and those plays that are usually classed under the title of *genteel comedy;* and these, with a

[1] III, 196–198. Travesties of Shakespeare manifest popular interest in the poet. See R. F. Sharp, "Travesties of Shakespeare's Plays," *The Library,* 4th series, I (1920), 1–20. They were not, however, common before the end of the eighteenth century.

few exceptions, continue my favourite entertainments. Regarding the theatre as the mirror of human life, I prefer such pieces as reflect in my notions the most agreeable representations of it: from hence arises my admiration of Shakespeare. I have no time to consider how he strains probability in his *events,* my attention is wholly engaged by the innumerable strokes of truth and nature in his *characters.* How amiable, how interesting are some of these! I am not going to write a panegyric on this immortal bard, but I shall for ever love and honour his memory, because he is the only poet (that I know of) who has delineated to perfection the character of a *female friend.* Now, if to this some *manly* critic should *wittily* object, that Shakespeare created many *imaginary beings,* I will readily allow *that,* because it does not affect this character. We *wonder* at the fairies, at the witches, at Ariel, at Caliban, but do we wonder at *Celia?* No, she is generally passed over with inattention, which alone is sufficient to prove that the character is not uncommon, at least not *unnatural:* but it often proves more, it proves a slowness in discovering the beauties of this matchless writer.

Pray, pray, now, good lords of the creation, let us do justice to my favourite heroine: while David and Jonathan, Pylades and Orestes, Damon and Pythias, are so triumphantly held up on your side, let us at least erect one standard of friendship on our own, and inscribe it with the names of Celia and Rosalind.

Consider then, in the first place, the *situation* of these two friends.

"Rosalind, the old Duke's daughter is not banished with her father . . . for . . . the new Duke's daughter, her cousin, so loves her, (being from their cradles bred together) that she would have followed her exile, or have died to stay behind her."

Observe, too, that *Rosalind* carried the palm of beauty; she was "tall and fair," her cousin "low and browner." "Thou art a fool;" says the Duke to Celia, "she robs thee of thy name; and thou wilt shew more bright, and seem more virtuous when she is gone."

And now let us recollect the conduct and sentiments of this magnanimous girl.

Cel. I pray thee, Rosalind, sweet my coz, be merry.

Ros. Dear Celia, I shew more mirth than I am mistress of; and would you I were yet merrier? Unless you can teach me how to forget a banished father, you must not expect me to remember any extraordinary pleasure.

Cel. Herein I see thou lov'st me not with the full weight that I love thee. If my uncle, thy banished father, had banished *my* father, so *thou* hadst been still with me, I could have taught my love to take thy father for mine.

Ros. Well, I will forget the condition of my own estate to rejoice in yours.

Cel. You know my father hath no child but I, nor none is like to have: and truly, when he dies, thou shalt be his heir; for what he hath taken away from thy father *per* force, I will render thee again in affection; by mine honour, I will;—and when I break that oath let me turn monster: therefore, my sweet Rose, my dear Rose, be merry.

I pass over her generous intercession with the duke, when his anger breaks out against Rosalind, and shall trouble you only with what immediately follows the sentence of her banishment.

Cel.　　O, my poor Rosalind! where wilt thou go?
　　　　I charge thee, be not thou more griev'd than I am.

Ros.　　I have more cause.

Cel.　　Thou hast not, Cousin;
　　　　Pr'ythee be cheerful; know'st thou not the Duke
　　　　Hath banish'd *me,* his daughter?

Ros.　　That he hath not.

Cel.　　No! hath not? Rosalind lacks then the love
　　　　Which teacheth *me* that thou and I are one.
　　　　Shall we be sunder'd? shall we part, sweet girl?
　　　　No;—let my father seek another heir.
　　　　Therefore, devise with me how we may fly,
　　　　Whither to go, and what to bear with us;
　　　　And do not seek to take your change upon you,
　　　　To bear your griefs yourself and leave me out:
　　　　For, *by this heaven,* now at our sorrows pale,
　　　　Say what thou canst, I'll go along with thee.

The heroic generosity of this resolution, and the fortitude, constancy, and cheerfulness that attended the execution of it, made a very early impression on my mind; and from the time I remember any thing, I remember a particular esteem for the character of Celia. You will pardon, therefore, my prolixity in speaking of it, and will allow too, I fancy, that the play in general abounds with moral, poetical, dramatic, and sentimental beauties.

I have now had the honour to acquaint you at large with my theatrical opinions; for you gather from what I have said concerning this comedy, that I prefer the flow of conversation to the pomp of declamation; and am more interested, more affected, and consequently better pleased by one Shakespearian touch of nature and sentiment, than by all the most florid and impassioned speeches of other tragedians. I have *laughed* at the sorrows of *Theodosius* and the ravings of *Roxana:*—I have *wept* at the generosity of old *Adam,* and the tenderness of *Miranda.*[1]

Twelfth Night was shelved from the early years of the Restoration till 1741, when it was revived at Drury Lane with Macklin as Malvolio, Woodward as Sir Andrew, Mrs. Pritchard as Viola, and Mrs. Clive as Olivia.[2] Since then it has persistently held the stage. From 1741 to 1841 it was only twice out of the repertory at Drury Lane for as much

[1] Pages 25–33. For the relationship of this novel to George, the first Lord Lyttelton, and Mrs. Apphia Peach, subsequently his daughter-in-law, see Rose M. Davis, "The Correspondents," *PMLA,* LI (1936), 207–221. The novel was reviewed for *The Monthly Review,* LII (1775), 430–436, by George Colman the Elder, who found "much novelty as well as elegance in the fair Commentator's criticism on the 'As you like it' of Shakespeare." The review quoted the passage above.

[2] The acting text is in Bell's *Shakespeare,* 2nd ed., 1774, V, 293–359.

as eight years at a time. Garrick did not himself act in it, but Peg Woffington and Mrs. Yates became famous as Viola, and Yates was a notable Malvolio from 1751 to 1775. It is curious that the novelists
failed to refer to it, aside from Matt Bramble's comment that his sister
Tabitha, once she is in London, "does nothing but smile, like Malvolio
in the play." [1]

Of *The Merry Wives of Windsor* there is notice, thanks to the excellence of James Quin as the fat knight in this comedy and in both
parts of *Henry IV*. Shakespeare's play [2] was restored to the stage in
1704 after the failure of John Dennis' vulgarized version, *The Comical Gallant; or, The Amours of Sir John Falstaffe,* at Drury Lane in
1702. Quin played Falstaff long and well after the revival at Lincoln's
Inn Fields in 1720, and the comedy has ever since had a continuous
stage history. Garrick never appeared in it; but Woodward as Slender,
Mrs. Pritchard as Mistress Ford, and Dennis Delane, James Love, Edward Berry, and Ned Shuter as Falstaff were rewarded with public
favor.

An early reference to *The Merry Wives* appeared in a novel in
1744, *The Travels and Adventures of Mademoiselle de Richelieu.* The
heroine, disguised as the Chevalier de Radpont, asks a friend to describe English theaters and plays. His reply with regard to the abun-
dant immorality of the repertory follows the main headings of Jeremy
Collier's notorious attack of 1698. Some plays are "full of Wit, but
many of them so smutty, that the Play Houses in *London* may be justly
said to be the Sources of Corruption." Women learn how to carry on
successful intrigues. Youth is familiarized with vice: "they swear,
game, drink, debauch Women, and fight." All that can be said of the
man of honor is *"that he is more genteelly wicked than the rest."* Particularly objectionable are the characterizations of clergymen in English plays:

Some of the Clergy . . . have severely lashed Play-house Poets, especially
those of modern Date, for their lewd Scenes, their Prophaneness and
Blasphemy, and are provoked to the last Degree by their bringing *Chris-
tian* Priests upon the Stage, only to expose them; as Parson *Bull* in the
Relapse; Roger in the *Scornful Lady; Say-Grace, Cuff-Cusheon,* and the
Spanish Fryar &c. nor does *Shakespear* himself escape them, whom they

[1] *The Expedition of Humphry Clinker,* 1771, Shakespeare Head edition, Oxford,
1925, I, 151. See G. M. Kahrl, "The Influence of Shakespeare on Smollett"; he
notes that Smollett's "Shakespearean allusions are . . . clearly drawn from the
stage" (p. 408).

[2] The acting text is in Bell's *Shakespeare,* 2nd ed., 1774, III, 71–138. Odell, II,
27, notes that "it is impossible, apparently, to give it without most of its Shakespearian matter."

James Quin in the character of Sir John Falstaff

reprove for bringing *Sir Hugh Evans* upon the Stage, in the *merry Wives of Windsor,* and making him a silly chattering Priest. . . . The whole Clergy . . . do not aim at abolishing all Theatrical Entertainments, but the Reforming them.[1]

Tobias Smollett's early acerbity towards James Quin is well-known to readers of *Peregrine Pickle* (1751). Angry with the actor because he had not patronized *The Regicide,* Smollett satirized Quin here more extensively than any other individual, including Garrick himself, who had refused the tragedy. In the second edition of the novel in 1758 the attack on Garrick was deleted, but rancor against Quin remained, and remains still, in the fifty-first and the ninety-fourth chapters, where a Knight of Malta and a College of Authors criticize in detail the old-fashioned tragic acting of Quin, which was outmoded by the new school of naturalism approved by Garrick. The rant and the "expressive" gestures of Quin are ridiculed to the point of caricature. He tears a passion to rags. He blusters and loses all decorum. However bad he may be in tragedy, the Knight concedes Quin's excellence in comedy: "Yet this man, in spite of all these absurdities, is an admirable Falstaff . . . and would be equal to many humorous situations in low comedy, which his pride will not allow him to undertake." [2]

Unquestionably Quin's best role was Falstaff, for which nature and his own gourmandizing had provided him with the requisite embonpoint. Even after his retirement to Bath in 1751, he twice appeared as Falstaff for Lacy Ryan's benefit, each time to overwhelming applause. In figure, repute, and humor, indeed, Quin was the incarnation of Falstaff. The mellowing of Smollett's attitude towards him as the result of illness and age is apparent in his last novel, *The Expedition of Humphry Clinker* (1771). Even the genial misanthrope Matthew Bramble's eyes sparkle whenever Quin makes his appearance. Jerry Melford, Bramble's nephew, writes to his friend Sir Watkin Phillips of Oxford, describing the actor's wit, good breeding, and companionship:

T'other day, the conversation turning upon Shakespeare, I could not help saying, with some emotion, that I would give an hundred guineas to see Mr. Quin act the part of Falstaff; upon which, turning to me with a smile, "And I would give a thousand, young gentleman, (said he), that I could gratify your longing." My uncle and he are perfectly agreed in their

[1] III, 301–305.

[2] 1st ed., II, 20–21 (Shakespeare Head edition, II, 122). For a full account of Smollett's opinions of Quin, together with a collation of the first and second editions of *Peregrine Pickle,* see Howard S. Buck, *A Study in Smollett, Chiefly "Peregrine Pickle,"* New Haven, 1925, chapter 3, "Smollett's Quarrels," pp. 65–81; Lewis M. Knapp, *Tobias Smollett: Doctor of Men and Letters,* Princeton, 1949, pp. 53–55, 125.

estimate of life; which, Quin says, would stink in his nostrils, if he did not steep it in claret.[1]

Further allusion to Quin's fame occurs in the picaresque *Memoirs of an Oxford Scholar. Written by Himself* (1756). Having left Oxford, the scholar visits London:

The first Place we proceeded to was the Playhouse in *Covent-Garden,* to see inimitable *Falstaff,* in *The Merry Wives of Windsor,* perform'd by Mr. QUIN. I was indeed entertained.[2]

When the play was done, he and an acquaintance adjourned to a tavern in the neighborhood, where in merry Falstaffian mood, they drank a bowl of arrack punch, and "as happy as young Fellows could be, . . . circulated the Glass 'till near One."

For the realistic or problem comedies, *Troilus and Cressida, All's Well That Ends Well,* and *Measure for Measure,* the novelists showed neither fondness nor aversion. They disregarded them. There is no reason why they should have been concerned with the first, for its theatrical history has always been meager. Although the record of performances of *All's Well* is brief and undistinguished, the comedy was known to Garrick's age after its first recorded performance at Goodman's Fields in 1741. From then on, it was occasionally acted at both houses with a succession of Helenas: Mrs. Woffington, Mrs. Pritchard (who was also a distinguished Countess), Miss Macklin, Mrs. Palmer, and Mrs. Mattocks. John Palmer and Lee Lewes acted Bertram, and Harry Woodward liked to act Parolles, which he played for thirty years at a time when the romantic story was made subservient to the comic roles of the braggart poltroon and the Clown, Lavatch.

Measure for Measure was familiar in Garrick's time after the low-comic roles, removed in Gildon's version (1700), were restored at Drury Lane in 1738. Susannah Cibber as Isabella and Quin as the Duke were seen fairly often at both theaters, and the play remained active in the repertory, though Garrick himself never played in it. Other Isabellas were Mrs. Woffington, Mrs. Pritchard, Miss Bellamy, and Mrs. Yates. Early in her career Mrs. Siddons played the role at Bath in 1779. Harry Woodward was a competent Lucio. After the desertion of the role of the heroine by Mrs. Cibber in 1758, the comedy was apparently less favored, for there are no further records until 1770. At any rate, the novelists ignored this group of comedies in their discussions of the theater.

[1] Shakespeare Head edition, I, 71–72.
[2] Page 51.

CHAPTER THREE

The Plays: The Histories

SHAKESPEARE'S history plays were more congenial to eighteenth-century taste than the romantic and realistic comedies. Consequently, the novelists paid them more attention. Writers were particularly impressed with that lurid favorite *Richard III* and with both parts of *Henry IV,* all of which were constantly performed at the patent houses.

From 1742 to 1776, *Richard III* missed only four seasons at Drury Lane and five at Covent Garden. Audiences have always had a weakness for the monstrous Machiavellian Crookback. Throughout the Garrick period, and indeed even after Samuel Phelps temporarily restored Shakespeare's text in 1845, the play was presented in the famous version of Colley Cibber (1700), which held the stage longer than any other alteration of Shakespeare.[1] From his intimate knowledge of the stage as actor and manager, Cibber provided an effective acting text. He cut out Clarence, Margaret, Hastings, and Edward IV, and greatly reduced and altered the dialogue, not hesitating to interpolate a number of lines from *Richard II, 2 Henry IV, Henry V,* and the first and third parts of *Henry VI.* He pointed up the role of the villainous protagonist by omitting scenes in which Richard did not appear. In the final act the eleven ghosts who bid Richard to despair at Bosworth Field were cut to four: Henry VI, the little princes, and Anne. These changes and curtailments reduced a very long play to

[1] For details of the stage history of *Richard III* and Cibber's "improvement" see Alice I. Perry Wood, *The Stage History of Shakespeare's King Richard the Third,* New York, 1909; Hazelton Spencer, *Shakespeare Improved,* Cambridge, Mass., 1927, pp. 335–338, and his edition of *The Tragedy of King Richard the Third,* Boston, 1933, pp. 237–239; Arthur Colby Sprague, "A New Scene in Colley Cibber's *Richard III,*" *MLN,* XLII (1927), 29–32.

presentable dimensions: the length of the adaptation is about half that
of the original play. Since Cibber was notoriously no tragedian, and
despite his later laureateship no poet, the dialogue is mangled and absurd. But the play was a wonderful vehicle for the talents of James
Quin and David Garrick.

Smollett, it is true, abused Quin for his ranting style. The French
Chevalier who discusses the English stage with Peregrine Pickle observes:

Yet one of your gracioso's I cannot admire, in all the characters he assumes.
His utterance is a continual sing song, like the chanting of vespers, and
his action resembles that of heaving ballast into the hold of a ship. In
his outward deportment, he seems to have confounded the ideas of dignity
and insolence of mien, acts the crafty, cool, designing Crookback, as a
loud, shallow, blustering Hector.[1]

Garrick made his first stage appearance at Ipswich in 1741, and on
October 19 of that year he chose Richard for his London debut at
Goodman's Fields.[2] For thirty-five years the stage history of this play
was brilliant, and no other actor could match Garrick's imitation of
the stupendous passions of Richard, his *vivida vis,* his deviltry. Novelists at once recognized the young actor's genius. We are fortunate in
having two fictional letters dated in February, 1742, a few months
after the debut, in *Memoirs of Sir Charles Goodville and His Family:
In a Series of Letters to a Friend* (1753). They provide an interesting
review of an early performance. Letter XVIII concludes:

I must suspend . . . having an Engagement, to that of *Richard* the Third,
at the Theatre, in *Goodman's Fields;* where a famous, new, Performer, appears in that Character; who, when I have seen, as I know you are fond
of Theatrical Entertainments, I'll give you my Sentiments.[3]

Letter XXVI continues:

I shall take this Occasion, of discharging the Promise, I made some Time
since, in giving you an Account, of the new Performer, whose Name is
not yet known, at the Theatre in *Goodman's-Fields.* His Stature is low, I
think, too low, for the Stage, his Voice, round, full, and manly; but not
strong in Proportion; for, toward the fifth Act, he grew hoarse—though,
possibly, that might be occasioned by Inexperience, and not judging the
proper Modulation. He has vast Spirit in his Manner, and Countenance,
which is greatly assisted, by a quick, piercing Eye, of which he often makes

[1] Chapter 51 (Shakespeare Head edition, II, 121).
[2] For an account of the reception of Garrick's novelties in interpreting the role
see Percy Fitzgerald, *David Garrick,* 1899, pp. 37–43. *The Daily Post* for October 20 reported that the "reception was the most extraordinary and great that was
ever known on such an occasion."
[3] I, 186.

a judicious Use, as indeed, of every other Feature, which seem all calculated, for the expressing, not only the Impetuosity and Fire, of *Richard's* Nature, but the Artifice, and Hypocrisy of it. His Action is less constrained, and awkward, than could be imagined, from a new Performer; and to me, it was manifest, great Time, and Care had been taken, to digest every minute Action, and Accent; though great Force of Genius, shewed itself, through the Whole; and, if he is not hereafter prevented, by Negligence, Vanity, or a too precise pedantic Use, of throwing in *Art,* where *Nature* alone, should do the Business, he promises, in my Opinion, to be a distinguished Player— Thus much, at present, for his Talents in *Richard*— since when, I saw him in a pert, flashy Character, in a Play, wrote upon the Novel, called *Pamela;* in which, he discharged himself, with great Life, and Smartness, suitable to what, I conceive, the Author intended; and, in the last Act, read a Letter, wrote by a *French* Valet de Chambre, little acquainted with *English,* in the drollest Manner, and with as high Marks of Comic Humour, as I ever saw executed.

If this Tragi-Comic Genius continues his Progress, the Town will be much obliged to the Proprietor of that Theatre, for so judiciously distinguishing, and giving Encouragement, to such promising Merit; which probably, by the *ipse dixit* Directors of the other Theatres, would have been haughtily overlooked, or coldly neglected; to say nothing of the Obstacles he might have met, from the jealous Apprehensions of the Performers. These are Difficulties, he has not been obliged to encounter; but I am informed, has received all the open candid Treatment, and Assistance, he wished or wanted, and his Merit demands.

I purpose making as frequent Visits, to that Theatre, as my Affairs will admit; when this new Adventurer, sets off either the Tragic, or Comic Drama.

The enthusiastic author concludes his letter with a defense of the stage against the virulence of its critics, who are "either Jacobites, Nonjurors, or precise, inveterate Schismaticks." [1]

There was dissent from this glowing appreciation, for in the first edition of *Peregrine Pickle* the Knight of Malta berates Garrick's Richard no less than Quin's:

I shall never cease to wonder that the English, who are certainly a sensible and discerning people should be so much infatuated, as to applaud and caress with the most extravagant approbation, not to say adoration and regard, one or two gracioso's, who, I will be bold to say, would scarce be able to earn their bread by their talents, on any other theatre under the sun. I have seen one of these, in the celebrated part of Richard the third, which, I believe, is not a character of ridicule sollicit and triumph in the laugh of the audience, during the best part of a scene in which the author has represented that prince as an object of abhorrence. [2]

Actually, this criticism "testifies to the relishing diablery of Garrick's Richard." [2] Happily, Smelfungus' view of the great actor sweetened

---

[1] I, 259–263.
[2] II, 138. See Buck, *A Study in Smollett,* pp. 89–90, 154–155.
[3] Buck, p. 90.

with time.[1] In *The Adventures of Sir Launcelot Greaves* (1760–1761), when the hero ascends the balcony of the townhouse to oppose the brutal Mr. Anthony Darnel in a contest for a seat in Parliament, "there was just such a humming and clapping of hands as you may have heard when the celebrated Garrick comes upon the stage in King Lear, or King Richard, or any other top character." [2]

Smollett's pamphleteering foe, the eccentric John Shebbeare, in *The Marriage Act. A Novel* (1754), could think of no more fitting illustration of astonishment than "Mr. *Garrick* in King *Richard,* when he wakes from his Dream," [3] that is, in the third scene of the last act of Cibber's version, when the ghosts of four of his victims appear to him.

Especially impressive to novelists were the scenes in the fourth act in which the young princes, Edward and Richard, are torn from their mother and murdered by Tyrel at their uncle's command. Cibber originally presented the murder *coram populo,* prolonging the children's terror by their waking before the entry of the murderers.[4] However, in later editions that scene was omitted and the murder was reported only, as in Shakespeare, though more briefly. The scene was perhaps too strong for souls of sensibility. It was powerful enough as revised. The heroine of the anonymous *Almira. Being the History of a Young Lady of Good Birth and Fortune, but More Distinguished Merit* (1762) went with her friend Cleone one evening to see "the tragedy of Richard the third;—the part of Richard was performed by Mr. Garrick; and was so admirably acted, that it gave pain, not pleasure, to them both. . . . Almira most sincerely felt, and wept, the horrid uncle's cruelty." [5]

A fuller account of the melodrama appears in *The History of Miss Pittborough. In a Series of Letters. By a Lady* (1767). The heroine's family are dead. Her education has been austere, but at the opening of the story she is in town, as she says, "fruzeed and furbelowed up to my very ears":

And where do you think I am going, butterfly-like, to unfold my gaudy wings—but to the play.—The old house is first complimented with my appearance—in compliment you must understand though, to my own judgment; for where else could I find a Garrick?

---

[1] See Lewis M. Knapp, "Smollett and Garrick," *University of Colorado Studies,* II, no. 4 (1945), 233–243, and his *Tobias Smollett,* pp. 53–57, 125–126, 196–202.

[2] Shakespeare Head edition, p. 35.

[3] I, 40. The second edition was entitled *Matrimony,* 1755.

[4] For a reprinting of the scene from the first edition see Sprague, "A New Scene in Colley Cibber's *Richard III,*" pp. 29–30.

[5] I, 17. LC.

My expectations are at their last gasp—I die with impatience.

She is captivated by Colonel Dingley, who in his turn writes to Mr. Brooksbank:

> Some hours leisure, and the appearance of Garrick in the character of Richard, induced me to engage a solitary place in the side-box, that I might indulge myself, free from all that impertinent interruption a party is too liable to produce.

Having seen Miss Pittborough, he thinks her appearance intelligent:

> With what delight did I observe the genuine operation of that variety of passions the performance naturally excited in her breast, unwarped by prejudice, and uncontaminated by affectation.
> Now her lovely bosom was agitated with horror; and now her tenderness was evinced by a falling tear—now disgust was also predominant—and now astonishment, for a moment, held even feeling in suspense:—the villainies, the artifices of Richard, occasioned many beautiful changes in her aspect.—Lady Anne's weakness and credulity had her highest disapprobation.—She even condemned the author for drawing so unnatural a character; and humorously insisted upon it "that no age could have furnished him with an original!"—But when that pathetic scene was exhibited, where the wretched queen is torn from her helpless, her beloved children; the soft sorrow of her heart became irrestrainable: in short,—she in that instant compleated her conquest; and your friend yielded himself a willing captive. . . .
> It is a queer sort of an affair though—to have one's head and heart thus turned topsy turvy.—I that was wont with Benedict to behold one lady fair—yet find myself well, &c. &c.—that could find charms in retirement and self-contemplation—to be so miserably reduced to the whiners' class, as not to be capable of one idea.[1]

Less lively are the moral reflections upon the theater made by the almost complete victim of sensibility, the exclamatory heroine of *Ermina; or, The Fair Recluse. In a Series of Letters. By a Lady* (1772). After the death of her mother (so many of the sentimental heroines are motherless!) Ermina is destitute of fortune and dependent on the bounty of her beloved Sir William Pembroke's sister. Living in town, she writes to her friend Julia Devereux that she cannot enjoy her contemplations in London, "this dissipated noisy place":

> I have been several times to the play, and must own, that, of all the amusements of the town, I look upon it the most rational; especially if the representation is the production of the tragic muse. With what lively sensations do I join in lamenting the wretched fate of poor Monimia; or in weeping at the untimely end of the two innocent princes in Richard the Third! How surprising is it to me to see the number of beings who frequent the theatre, without any other view but that of seeing, and being

[1] I, 9, 19–24. BM.

seen; and can behold, unmoved, the most melting and pathetic scene! How incapable are such minds of receiving intellectual improvements! To me the chief end of theatrical amusements seems calculated to inspire the mind with a love of virtue (if possessed of a sufficient share of sensibility to receive the impressions); but to those who can, without any emotion, be witness to the misery of others, they serve only as an incitement to vice. There are but a few pieces from which may not be drawn an instructive moral, if the spectators have judgment enough to point out the beauties, and cast aside the imperfections. But where am I rambling?[1]

Of Thomas Sheridan's performance of Richard, in which, according to Francis Gentleman, he displayed "much judgment" but required "more harmony, with less stiffness," [2] there is a side-glance in George Wollaston's picaresque *Life and History of a Pilgrim* (1753). Sheridan competed with Garrick also as Hamlet. At a native play in Cadiz the hero describes the improvisation of the bewhiskered buffoon, which, "let it be never so stupid is attended with an universal Shout, and a Pair of Spectacles, with Glasses of the Size of our Penny Loaves properly clapped on his Nose on a sudden, have occasioned a longer and louder Clap than ever Mr. *Sheridan* got by acting the Part of *Hamlet* or *Richard the Third;* though I know no one that can excel him in that or any other Character he appears in." [3]

It was Garrick's performance, however, which inspired the hero of the vivacious *Adventures of a Valet, Written by Himself* (1752) to theatrical ambitions, and possibly the emotions of this young aspirant resembled Garrick's at the time of his debut. In this interesting and very rare novel the lad, deserted by his parents, finds employment in the custom house when he is fifteen or sixteen. He and his friends attend many places of diversion. His companions favored the entertainments at Sadler's Wells and the equilibrist at the Haymarket. But his taste was more classical:

For my own Part, the Playhouses were always my Favourites: I attended them at least four times a-week, and very often was not absent one Evening in a Fortnight.

Envious of the players, he craves a career on the stage:

Mr *Garrick,* just at this period of time, appeared on the Stage at *Goodman's Fields:* The first Notice of a Person of Merit in the theatrical Way, could not fail to hurry me to be an Admirer of it, I neglected *Drury-lane* and *Covent-Garden* to attend at this obscure Theatre every time he appeared; and from what I constantly observed of his Manner in performing, I convinced myself I had discovered that what I had been used to admire

[1] II, 7–8. BM.
[2] *The Dramatic Censor,* I (1770), 12.
[3] Dublin, p. 502.

David Garrick in the character of Richard the Third

as the Effect of hard Study, was, in its utmost Perfection, nothing but mere Nature; that Mr. Garrick, while he commanded his loudest Thunders of Applause, did no more than just what the Person he represented would have done in real Life on the same Occasion, and that, consequently, every Man who had a Heart to feel, a Genius to comprehend, and Organs to execute what should be dictated by these Means, might do just the same.

Full of this Persuasion, I went the next Morning to Mr. *Rich,* and begged it as the greatest Favour that he would give me leave to play King *Richard* for him: He desired me to give him a Specimen of my Abilities in the first Speech; but I told him honestly I had not got it by Heart; He stared upon me with a Mixture of Astonishment and Contempt, and asked me what Reason I had to suppose myself qualified for so difficult an Undertaking? To this, upon my answering that I had minded sufficiently what Playing was; and that if he would give me leave to come among them upon the Stage, I would engage for the executing my Part as well as the rest of them; he ordered the Footman to bring his Hat and Sword, told me he was engaged that Morning to the Practice of a new Entertainment, and so ended our Acquaintance.

Rich's abruptness nettles the hero, who plays over some part of King Richard, his favorite character, every day in his bedroom. There an actor acquaintance, after watching him perform, is enraptured with his powers and invites him to act a part at his benefit. The hero readily accepts:

The only Objection I made was, that my favourite Character was this of *Richard;* he immediately agreed to alter his Play, and I gave him an absolute Promise of performing in it.

He is given a month to master the role:

The Bills were printed for it, with Notice that a Gentleman who had never appeared on any Stage before was to play the Part, and the Expectation of the whole Town was raised to a very considerable Pitch, by the Account given of my Abilities by People who had, and who pretended to have seen me rehearse it, while so faithful a Secrecy was kept on my own Part, as well as on that of the Person who was to be profited by it, that not the most intimate Acquaintance I had in the World had the least Idea that it was me they were to see upon the Stage.

Perhaps it is absolutely impossible for any Man, who has not been instructed by some Person accustomed to the Stage, to perform a capital Character successfully in his first Attempt before an impartial Audience; but the Case with me was otherwise: the Audience at a Benefit is always a favourable one, the Player had said a vast deal in my Favour, and begged every body to support and encourage me with Applause, wherever he had delivered his Tickets; so that two Thirds of the Audience were prejudiced in my Favour: If we add to this the infinite Pains I had taken for the last Month to qualify myself for the Undertaking, and the Length of time I had been practising the Part, with some other favourable Circumstances that will be mentioned in their Place, it will not be esteemed a Miracle that I did not totally fail in it.

The Panics I suffered during the Interval between the first Music and the drawing up of the Curtain, are not to be expressed. . . . At length the Moment came for my appearing. I threw myself boldly on the Stage, and was received by a Clap that gave me Time to breathe and look about me, before I entered on my Speech. The Friends of the Person whose Benefit Night it was, had set this on foot the Moment I entered on the Stage; but I had no sooner advanced three or four Steps on it than my Face was known to a dozen or more of my Intimates, who never missed any thing new at the Theatres, and who had been seeking me through the whole Town to be one of their Party.

These Gentlemen, and their Adherents, formed a very considerable Part of what Authors and Players call the Town; they revived the Applause with tenfold Ardour the Moment they discovered me, and continued it so long as to persuade a very considerable Part of the unbiassed among the Audience, that I must be some very extraordinary Person.

People who are willing to be pleased easily find Occasions of being so; almost every Sentence I pronounced produced a Clap during the first Act, and hardly a Speech during the whole Play that had not the same Tokens of Applause at its Conclusion.

It was not only the Audience in general that was deceived by this Applause, the true Source of which they did not know; the People behind the Scenes were led into the same Sentiments by it; they received me every time I came off the Stage with the highest Encomiums, and told me there was nothing I might not, if I pleased, arrive at as a Performer.

The Manager of *Drury-lane* Playhouse, at this time, had many Reasons against appearing in Person at the House; but he had so many Emissaries to give him an Account of every thing that passed there, that I had not got through the Second Act before I received a very polite Message from him requesting to see me the next Morning at his Lodgings: In the fourth Act I was put in mind of this Invitation; and before the End of the fifth, a fresh one was delivered to me, desiring our Meeting might be that Night after the Play was over.

The Prudence that inspired the Resolution of sending this second Message to me was not without its Foundation: My Success in the third Act was such, that he suspected the Master of the other House might otherwise have been before-hand with him. I did indeed receive a Hint of that kind behind the Scenes, tempered with the Conditions, if I had no immediate Connection with the House I was then at; but had Mr. *Rich* known that the Person he sent to, was the same he had so lately refused, or had Mr. *Fleetwood* known my resentment of that Treatment, there would have been a short End of the Hopes and Fears on the two different Sides about it.

I finished my Part, as it appeared to my own Judgment, more to the Satisfaction of the Audience than I deserved.

The young hopeful enters Mr. Fleetwood's apartment:

The Manager, after many Compliments, desired me, as the Gout had prevented him from being able to see me on the Stage, to repeat any Speech that I liked, in private to him: the Applause that I was at this time flushed with, gave me one of the first Requisites to a player, great Spirit, by the Assistance of which I pronounced one of the principal Speeches in that Part better, I am confident, than I had done any of it on the Stage.

Fleetwood is so impressed that, with the aid of a supper and "Bergundy," he signs a contract with the boy for five hundred pounds a season. The boy spends the summer studying several new parts recommended by his new master. When the playhouses had been open about three weeks,

there appeared Notice in the Bills, that on such a Day would be acted the Tragedy of *Hamlet,* the Part of *Hamlet* to be performed by the Gentleman who had acted King *Richard* the Season before with so great Applause. . . . Whether it was, as I first suspected, that I owed my Success in *Richard* to the Partiality of the Audience, more than to any Merit of my own; or whether like the Button maker, who some years ago succeeded in *Othello,* and failed in every thing else, I had so deeply and indelibly impressed my Sense of the Character and Manners of my first Part, *Richard,* on my Mind, that I could never divest myself of them afterwards, and consequently was *Richard* in every thing; whether the World had been talked into too great an Opinion of me; or to what other Cause it was owing I know not, but certain it is, that my Success in *Hamlet* was by no means equal to that in *Richard.* The Manager, who was not easily to be persuaded out of his own way of thinking, forced me a second Night upon those who had been dissatisfied with the first, and the Consequence was, that I was received with that noisy Disapprobation which People seem to have very well understood what the Person who is the Subject, feels from it, when they gave it the Name of Damnation.

Those who had been the warmest in their Applause began now to cool upon me; but not one of them so much as my late dear Friend the Manager: He sent me a Letter in a Day or two, however, desiring me to rally all my Force against a certain Day at about a Week's Distance, on which he would give me another trial in *Richard.* Anxiety and Vexation added tenfold Strength to my Endeavors of excelling in this great Task, but they failed. I was hissed off the Stage by the unanimous Voice of the Audience, and every body declared there was no Expectation of my ever making a first-rate Player: Most gave it as their Opinion that I should never be able to make anything of it at all.

The valet's theatrical episode has an unhappy ending. Like many another frustrated artist he falls into the paths of evil. He takes up company with the lower class of players, "till by continual Conversation with them I had fallen into all their Vices. I found myself, instead of the sober, decent, innocent, and consequently happy Youth I remembered at the Custom-house, a Sot, an Atheist, and a prostituted Rake," thanks especially to an avaricious figure-dancer, "whose Views upon my plentiful Salary had made her imagine it no undesirable or unprofitable Thing to be under my Protection." He lands in jail for debt, but is rescued by an unknown benefactor.[1]

Richard III was in every way a splendid medium for the strolling

[1] I, 7–35. BM. Ralph Griffiths in *The Monthly Review,* VI (1752), 110–123, praised this novel for its lively style and quoted liberally.

players, and since novelists wrote many of their happiest chapters about the Shakespearean repertory of these "robustious fellows," a description of their habits of life will aid in understanding the peculiar and delightful accounts of their productions. It has not, perhaps, been sufficiently recognized that strollers played an important part in the history of the drama and theater.[1] It has been observed that they were "the most conservative of all players," for they continued the Elizabethan traditions long after the established theaters, new types of drama, and new styles in acting had dimmed them.[2] Garrick himself commented on their conservatism in a letter to his brother Peter, after he had seen a traveling company at Lichfield:

I don't know how it is, but, the Strollers are a hundred years behind hand— we in Town are Endeavouring to bring the Sock & Buskin down to Nature, but *they* still keep to their Strutting, Bouncing, and Mouthing, that with whiskers on, they put me in mind of ye late Czar of Russia who was both an Ideot & a Madman.[3]

In another letter he expressed his aversion for provincial actors:

I dread a Stroler, they contract such insufferable affectation that they disgust me— I never could account for the Country Actors being so very wide of ye mark.[4]

The rugged life of these volatile barnstormers, their want of security and social standing, their trickery, their vagabondage, and their ragtail existence subjected them to continuous gibes; but (except to mayors and justices) they were welcome when they appeared in the country, because they brought old and new plays to the remotest hamlets. And their ranks contributed many a notable player to the London theaters: Macklin, Quin, Garrick, Foote, Henderson, Holcroft, Mrs. Siddons, Mrs. Inchbald, and many others learned their art in the nur-

---

[1] See Alwin Thaler, "Strolling Players and Provincial Drama after Shakespeare," in *Shakespeare and Democracy,* Knoxville, 1941, pp. 185–223, reprinted with additions from *PMLA,* XXXVII (1922), 243–280, the best general account of eighteenth-century strollers; Elbridge Colby, "A Supplement on Strollers," *PMLA,* XXXIX (1924), 642–654; F. T. Wood, "Strolling Actors in the Eighteenth Century," *Englische Studien,* LXVI (1931), 16–53; Herschel Baker, "Strolling Actors in Eighteenth-Century England," *University of Texas Studies in English,* 1941, pp. 100–120; Sybil Rosenfeld, *Strolling Players and Drama in the Provinces, 1660– 1765,* Cambridge, 1939.

[2] Thaler, pp. 185–186.

[3] Manuscript at Harvard University, quoted by G. W. Stone, Jr., "The God of His Idolatry," *J. Q. Adams Memorial Volume,* Washington, D. C., 1948, p. 120.

[4] Letter to Thomas Love, a Drury Lane actor, dated March 3, 1765, in Paris; printed for the first time by C. R. Williams, "David Garrick: Actor-Manager," *The Cornhill Magazine,* new series, LXVI (1929), 294.

Strolling players rehearsing in a barn

sery of the strolling companies, of which there were two kinds, the greater and the lesser. The greater were composed of established players from London who were licensed for the road. The lesser (and more colorful), as in Ben Jonson's day, still traveled with their pumps full of gravel, after a blind jade and a hamper, and stalked upon boards and barrel-heads to an old cracked trumpet.[1] These actors were "unlicensed vagabonds in the eyes of the law, subject to prosecution, impressment, and hunger, and many of them without hope of ever making their bow" on city stages.[2] Members of these itinerant companies, branded in 1572 as "rogues, vagabonds, and sturdy beggars," fascinated the novelists with their eccentric and comic humors, which were often beyond the law. The contempt of professional critics is well exemplified in the description of the poorer strollers by James Ralph in *The Taste of the Town* (1731):

To form a true Idea of these itinerant Players and undeceive that Part of the World which may expect mighty Matters from them, I am inclinable to think that most of them were got under Hedges, born in Barns, and brought up in Houses of Correction: nor should they ever dare to shew their faces in any Place but a wooden Booth.

For undoubtedly, the buskin'd Ragamuffins that Thespis first carted about the World, must have been Demi-gods and Heroes, to these Pedlars in Poetry and Gipsies of the Stage.

It is impossible to enter into a regular Criticism either on their Action or Drama; to get thro' such Heaps of Rubbish would require more than Herculean Help: the Confusion of such Nonsensical Scenes cannot be view'd forwards, they will not bear the least Light; nor have they the Merit even of a Witch's Prayer to be read backwards.[3]

Since the manager of a strolling company appears persistently in the novelists' accounts, it should be noted that, although the ancient sharing system still persisted, he was an economic czar with almost absolute command, as is clear in the memoirs of Thomas Holcroft, himself a stroller:

A company of traveling comedians then is a small kingdom, of which the manager is the monarch. Their code of laws seems to have existed with few material variations since the days of Shakespeare, who is, with great reason, the god of their idolatry. The person who is rich enough to furnish a wardrobe and scenes, commences manager, and has his privileges accordingly: if there are twenty persons in the company, for instance, the manager included, the receipts of the house, after all incidental expenses are deducted, are divided into four and twenty shares, four of which are called *dead* shares, and taken by the manager as payment for the use of

[1] See Ben Jonson, *Poetaster*, III. i.
[2] Thaler, pp. 188–189.
[3] Page 223.

his dresses and scenes; to these is added the share to which he is entitled as a performer.[1]

About the witchery of the strollers Holcroft is lyrical, sharing the common mood of other novelists, for these straggling parties exerted a peculiar magic which could metamorphose an old stable, outhouse, maltkiln, or slaughterhouse so wonderfully that it became now a palace, now a peasant's cottage.

What is still more wonderful, they carry all their spectators along with them. . . . These necromancers . . . give a kingdom for a kiss, for they are exceedingly amorous; yet, no sooner do their sorceries cease, though but the moment before they were revelling and banquetting with Marc Antony, . . . it is a safe wager of a pound to a penny that half of them go supperless to bed. A set of poor, but pleasant rogues! miserable, but merry wags! that weep without sorrow, stab without anger, die without dread, and laugh, sing, and dance, to inspire mirth in others, while surrounded themselves with wretchedness. A thing still more remarkable in these enchanters is, that they completely effect their purpose, and make those, who delight in observing the wonderful effects of their art, laugh or cry, condemn or admire, love or hate, just as they please; subjugating the heart with every various passion: more especially when they pronounce the charms and incantations of a certain sorcerer, called Shakespeare.[2]

The repertory of traveling companies was mainly classical. The records specifically prove their fondness for Dryden, Lee, Otway, Southerne, Congreve, Wycherley, Vanbrugh, Farquhar, Rowe, Addison, Steele, Cibber, Lillo, and Fielding, as well as the popular revivals of Elizabethan and Jacobean plays.[3] In this respect the non-fictional record is confirmed by the fictional, just as the novelists' vigorous scenes of fires, uproars, riots, drunkenness, and amours in barns are corroborated by non-narrative sources. Beyond a doubt Shakespeare was the strollers' idol, and fiction was seldom stranger than truth in depicting these shabby regiments of parti-colored impersonators of Richard III, Julius Caesar, Romeo, Lear, Hamlet, Macbeth, Falstaff, or Cymbeline.

> In shabby state they strut, and tatter'd robe;
> The scene a blanket, and a barn the globe.
> No high conceits their mod'rate wishes raise,
> Content with humble profit, humble praise.
> Let dowdies simper, and let bumpkins stare,

[1] *Alwyn*, I, 130–132; the passage was incorporated in *The Life of Thomas Holcroft Written by Himself*, ed. Elbridge Colby, 1925, I, 153–155. For an interesting account of the avarice of the managers see [John Potter], *The History of the Adventures of Arthur O'Bradley*, 1769, I, 129–131.

[2] *The Life of Thomas Holcroft*, I, 181–182.

[3] See Thaler, p. 215. The novelists devote many pages to country productions of plays by these dramatists.

The strolling pageant hero treads in air:
Pleas'd for his hour he to mankind gives law,
And snores the next out on a truss of straw.[1]

The poverty of the "barn-treading princesses and bestabled monarchs"[2] is well described by Robert Lewis, in his excellent *Adventures
of a Rake. In the Character of a Public Orator* (1759). The hero joins
a company whose success is so bad that they do not take in above thirty
shillings a night. The manager does not expect to be able to keep them
together for more than another week.

Some of them had pawned their Shirts, others their Stockings and Waistcoats, and others even their Coats, such bad Luck had they at the Place,
and the greatest Part of them were so Poverty-struck, that they could not
afford to buy a Dinner—in short, this Itinerant Company of Comedians,
were yet in a worse Condition than those described by the inimitable
Scarron, and only equalled, by those who have performed the last and
present summer at *Chatham.*

Visiting the barn where *The Fair Penitent* is in rehearsal, the youth
discovers a "Couple of miserable Objects, scrawling out their Bills."
They are actors.

Shortly after, entered the Rest of the Company, but sure such a despicable
Groupe of Figures were never before seen. Some of them had no Shirts
on, some no Waistcoats, some no Hats; and others, with Shirts which
formerly had been white. . . . Others with great Holes in their Stockings,
large enough to put one's Hand in, and others, more neat, whose Stockings
were one continued Darn. Their Cloaths in short were either ragged, or
wretchedly mended from Top to Toe: And yet did they dress in Taste,
wore laced Hats, Bag Wigs, ruffled Shirts, and all their Cloaths were cut
a la Mode de Paris, though something Worse for Wear, and entitled to
that expressive Term *Shabby Genteel.* The Actresses indeed, who soon
after entered *the House,* made quite a different Appearance; for they were
dressed very neat, very clean, and very genteel. In particular, one of them
who seemed to be about one and twenty years of Age, and who was excessive pretty, was dressed quite grand. The Reason of their appearing
thus different from the Actors, I could not at first comprehend, but which
I soon after learnt, and which is more proper to be guessed at than told.[3]

[1] Charles Churchill, *The Apology,* ed. R. W. Lowe, 1891, p. 69. In addition to
novels about strollers mentioned in the course of this study, the following contain
material about drama in the provinces: *The Adventures of Mr. Loveill,* 1750; *Virtue Triumphant, and Pride Abased; In the Humorous History of Dickey Gotham
and Doll Clod. By R. P. Biographer,* 1753.
[2] See *Memoirs of Harriot and Charlotte Meanwell, Written by Themselves,*
1757, p. 102. The copy of this novel in my possession seems to be unique.
[3] I, 141–147. Bodleian. The level of society which furnished actresses to the
strollers is apparent in the title of a short novel of about 1750: *The Secret History
of Betty Ireland, Who Was Trepann'd into Marriage at the Age of Fourteen, and
Debauch'd by Beau M—te at Fifteen . . . the Vile Injury She Did to the Gentleman, and Her Turning Prostitute. Her Amour with the Lord M—d . . . Her*

The efforts of the poor strollers to produce brave effects in costuming and scenery are noted in *Female Friendship; or, The Innocent Sufferer. A Moral Novel* (1770), in which a *valet de chambre* describes his early life. On his way to London, he crawls exhausted into a barn.

I was almost struck dumb with astonishment at what I saw before me. In a corner, on one poor melancholy truss of straw, sat a tall, genteelish woman; in her hands she held an old scarlet coat, lin'd with blue, of which she had turn'd the inside out; and was industriously trimming it with white paper, in so artful a manner, as ingenuously to conceal all the patches, which, from length of time, and constant wear, were pretty numerous: near her was another woman, more inclining to the girl, in whose face were strongly pictur'd all the marks of vanity: nor did her actions contradict my suspicions; as she was washing about ten or a dozen pieces of old lace, and some other ornamental trifles, which she afterwards very curiously joined together, and made into a most superb head-dress, splendidly decorated with bits of Bristol-stone, glass, &c. *thinly scattered to make up a shew,* to please that part of the world, whose sole ambition is to feast their sight. Not far from them, on the ground, lay two men, fast lock'd in slumber, forgetting misery; and, at a little distance, sat a man and a woman; who, by the dismal light of a single solitary candle, were reading out of the same book: at the other end of the barn, was a person very busy in ornamenting and fitting up, what I afterwards found to be the stage, where kings and princes march'd in all theatric pomp; though at that time it was occupied on one side, by a cow and a calf, and on the other, by two jackasses. Notwithstanding I had seen so very little of the world, I did not want to be informed, that these were a company of strolling comedians, preparing for their next night's task.[1]

Despite the rigors of a hard-bitten existence, the life of the road recruited the veriest tyros from the ranks of young London spouters, who were more often blinded with hayseed than with stardust. In Thomas Mozeen's satire on the strollers, *Young Scarron* (1752), we read that "the Strolling-Companies are commonly a Set of undutiful 'Prentices, idle Artificers, and Boys run mad with reading what they don't understand."[2] And when Ned Shuter, the inimitable comedian who appears as a character in the popular topical novel, *The Adventures of a Hackney Coach* (1781), inquires of a stroller whether there has been "any thing of the *vis comica*" in his last campaign, his friend replies:

Incest with Her Own Son, by Whom She Conceiv'd and Brought Forth a Daughter . . . *Her Amours with a Jew* . . . *Her Taking a House and Intriguing with Smutty-Will* . . . *Her Associating with Shoplifters* . . . *Her Turning Strolling-Player,* etc. BM.
[1] I, 211–213. For other descriptions of strollers' theaters, scenery, properties, and costumes see [John Shebbeare], *Lydia; or, Filial Piety,* 1755, IV, 62–64; *Du Plessis's Memoirs; or, Variety of Adventures. . . . With a Description of Some Strolling-Players,* Dublin, 1757, II, 80–90; Mrs. Anne Skinn, *The Old Maid; or, The History of Miss Ravensworth,* 1770, II, 188–190.
[2] Page 63.

"Yes, faith, a great deal; . . . some silly youths left their solid pudding in London, for the empty praise of a barn; mad to put the buskin'd muse out of countenance; we had a whining Romeo—a ranting Richard, a very dolorific Hamlet, and a Lear of sixteen years old.—Bob gave the cries of London, after the manner of the inimitable Mr. Shuter, they were so well pleased they would have given any price to have heard the original.—We shared pretty well, with tolerable benefits." [1]

The first novel of importance about strollers, *Young Scarron,* which Mozeen dedicated to the managers of both theaters, presents much information about the personnel and conduct of a traveling company, as well as about their Shakespearean offerings, which include *Richard III.* Will Glitter, an old stroller, and Young Scarron form a company to act in the north during the summer. They engage Miss Whiffle, a good actress, and a good intriguer who will attract all the young fellows for ten miles round the country. They hire also Mr. Spruce, "whose Performance was just good enough to make him of Consequence in a strolling Company." He is little better, however, than a conceited woman-chaser. Others are Mr. Grammar, a tolerable comedian when sober, but a "Sort of Monster in Morals"; and Mr. Humphry Loveplay, a stage-struck youth who wants to act *"Mr.* Barry's *Way entirely; for I am tall and thin, you see, and should make no Figure in Mr.* Quin's *or Mr.* Garrick's *Parts."* Mrs. Meggot, a useful actress, "perfect in almost all the common Plays," introduces Scarron to Mr. Valentine, aged twenty-three, who advances money for the expedition. Frustrated in love, Valentine joins the company as "Ramble."

We learn of the difficulties in fitting the actors with clothes and parts. Since the dress for Richard III is the handsomest, all the men crave to be cast in that role. The women are, of course, even more difficult to please. When Mrs. Broad covets all the clean dresses, Miss Whiffle sneeringly remarks that Mrs. Broad has more clothes than ability:

But, continu'd she, *you may put up what you please for me; I shall distinguish myself enough by my Performance.* With these Words she swam out of the Room, and gave Mrs. *Broad* an Opportunity of venting her Rage, which she threw all at Miss *Whiffle's* Character. She reckon'd up all the Amours she had had, how many Gallants she had jilted, and young Fellows taken in: In short, recounted her whole Life; and, in so scandalous a

---

[1] 3rd ed., 1781, pp. 84–85. See the caveat entitled "Dissertation on the Country Stage," a letter to the editor from a strolling player to "rescue from misery several young people who are possessed with high notions of the happiness attending upon the profession," in *The European Magazine,* XXII (1792), 230–231. See also George Crabbe, *The Borough,* 1810, Letter XII, "Players."

Manner, that the Actors blush'd to hear her. . . . To my great Surprize, I found Mrs. *Broad* drinking Tea at Miss *Whiffle's* the next Day.[1]

Having gained the mayor's permission, Glitter and Grammar hire a handsome barn at eight guineas for the summer. Casting problems rise, and the dispute between Mr. Pepper and Mr. Spruce as to which shall act Lothario is bitter, but not beyond words, for as the argument grows higher Spruce taunts his rival: *"You do* Lothario! *why* Calista *ought to be damn'd, for having any Thing to do with such a bandy-legg'd Bastard as you are."* His reward was a glass of wine in the face. But having tossed for the part, Spruce wins. After great bickering nine plays are cast, and the author comments on the "unaccountable Opinion this Class of Actors have of their own Merit, which is never seen while they are under the Direction of a regular Theatre; but as soon as they engage in a Summer Expedition, it breaks out most extravagantly, and hardly one but what would sacrifice his best Friend, rather than give up a Part."[2] The comedians crave tragic roles, and the tragedians insist on comic.

For Example: Mr. *Pepper,* who is really a good Comedian, and may in Time rise to the Fame of a *Johnson* or a *Griffin,* could not be satisfy'd without playing King *Richard;* and is better pleas'd when strutting in Tragedy, with the Contempt of the Audience, (which indeed his Vanity won't let him see) than he would be in playing a *Fondlewife* or a *Manuel,* to their entire Satisfaction and Approbation.[3]

With differences temporarily surmounted, the actors set out, but the alarums and excursions are many. There are coach accidents, sick lap dogs, Grammar's drunkenness, and Miss Grin's coquettish attempts to attract Mr. "Ramble." But they arrive, and the first play to be presented is *Richard III,* for *"it is the opinion of the whole Company, that it is the strongest Play we can open with."*[4] The rehearsal starts, with "Ramble" as Richmond. Although the performance is scheduled for seven o'clock, at half-past six not a single spectator has appeared except those with orders from the actors. Spruce has been cast as Richard, an assignment which moves Mr. Pepper to violent rage. He knocks down Mrs. Pepper, who is dressed for Queen Elizabeth, and gives her "the additional Ornament of a Black Eye,"[5] a wanton act of cruelty which enlists all the women against him.

[1] Page 62.
[2] Page 82.
[3] Page 83.
[4] Page 111.
[5] Page 113.

Lady *Ann* (Mrs. *Broad*) attack'd him with one of the Guard's Haltberts. Mrs. *Meggot* (the Dutchess of *York*) seiz'd a Tragedy-Dagger, and swore she would stick it to his Heart.[1]

In the ensuing melee Spruce is obliged to yield his robes to Pepper. The damage was so great that it was the general opinion to defer the play until the next night, but Pepper swore that he would go on that night, if only for his own diversion.

And for my Wife's Eye, she may keep her Handkerchief to it all the Time she's on, and as the Queen is a crying Character, it will look rather natural than otherwise.[2]

The Tragical History of King Richard the Third begins, in which everyone is perfect except Pepper himself, who "could not speak one Speech without the Assistance of Mr. *Idle,* the Prompter." Since a decent audience has appeared, the evening goes well, except for Pepper.

[He] seem'd more concern'd to preserve his Character as a Husband, than his Reputation as an Actor; for in all the Scenes with the Queen, instead of minding his Part, he was whispering, *Hold up your Handkerchief—the People will see your Eye*—which she so nicely observ'd, that her Royal Face was scarce visible the whole Night.[3]

The only other Shakespearean offering of this company was *Othello,* an account of which will be given later.

Strollers who featured *Richard III* figure prominently and entertainingly in *The Adventures of Jack Wander* (1766). The unknown author of this picaresque story of fortunes by land and sea, in England and abroad, introduces his hero and an Irishman whom he has met near Coventry to a stranger during a storm. The two wanderers have taken refuge in a hovel. Jack writes:

We observed a man advancing in the path we had left; his singular actions rouzed our curiosity and attention, and we presently heard him apostrophy thus— Blow on ye winds, spout cataracts, and waters roar, ye suit the present temper of my soul.—These words . . . amazed us; however we hollowed to him, and advised him to shroud himself from the storm, in our hut; he came directly towards us, and entered.[4]

He is a Welshman named Jones. In an interpolated narrative he tells his history. Transported with pleasure at a miserable performance by strollers in a ruinous barn, in which, however, "the beauties of the author were still visible," he offers his services to the manager. An old

[1] Page 113.
[2] Page 115.
[3] Page 115.
[4] Page 14. Jones is not letter-perfect in his rendition of Lear's great speech at the opening of III. ii. This is not even good Tate.

actor, Mr. Canker, describes the "almost insuperable difficulties" in attaining success as an actor:

Few, very few, says he, acquire reputation on the stage; few possess the many requisites necessary to form a complete player, as voice, action, a pleasing person, and a liberal education: however, if notwithstanding these discouragements, you resolve to proceed, I will give you my assistance; you see I play the first characters, and am grown old in the business. . . . I asked his opinion of a personable young man, who play'd Richmond, and appear'd with great advantage in the entertainment: all that glistens is not gold, replies Mr. Canker, when I enter'd this company he only play'd messengers, and other trifling parts, how should he excel? he has had no experience, and there is no growing a comedian like mushrooms.[1]

Canker's acrimonious tongue, indeed, spares none of the company. The manager, Sawpit, is an ignoramus who aspires to the role of the "haughty, gallant, gay Lothario; though there is not a more awkward wretch existing. . . . He was originally a journeyman carpenter, whose uncle, an old publican, dying, he became possess'd of a few hundreds, and set up manager." The heroine, Miss Mincing, was a lady's maid, who "quitted her mistress's service, to shine in Juliet." She is a wretched creature. "However, she may subsist: a young actress, though an execrable performer, may live where a man of superior talents would starve; you understand me?" There is in addition a woman who plays small parts, washes linen, and is a Doll Common to the entire company. Occasionally, an old man and his wife are useful in some characters. He "snuffs the candles, beats the drum, shifts the scenes; and being an excellent po[a]cher, often treats us with some game." In short, Canker is a misanthrope whose wit consists in universal ridicule. As young Wilding, the actor of Richmond in *Richard III,* tells Jones:

His malice is more particularly directed to the most excellent in our art, even Garrick, the inimitable Garrick, cannot escape his cynical remarks; those amiable pauses, "that broken voice, and ev'ry function suiting," are in his opinion carried to a faulty extreme; the sententious Sheridan, the articulate sprightly Smith, and truly comic Yates, are food for his envy.[2]

Undiscouraged, Jones joins Sawpit's company. When a mad Methodist raves at them, Jones defends his profession of actor, "merely as an antidote against that gloomy fanaticism, which extends itself over England," and Jack Wander begins to entertain a better opinion of strollers, "who with all their vices, can never injure religion, so much as low minded, self-interested enthusiasts, who desire the benevolent

[1] Page 20.
[2] Pages 24–25.

deity, should be an object of universal horror, that they may become more necessary; and extort the effects of their deluded disciples, under the specious pretence of charity." [1]

Jack attends a tragedy under Sawpit's direction, in which his friend Jones plays three different parts.

I could not forbear smiling, to see him appear with a pompous plume, and a glittering habit; while he still wore his shabby breeches, and dirty shoes and stockings. The heroine was badly equip'd, and gave me an idea of misery beyond description: her robes were a tatter'd lutestring, lac'd down the seams with tinsel; the wide sleeves of this garment, discovered a shift, black as jet; and every step she took, a large hole became visible in the heel of a greasy pink stocking. When the play was over, Mr. Jones receiv'd his share, which amounted to one shilling and sixpence. I condoled him for his ill fortune; when he laugh'd aloud, and cried out, not so bad, not so bad; I've shar'd only six-pence before this, for playing Richard the Third, and the Lying Valet. [2]

After traveling abroad, Jack meets Jones again one night at Drury Lane, "where we saw Cymbaline, with great satisfection [sic]." Jones invites him to a performance at Covent Garden: "Mr. Woodward shines to night in Bobadil, and Smith rivals Garrick in Kitely." After the play, "which gave us entire satisfaction," the two visit a spouting society across the way:

> Where Alexander cries I burn! I freeze!
> While gentle Romeo eats his toasted cheese;
> And mighty taylors, barbers, bakers,
> Act heroes, cowards, beaus, and quakers.

One learns at this point something about the contemporary makeup of Richard III as conceived by this curious assemblage:

We follow'd [Jones] up stairs into a room full of young fellows, paid our quota, and sat down; when a monstrous figure stalk'd from behind a screen, whose upper lip and eyebrows were daub'd with lamp-black and oil; we found by a soliloquy he utter'd, that he represented the tyrant Richard, while he pronounc'd some words in an accent hedious [sic] as his person: a young man who sat near us, finding we laugh'd at this singular appearance, whisper'd us, did you ever see such action! gentlemen, did you ever hear such a voice! very shocking indeed, says Jones. [3]

This evening concluded Jack's theatrical adventures.

There is a long chronicle of strolling players in Wales, whose repertory includes *Richard III,* in the excessively scarce novel by James Thistlethwaite, *The Child of Misfortune; or, The History of Mrs. Gil-*

---

[1] Page 34.
[2] Pages 35–36.
[3] Pages 156–157.

bert (1777). At the opening of the story, a Welsh antiquarian and a curate meet two men and a woman in a public-house in Glamorganshire. The woman is the heroine, Mrs. Louisa Gilbert. Well read in Shakespeare, she observes the gloomy countenances of her companions, throws herself into a theatrical attitude, and exclaims, "Why does the great Duke Humphrey knit his brows?"[1] They are worried because the local Justice has refused them permission to act. Mr. Lloyd, one of the newcomers (who turns out to be her uncle), explains the popular opposition to the stage. Acting is a profession which "in the eyes of the Law, is considered infamous, and whose followers are denominated vagrants."[2] In the great days of Greece the drama was a school of virtue:

But now, since every species of the Drama evinces such manifest corruption; since Tragedy is degenerated into bombast, Comedy into an amorous vehicle to convey loose description, and Farce into absurdity; and moreover, since theatrical performers, instead of that humility which should ever appear in them, affect the coxcomb and dishonour their Betters by an usurpation of the word Gentleman; it is highly necessary to bring such persons to a right knowledge of themselves, by shewing them what they really are in their proper colours.[3]

A riot ensues, during which the two male performers, the manager and Mr. Rattle, are hauled to jail by a justice of the peace. Mr. Lloyd takes the lady to his home, where she relates the story of her life. From youth she had been fond of the theater. "The fire of Shakespeare, the pathos of Otway, the wit of Congreve, got such a prodigious hold of my inclinations, that at every leisure moment I was perpetually amusing myself with a repetition of some speech out of these favourite Authors."[4] She admired *Hamlet.* Since she was an orphan obliged to seek her fortune, she went to London, where she met Mr. Sefton, author of a play. Like so many virginal efforts, *The Smithfield Tragedy; or, The Life and Death of Wat Tyler* made its "literary exit, amidst the united groans of the critics and the curses of the actors," and Sefton and Louisa went to a debtors' prison. When released, they joined a company of traveling players in Warwickshire. It was a poor company. "They seldom shared more than half a crown on the nights of performance, and oftentimes not even so much."[5] Assigned the role of Crookback in *Richard III* for his debut, Sefton failed miserably:

[1] *2 Henry VI,* I. ii. 3.
[2] I, 12. UP.
[3] I, 13.
[4] I, 26.
[5] I, 229.

Before the conclusion of the very first soliloquy, owing to his ignorance in the art of modulation, he unfortunately carried his voice to such an amazing pitch, that, unable to confine it, he thereby created a dissonance at once painful to himself and disagreeable to his audience. Nor was this the only inconvenience that arose from the violence of his exertions. The manager, who had undertaken to represent the part of Buckingham, and who had drank somewhat more than sobriety could well justify, hearing an uncommon noise upon the stage, and such as his ears had for a long time been unaccustomed to, concluded that the house was on fire, and under this persuasion instantly gave the alarm.

The audience, many of whose imaginations were fertile at multiplying danger, were presently thrown into the most violent commotion. Unmindful of the fate of the unfortunate Richard, every one was solely intent on the preservation of himself. The cry of *fire* prevailed, and as it was impossible to undeceive them, poor Sefton, to his unspeakable mortification, and to the everlasting disgrace of his hopes, found himself forsaken by his auditory, and the instrument of mirth to the unfeeling minds of his brother actors.[1]

Although Louisa's debut as Jane Shore was almost fatal when a falling chandelier set her ablaze, she was later a successful performer, and it is pleasing at the denouement to learn that the various scenes of her life had not destroyed her beauty and that she regains her husband. She describes the hard life of the stroller:

Friendless, hopeless, and often pennyless, we have to combat with the wantonness of the world and the insults of ignorance and prejudice, procuring to ourselves a miserable existence by means which prudence would turn from and delicacy blush to own.[2]

Despite hardships in Warwickshire, Worcestershire, Shropshire, and Lancashire, she affirms that the stage is not a "seminary for vice" but a "moral mirror; where by a faithful representation of undisguised nature, virtue is invited and encouraged to perseverance, and wickedness and folly meet the punishment they so justly merit, by a timely application of the sword of reproof, severely sharpened by the powers of wit and ridicule."[3]

Her description of the strollers' "theater" and *mise en scène* bears witness to their pathetic efforts to provide comfort and atmosphere. The theater was converted out of the ruins of an old barn.

The scenes, 'tho no ways gaudy in exterior ornament, were however such as served to decorate the natural rudeness of the walls, and to impede the passage of the wind, which otherwise had free egress from numberless

---

[1] I, 232–233. Shakespeare opens the play with Richard's famous soliloquy, an abridgment of which ends the first scene in Cibber's version.

[2] I, 252.

[3] I, 238.

chasms and apertures which disgraced the edifice and were productive of inconvenience to the spectators.

The seats were such as well corresponded with the other parts of the building: a few rough deal boards, ornamented upon top with coarse red baize properly set off with the addition of a number of brass nails, presented to the rustic spectators no incompetent notion of genuine finery, and preserved an idea of uniformity, which tended to the satisfaction of the audience and the credit of the manager. Our chandeliers were composed of two small hoops suspended over the stage by means of a string, and round which were disposed at equal distances several small candles supported in clay sockets, no less remarkable for their simplicity than for the utility they manifested.[1]

A strolling performer of humble roles in Shakespearean and other plays presents himself as a possible husband in the rare anonymous novel, *The News-Paper Wedding; or, An Advertisement for a Husband* (1774). The heroine, Mrs. Eliza Sommers, has advertised in the papers for a husband. One of the applicants is a stroller, "but his abilities in that station were so small that they had not been able to procure him an engagement in any of the companies which had gone on the Summer campaigns."[2] The heroine's go-between, Charles, having asked what parts he had performed last season (1771), is informed: "Why I always acted a soldier in Richard the IIId. and one of the bearers in *Romeo and Julet* [*sic*]; and one of the *gang* in the Beggar's Opera; and a devil in Dr. Faustus; but besides all this, I sometimes helped to shift the scenes, and to sweep the stage."[3] This incompetent is unsuccessful in his suit, for the heroine has no high opinion of itinerants. In her early years she ran away from home with her lover, Charles. When their money was stolen on the road, the couple took shelter during a storm in a barn occupied by an acting company. There they met a theatrical couple who thus described their life:

The profits of our labours are so trifling, and the insolence of our tyrannical employer so great, that our situation would have been wholly insupportable, had we not been rendered, in some measure, independent of him by a liberal benefaction from some unknown friend. It is worth observing, that, by far the greatest part of travelling comedians, differ from the rest of the world in the following particular: men, in general, endeavour to conceal their vices, and shew the most favourable parts of their characters: but actors defy all censure, and, with such pleasure boast of the villainies they have perpetrated, that one would imagine, they wish to be distinguished by something; and, despising the opinion of the world, follow every vicious suggestion of their depraved minds, as much for the sake of singularity as self-gratification. In short, a company of strollers

[1] I, 240–241.
[2] II, 4. BU.
[3] II, 12.

may be aptly compared to the ship's crews that trade on the coast of Guinea; for the troop is principally composed of the most prostitute and abandoned wretches, who having rendered themselves obnoxious to mankind, form themselves into little republics, and gain a transitory reputation by assuming a variety of characters: so that they are esteemed not for any intrinsic merit centering in themselves, but according to the degree of art they possess, in appearing to be what they really are not.[1]

Richard III was a favorite role of "the Margate Roscius" in *Letters of Momus from Margate, Describing the Most Distinguished Characters There, in What Was Called the Season of . . . 1777* (1778).[2] In the manner of Matthew Bramble this short Smollettian piece exposes social follies at the Kentish seaside resort. The first letter describes the playhouse:

The play-house is much on the plan of your theatres in London, and in another letter I may give you an account of our Margate Roscius. As Roscius's are now springing up like mushrooms, you may let Mr. Garrick know *from me* (and I am sure he will take my word) that his reputation and fame is full as much in danger of being eclipsed by the Margate Roscius as by any other Roscius whatsoever. You will think so when I describe him. As an instance of the manager's judgment, which I desire you will communicate to Mr. Colman, . . . I must tell you that the play-house is built over a stable, in order to give a peculiar effect to that striking part in Richard the Third, where he calls out "A horse, a horse—a kingdom for a horse." I cannot describe to you the amazing effect produced by the peculiar manner of the actor, and the combustion among the grooms and horses. I mean to write a tragedy on the story of Darius's horse; to pay a principal attention to this circumstance, as you do in London to closets, trap-doors, and skreens; and to bring it on at Margate.[3]

At the conclusion of the period under study, Thomas Holcroft, who knew profoundly the economy of wandering companies, gives in *Alwyn* a list of some of their properties. The old actor Stentor and his wife have arrived at Kendal with few of their requisites for performing, for their landlady has withheld them. Writing to his friend Jemmy Drumshandrugh, Stentor lists the indispensable missing articles:

My grey hairs, and my wife's tie wig; the coronet I wear in Lear, with the George and garter for Richard, Banquo's bloody throat, that you painted on flesh-coloured callimanco; my shirt-shams, new Basil buskins, never worn but one night in Mark Anthony; Mrs. Stentor's tate, her witch's high-crowned hat, and Hecate's spectacles; the boots and belt in which she plays John Moody, together with the manager's thunderbolt in Midas,

[1] II, 97–99.
[2] The preface states that these letters were reprinted from *The St. James's Chronicle*. The only copy of the novel which I have traced is in the British Museum.
[3] Pages 3–4.

and my last new sett of teeth, for which I paid half a guinea to our
French dancing dentist; the black stockings with spangled clocks, that I
wear in all my Kings . . . and a thousand other things that I shall want
every night, all stopt.—I'm in a pretty pickle.[1]

Novelists, with reason, noticed *Richard III* more than any other
chronicle play. Of *King John,* which offers effective acting roles in the
King, Faulconbridge, and Constance, together with an abundance of
strong dramatic situations, they wrote virtually nothing, despite the
fact that the play was often presented and treated (except by Colley
Cibber) with respect.[2] Probably to rival Cibber's political and anti-
papal version, *Papal Tyranny in the Reign of King John,* at Covent
Garden in 1745, Garrick simultaneously revived Shakespeare's play,
acting the King to Mrs. Cibber's Constance, a role which was regarded
as her masterpiece. But after a number of performances that spring,
the play was dropped at Drury Lane until 1754, when Garrick won no
success as Faulconbridge. He never acted in this play after 1760. However, there were many performances at one theater or the other during
the sixties and several revivals during the seventies. The finest actors
participated throughout the era: Quin, Thomas Sheridan, William
Powell, and Samuel Reddish acted John; Spranger Barry, Charles Holland, and John Palmer acted the Bastard; Mrs. Yates and Mrs. Barry
played Constance. But it was not a favorite play with writers of fiction,
and the only reference to it of any interest reveals more about the nefarious methods of strollers than about Shakespeare.

In *The Adventures of Jack Wander* (1766), which, as we have
seen, treats at length of the itinerant gentry, an old and toughened
stroller, and a sharper to boot, Mr. Shift, bilks a group of young spouters in order to obtain equipment for his forthcoming expedition:

He began by employing a drunken painter, to daub him a few scenes,
for ready money; his next step was to persuade some young spouters that
they had great merit, and advis'd them to exhibit a play among themselves,
offering to provide a proper place, dresses, scenes, and every other requisite, if they would advance half a guinea each; the bait took, and they
all applauded the scheme; the next point was to chuse them a play full of
characters, he propos'd King John, they approve of his choice, and advanc'd
their subscription, which amounted to ten guineas; besides, he avail'd
himself of their good opinion, and borrow'd, or got credit of them, for
several valuable things. His remaining business was to get an old curtain,
and some paultry dresses of Mr. H—m, at a cheap rate, advancing half
cash, and giving a note for the rest. When the painter brought home the

[1] I, 135–136. Mark Antony, in *All for Love,* acted 111 times from 1702 to
1776. John Moody, in *The Provok'd Husband,* by Vanbrugh and Cibber.

[2] For its stage history see the full account by Harold Child in the New Cambridge *King John,* ed. J. Dover Wilson, Cambridge, 1936, pp. lxiii–lxxix.

scenes, he made the poor fellow drunk, and then sent him home, appointing next day for payment; taking care that evening to discharge his lodging, and sent his moveables to an inn, where he had a waggon ready, which convey'd all into the country early next day.[1]

Of *Richard II* the novelists wrote nothing. Its stage record during the eighteenth century was slight. After revivals of the original play at Covent Garden in 1738 and 1739, neglect fell upon it, and though Garrick planned to produce it with magnificent scenery, he never did. "The criticks," wrote George Steevens, "may applaud, though the successive audiences of more than a century have respectfully slumbered over it as often as it has appeared on the stage."[2] Only in the twentieth century has this weak but poetic monarch found sympathetic interpreters and audiences.

The Falstaff plays, on the contrary, were favorites of eighteenth-century theater-goers, and the popularity of both parts of *Henry IV* then reached its height. The versions employed were cut rather than altered, on the principle of emphasizing the Falstaff scenes at the expense of the historical passages, which were considered long and prolix, if not tiresome. The number of performances was great. For the first part of the play there were at least two hundred twenty during the first half-century; for the second part there were eighty from 1720 to 1750.[3] Garrick himself took little interest in the two plays, although he acted briefly in both. After 1738, till well past the middle of the century, Covent Garden enjoyed a virtual monopoly on them. Quin was the favorite Falstaff in both parts from 1730 to 1753, as well as in *The Merry Wives of Windsor*. Until his retirement he enlivened the fat rogue, as we have seen. He appears to have made his own version, of which his manuscript part of Falstaff is extant.[4]

Such continuity of performance as *Henry IV* enjoyed, to say nothing of the sheer delight radiated to all but Puritans and moral precisians

---

[1] Pages 144–146.

[2] *Supplement to the Edition of Shakespeare's Plays Published in 1778 by Samuel Johnson and George Steevens*, 1780, II, 677.

[3] See A. H. Scouten and Leo Hughes, "A Calendar of Performances of *1 Henry IV* and *2 Henry IV* during the First Half of the Eighteenth Century," *JEGP*, XLIII (1944), 23–41; E. L. Avery, "*1 Henry IV* and *2 Henry IV* during the First Half of the Eighteenth Century," *JEGP*, XLIV (1945), 89–90. See also the stage history of both parts by Harold Child in the New Cambridge *Henry IV: Part 1*, ed. J. D. Wilson, Cambridge, 1946, pp. xxix–xxxvii. The good acting versions of both parts are in Bell's *Shakespeare*, 2nd ed., 1774, IV, 63–132, 133–206.

[4] In the Folger Library. See Samuel B. Hemingway, ed., *1 Henry IV* (New Variorum edition), Philadelphia, 1936, p. 502; Harold Child, p. xxxvi. Quin reduced Falstaff's participation in the Gadshill scene and was the first to omit the extemporaneous play with Prince Hal in II. iv.

by Shakespeare's greatest comic achievement, could not fail to be reflected by the novelists. Falstaff, Ancient Pistol, and Hotspur were favorite characters. When Fielding, in *The Adventures of Joseph Andrews* (1742), wished to convey the notion that the odious, hypocritical, and well-fed Parson Trulliber was as gross as his own pigs, he described him as "indeed one of the largest men you should see, and could have acted the part of Sir John Falstaff without stuffing. Add to this, that the rotundity of his belly was considerably increased by the shortness of his stature, his shadow ascending very near as far in height, when he lay on his back, as when he stood on his legs." [1] The impression of Falstaff's enormousness continues in Thomas Bridges' crude and vigorous *Adventures of a Bank-Note* (1770–1771), when the bank-note describes itself:

Small as I am in my own eye, I chuse to step forth in my natural shape, rather than suffer myself to be cramm'd with other folks reasons; and by that means cut as bad a figure as the starv'd apothecary in Romeo and Juliet would, should they stuff him with cushions, and oblige him to personate sir John Falstaff. [2]

Ancient Pistol, familiar to audiences in Theophilus Cibber's famous portrayal, was remembered by novelists for his flamboyance and his bombastic jargon. In *Roderick Random* (1748) the practical-joking hero meets an actor, Ranter, at a tavern. When Ranter tries to involve Rod in trouble with another guest, Rod orders him to jump over a sword held three feet from the floor:

Instead of complying with my command, he snatched his hat and hanger, and assuming the looks, swagger, and phrase of Pistol, burst out into the following exclamation: "Ha! must I then perform inglorious prank of sylvan ape in mountain forest caught! Death rock me asleep, abridge my doleful days, and lay my head in fury's lap. Have we not Hiren here?" [3]

The sword is applied to the player's posterior with such success that he vanishes in a twinkling.

The motto (somewhat misquoted) of the hero of the crude precursor of *Tristram Shandy*, *The Life and Memoirs of Mr. Ephraim Tristram Bates, Commonly Called Corporal Bates, a Broken-Hearted Soldier* (1756), was that of Ancient Pistol: *"Si fortune me tormento, spera me contento."* [4] Mistaken for a "vagabond Shew-fellow" by the

---

[1] Book 2, chapter 14.
[2] I, 4–5.
[3] Chapter 46. Compare *2 Henry IV*, II. iv. 173, 189, 211.
[4] Page 78. Compare *2 Henry IV*, II. iv. 195. See the interesting critical analysis of this novel by Helen S. Hughes, "A Precursor of *Tristram Shandy*," JEGP, XVII (1918), 227–251. The novel has eighteen quotations from, or allusions to, Shakespeare.

old soldier Bayonet, whom he has hired to instruct him in gunnery, Bates "could not help wond'ring at the general Contempt for Play'r-Men, as *Bayonet* call'd them,—a Profession, says he, that in general requires the best Talents of every particular one, Voice, Address, Figure, Memory, Application, Judgment, and what not? I own, I honour and pity them; honour their Abilities, and pity them for the Slights they endure."[1]

Pistol's propensity for quoting (or misquoting) tags from old plays was not unique. It was considered part of the typical humor of actors who carried over into real life what the Shandean author of *The Life, Travels, and Adventures of Christopher Wagstaff, Gentleman* (1762) calls "a kind of stage-pedantry," which "almost totally infects their looks, manner, voice, and common conversation."

The affectation I am speaking of is, by the way, very observable in players themselves, in whom it is, for the most part, rather diverting than offensive; and may in a great measure be accounted for *habitually*, as it were, from principles and attachments common to all professions.

The author illustrates this "histrionic quaintness" by appropriate quotations from Lee, Otway, and Shakespeare. When an actor so affected "is at dinner, he will frequently address himself to a fricasee, or a pudding, in the following terms,

> Thou com'st in such a questionable shape
> That I will speak to thee. . . .

If a single string of a fiddle is touched, or a key of a harpsichord, he immediately cries,

> If music be the food of love, play on. . . .

When he takes his leave of his friend, he does it with the tenderness and solemnity of a *Brutus:*—

> For ever, and for ever farewell Cassius!
> If we should meet again, then we shall smile,
> If not, why then this parting was well made.

He has frequently disturbed a whole neighbourhood, in the dead of the night, by bellowing thro' the streets,

> —What hoa, Brabantio!
> Look to your house, your daughter, and your bags! . . .

Or, if he calls for his horse at an inn, it is in the stile, and with the impetuosity, of King *Richard* in the tragedy:—

> A horse, a horse, my kingdom for a horse.

[1] Page 39.

If a lady looks out of a window, as he is passing by,

It is the east, and Juliet is the sun! . . .

Every country looby he meets is one of *Shakespear's* clowns; . . . and every landlord is *mine host of the Garter!* In short, he appears in more characters within the compass of a dozen hours, than *Garrick* himself does in a twelve-month, and of all men living has the best title to that old theatrical motto—

Totus mundus agit Histrionem.[1]

Hotspur's fine speech on honor, so nobly contrasted with Falstaff's pragmatic concept, was inaccurately recalled by the good Colonel Bath in Fielding's *Amelia* (1751):

"That Shakespeare . . . was a fine fellow. He was a very pretty poet indeed. Was it not Shakespeare that wrote the play about Hotspur? You must remember these lines. I got them almost by heart at the playhouse; for I never missed that play whenever it was acted, if I was in town.

'By Heaven it was an easy leap,
To pluck bright honour into the full moon,
Or drive into the bottomless deep.'

And—and—faith, I have almost forgot them; but I know it is something about saving your honour from drowning.—O it is very fine! I say, d—n me, the man who wrote those lines, was the greatest poet the world ever produced. There is dignity of expression and emphasis of thinking, d—n me."

Booth assented to the Colonel's criticism.[2]

In the next year, William Goodall, a professed admirer of Fielding, quoted Hotspur's lines in *The Adventures of Captain Greenland,* an interesting novel about Silvius Greenland's nautical adventures and his life on an island after shipwreck. Silvius loves Angelica. Captain Flame, attracted by the heroine, declares that he would fight any rival for the lady of his choice:

"By Heaven! Madam, replied the Captain, but before I would see myself rival'd in you, I would lay the wide World waste! waste as are the burning barren Sands of *Afric!*—Sir, said *Silvius,* smiling, you put me in mind of a fine and valiant Speech in *Shakespear,* that seems to suit your Sentiments extremely well; and which are these:

By Heav'n! methinks it were an easy Leap
To pluck bright Honour from the pale-fac'd Moon,

---

[1] II, chapter 37, pp. 174–181. BM. There is a character of the same humor, a strolling player in jail for the nonce, who quotes liberally from *Hamlet,* in Samuel J. Pratt's *Liberal Opinions; or, The History of Benignus,* 1783, IV, 216–235. BM.

[2] Book 10, chapter 5.

Or dive into the Bottom of the Deep,
Where Fathom-line could never touch the Ground,
And pluck up drowned Honour by the Locks.

Sir, returned the Captain to *Silvius,* that *Shakespear* was a very pretty, tolerable sort of a Fellow, and had indifferent good Notions: He wrote very well for the stupid Age he lived in. I think he was a Cotempory with *Virgil* and *Cataline,* and *Harry Stottle* in the Reign of *Pompey the Great,* a little after the Siege of *Troy,* or thereabouts. I remember to have read some of his Works in Greek, when I was at the University of *Canterbury;* but I forget all their flashy Stuff now: For you must know, Madam, continued he to *Angelica,* that one forgets a good deal of one's Learning in the Army." [1]

There is an account in Holcroft's *Alwyn* (1780) of the misadventures of *Henry IV* as performed by strollers. The jealous old villain Stentor writes his friend J. Drumshandrugh about his troubles with his autocratic manager, whom he dislikes because he has been demoted from Hotspur to Worcester:

A blunder of his, the other night, in the play of Harry the Fourth, will give you an idea of his capacity.

His eldest son Daniel, who looks as stupidly good-natured as a half grown mastiff, played Sir Walter Blunt, and his fat-headed father personated Douglas. The termagant Scot, as Falstaff calls him, is to kill Sir Walter; but when our pudding-headed director entered, instead of slaying the knight his son, he only stood to receive one thrust from him, then tumbled upon the stage, like an overgrown porpoise, gave a belch, instead of a groan, and pretended to expire. It would have done your heart good to have beheld the stupid look of the cub Daniel, who knew *he* ought to have fallen. The prompter began to swear, the people behind the scenes to laugh, and the mother, who lisps delightfully, hearing an uproar, waddled to see what was the matter; she found the mistake, and clapping her mouth to the side of the scene, began cursing her husband Roger in curious and well-chosen language:—"Get up," says she, "Godth cuth your showl, you old rogething rathcul, get up, don't you know the child ith to die?"—"You lie you b——," says Roger, "I am to die." "Godth cuth your thoul, I thay, get up, the child ith to die. Dothn't the child do thir Walter, and ithn't Douglath to kill him?"—Roger, however, persisted, that he was to die, and swore he would not get up. After a while the spectators began to smoke the blunder, and listen to the curious dialogue that was passing between the dead man and his persecuting wife. You may be sure they enjoyed it, and the house was presently in an uproar of laughter; this rouzed the butter-brained Roger's recollection, when, finding himself in the wrong box, he opened his eyes, and, after a tolerably stupid stare, which again incited the risibility of the audience, assayed to get up. But this was a task that he was not able to perform, for he was little less than dead drunk, so, after two or three unsuccessful efforts, he cast a maudlin look towards the wing, and called, in a kind of dismal hollow tone, "Moll! Moll! I can't get up, Moll!" "Godth cuth your old rogethin

[1] II, 34–35. LC.

rathcul's thoul," answered Moll, "Then lie there till the day of resurrection for what I care." "Moll, Moll,—do send the Prompter on, and let him give Dan a lift with me." "Godth cuth your thoul, I'll crack your th'kull, I will," replied Moll, irritated at the shouts that were heard through the house— The prompter, however, went on, and Dan and he once more set him on his feet; after which another battle ensued between Douglas and Sir Walter, to the great diversion of the beholders; and Dan was slain, amidst the clamour and acclamations of canes, hands, heels, and voices.[1]

Although *Henry V* was often played, mainly at Covent Garden, with few lapses after 1742, only one novel seems to have mentioned it with esteem.[2] In 1747, 1748, and possibly in 1752, Garrick, attired in court suit with sword, recited the Prologues as Chorus. The Prologues were appreciated by Sarah Fielding and Jane Collier in *The Cry* (1754):

Those inimitably beautiful chorus's to *Shakespear's Harry* the fifth, where he desires his audience *to play with their fancies,* and to suffer him to bear them on the lofty wings of his own sublime imagination, over the expanded ocean to different countries and distant climates, we should have thought might have warm'd the morosest cynic into a taste of pleasure, and have baffled the ill-humour of the severest critic.[3]

And yet the authors have heard a gentleman say that these choruses are "contrary to all form and order," and only the "wild reveries of an unbridled imagination."

By all odds the novelists' favorite characters in the historical plays were Richard III and Falstaff. Impressed with the dynamic natures of these two, the one for supreme villainy and the other for supreme comedy, writers were attracted by them more than by any character at all in the comedies. They reserved their best powers, however, for the immortal characters of the tragedies, who challenged their imaginations, as *Romeo and Juliet, Julius Caesar, Hamlet, Othello, Lear,* and *Macbeth* have challenged actors, audiences, critics, and novelists ever since. Tirelessly they conduct the creatures of their own imaginations to tragic spectacles in legitimate or occasional playhouses. The approach may be sentimental or ironic; the reaction may produce awe, tears, a fainting spell, grotesqueness, laughter, or bawdry. But homage to Shakespeare is always implicit in their work, for was it not he who inspired the scene? Was it not genius alone which could so fire the talents of lesser men and women, all eager to write in the unexacting and popular new medium?

[1] II, 16–20.
[2] For its stage history see C. B. Young in the New Cambridge *Henry V,* ed. J. D. Wilson, Cambridge, 1947, pp. xlviii–lvi.
[3] I, 3, Introduction.

CHAPTER FOUR

The Plays: The Tragedies

1. *Introduction*

IT IS only natural that in an age of great tragic acting the tragedies
of Shakespeare received most acclaim from novelists. At both London houses the tragedies were persistent, and it is necessary only to
outline the stage fortunes of each play. Allusions to *Romeo and Juliet,
Hamlet, Othello, King Lear,* and *Macbeth* are common. *Julius Caesar*
and *Antony and Cleopatra* received little attention, for reasons which
will be considered later, while *Timon of Athens* and *Coriolanus* received none whatever. *Romeo and Juliet,* after the revival at Drury
Lane in the season of 1748–1749, was seldom allowed to lapse. At
Garrick's theater until his retirement in 1776 it missed only three seasons. At Covent Garden it missed only one. *Hamlet* was acted at Drury
Lane every year from 1742–1743 until Garrick's departure, and every
year except two at Covent Garden. *Othello,* during the same period,
missed ten seasons at Drury Lane, but only seven at the rival theater.
King Lear was more persistent at Drury Lane because of Garrick's superiority as protagonist: there it missed five seasons, at Covent Garden
fourteen. From the time of Garrick's debut until his farewell, *Macbeth* missed only four seasons at his house in comparison with ten at
Covent Garden.

2. *Romeo and Juliet*

SHAKESPEARE'S early tragedy, *Romeo and Juliet,* became a favorite with writers of fiction. The play was known to the eighteenth
century in several versions. Otway's *History and Fall of Caius Marius*
(1679–1680), that remarkable mingling of ancient Rome and the
Renaissance, banished Shakespeare's *Romeo and Juliet* from the stage

until Theophilus Cibber's not quite so bad version appeared in 1744. Like Otway's, Cibber's play reunited the lovers a few moments before their death. Garrick presented his own rendering in 1748, with Spranger Barry as Romeo, Susannah Cibber as Juliet, and Harry Woodward as Mercutio.[1] His version long remained popular. He rewrote the scene in the tomb in order to provide a moving dialogue between husband and wife, an "improvement" praised by contemporary professional dramatic critics.

By writing in *Tom Jones* the scene in which Tom and Partridge behold Garrick as Hamlet, Henry Fielding gave other novelists the idea of similarly describing the action of plays as seen through the eyes of their characters, noting their emotional and critical responses, and recreating dramatically the actual scene in the playhouse during the performance. There is a meritorious description of this kind about a performance of *Romeo and Juliet* in *The History of Lucy Wellers. Written by a Lady* (1754), attributed to Miss Smythies of Colchester.[2] Jack Shooter, an ignorant, good-natured, horsy country squire, from Topewell Hall, visits London for the first time. The young fellow has a confused but pleasant time at the Mews, Westminster Abbey, and St. James' Park. During a call on Lucy Wellers, Jack accepts her guardian Mrs. Goodall's proposal that they all attend the theater, "as Romeo and Juliet was that night to be acted." Lucy's best friend, Mr. Godfrey, whom she subsequently marries, accompanies them:

It afforded Mr. Godfrey and the ladies great diversion, to hear honest Jack's remarks on that excellent performance. He seem'd much pleased with that merry fellow, as he call'd Mercutio, and commended Romeo for not standing shilly shally, but breaking his mind at once to his sweetheart: —was delighted with the conversation he held with Juliet from her chamber window; when Romeo mention'd his passion to the friar, said he, "I never saw a poor fellow so cut up in my life." At the mention of the cord ladder, he jogged Mr. Godfrey, and whisper'd, "Now, there I think the gentleman is to blame; if I was he I would tarry a while, and not venture my neck about the young woman."—At Mercutio's death he was sadly disturb'd, and said, 'twas pity such a clever fellow should lose his life in a quarrel, which by what he could understand, was begun long ago; adding, it was the part of a christian to forget and forgive: all along observing, it was a foolish thing for parents to be so cross; and he did not question but they wou'd repent on't. When they were married, Jack protested he wished them happy with all his heart; because they seem'd so much in earnest, and

[1] *Romeo and Juliet. With Some Alterations and an Additional Scene,* 1748; reprinted in *The Dramatic Works of David Garrick, Esq.,* 1768, II, 5–78. The text of the final scene is in Odell, *Shakespeare from Betterton to Irving,* I, 345–346.

[2] See Frank G. Black, "A Lady Novelist of Colchester," *The Essex Review,* XLIV (1935), 180–185; "Miss Smythies," *TLS,* Sept. 26, 1935, p. 596.

had such a value for one another. At the funeral procession, he look'd extremely solemn, and wished himself away, for he did not like it by any manner of means; 'twas for all the world like a burial. When he observed Romeo's affliction, at the news of Juliet's death, he vented a deep sigh, and said, in a whisper, it grieved him to the heart, to find that bald-pated fellow had been so careless about the letter; for the young gentleman seem'd so grieved, he question'd whether he wou'd ever get over it. Then blamed the *skinny* apothecary for selling poison.—The meeting between the lovers amongst the tombs, shocked him prodigiously, and he burst into tears. However, recovering himself, and wiping them away, he said, he was asham'd to behave so like a boy, but indeed he must needs say, he was vex'd for the young couple. Mr. Godfrey assured him there required no apology for discovering so laudable and humane a disposition; that the heart, devoid of such tender sensations, deserved the epithet of stubborn rather than manly. At the entertainment, Jack's features brightened up; and he laugh'd heartily at the agility of Harlequin and Columbine; tho' he declar'd, it seem'd to him to be all *witchcraft*.[1]

The "macaroni parson," William Dodd, who knew the London underworld so well that he was hanged at Tyburn for forgery, in his loose novel, *The Sisters; or, The History of Lucy and Caroline Sanson, Entrusted to a False Friend* (1754), tells the story of two country girls of good parentage, who journey to London to take jobs offered by their wretched cousin Dookalb. Dookalb is actually a pimp to the nobility. Lucy falls from virtue when invited by Beau Leicart to see the Romeo of "the inimitable Garrick," "that soul of fire, that wonder of wonders, that child and ape of nature. . . . D—— me, Madam, if he does not play *Romeo!*"[2] The Beau has sinister designs on the simple country

[1] II, 130–132. The skinniness of the apothecary is emphasized in Charles Caraccioli's *Chiron; or, The Mental Optician*, 1758, I, 177: "Well, to be sure, of all professions that tend to the starving quality, physic is the most hateful: what think you of that very thin, lean gentleman, who, by the way, would shine in the character of the starv'd apothecary in Romeo and Juliet, lounging every morning for hours at a bookseller's shop, or coffee-house . . . ? His father was an honest and pains-taking apothecary." The apothecary appears again in the *Memoirs of the Celebrated Miss Fanny M——* (2nd ed., 1759), a story similar to, but not so indecent as, John Cleland's *Memoirs of Fanny Hill*, 1749. Mr. H—— describes the hardships of his father, who, though better educated in elocution than Betterton, Booth, or Wilks, "was so thin as not to be a figure for any part but the apothecary in Romeo, and as that play then never had a run of sixteen nights successively at both houses at once, he was obliged to give up his pretensions to acting" (I, 128). This passage alludes to the *"Romeo and Juliet* War" at the two theaters in 1750, when Covent Garden gave twelve performances with Barry and Mrs. Cibber in the name roles, while Garrick and Mrs. Bellamy played them simultaneously at Drury Lane. In 1769 allusion was made to "the starved apothecary in Romeo and Juliet" in *Private Letters from an American in England to His Friends in America*, p. 132. Compare *Romeo and Juliet*, V. i. 69–71. The apothecary was acted at Drury Lane by Simpson, Waldron, and Castle.

[2] I, 76. See the account of Dodd and the analysis of this "coarse and crude" novel in J. R. Foster, *The Pre-Romantic Novel in England*, pp. 100–103. Dodd published in 1752 an anthology, *The Beauties of Shakespeare*, often reprinted.

miss. Before the performance they have supper, during which Leicart plies the as yet innocent girl with alcoholic liquors:

Why should we add the rest? The experienced will soon read the consequences; from the raw and ignorant it may, not improperly, be concealed: suffice it therefore to add, they enter'd not into the house 'till *Juliet* was preparing to drink the fatal draught, and silence sat closely attentive to the plaintive voice of piteous *Bellamy*.[2]

Caroline, befriended by Mr. Jaison, is wiser and more fortunate than her sister. The pert, airy, and garrulous Miss Stevens urges her to get ready for the play:

"that we may be time enough . . . because you know, if we are not at the play-house by half an hour after three we shall never get into the pit; for there's no getting in after that time, when that little, tiddy, pretty, dapper man Mr. *Garrick*, my sweet *Romeo*,

> *Oh* Romeo, Romeo, *wherefore art thou* Romeo!

how charming— I say, there's no getting in, if one does not go soon, when he acts; and so pray let me beg of you to be ready, for I must not go without you for the world. And pray now, my dear Mr. *Jaison*, won't you go too? Do, go with Miss *Caroline:* I am sure we shall all be vastly glad of your company, shan't we, Miss *Caroline?*" "Well, and my little, pretty, tiddy, dapper *Jenny*, said Mr. *Jaison*, laughing, to her, if Miss *Caroline* and *you* to be sure, desire my company, I am entirely at your service, what say you, Miss *Caroline?*" *Caroline* and he were both as much pleased with this interruption, as an old miser would be at the approach of a thief to carry off his gold as he was counting it over.

Jenny Stevens prattles on:

"Lord, Mr. *Jaison*, 'tis *Romeo* and *Juliet* to night. Had you never any inclination to act? I do think now, if you would do *Romeo*, I could do *Juliet* vastly well.

> *Give me my* Romeo, *ye gods; and when he's dead—*

Stay, stay, how is it? something about stars and cutting—

> *I'll cut him out in little* tiddy *stars,*
> *And he shall make the face of heaven so vastly fine,*
> *The birds shall sing, and think it is* not *day.*

Don't you think there's a good deal of Miss *Bellamy's* manner in that now?" Though their Spirits were very low, neither *Caroline* nor Mr. *Jaison* could refrain laughing at the girl's giddy lightness and impertinence; and as they knew not how to get shut of her, *Caroline* desired her to entertain Mr. *Jaison* below, while she drest, in which she promised to be as expeditious as possible.[2]

[1] I, 80.
[2] I, 237–239. Compare *Romeo and Juliet*, III. ii. 21–25; II. ii. 22.

David Garrick and George Anne Bellamy in the characters of Romeo and Juliet

The experience of this company at the playhouse was not happy, for Caroline's pleasure was quickly damped in the third act, when a couple of elegantly dressed ladies "made their appearance in one of the *flesh-boxes.*" Caroline no sooner looked than she perceived one of them to be her sister Lucy, "and on the sight fainted away." Caroline is removed to the Shakespeare's Head nearby for rest, while Jaison returns to the theater to persuade Lucy to accompany him to her ailing sister. Meanwhile, bailiffs have taken Caroline away. "Mr. *Jaison* could not support the heavy tidings, but dropt down in a fainting fit." [1]

Appropriately, perhaps, *Romeo and Juliet* was a utilitarian vehicle for those minded towards love or seduction, for in *The Invisible Spy* (1755), by Mrs. Haywood, Selima writes to her friend Belinda that one of her pursuers, Dorantes,

begg'd I would favour him with my company to the Theatre in Drury-Lane, where he had already sent a servant to keep places in the box;—I consented, and went with him in his chariot,—the play was Romeo and Juliet; —he apply'd all the tender things spoke by the former of these lovers to his own passion, and press'd my hand with a vehemence of fondness, whenever he had an opportunity of doing so unperceiv'd by the audience. [2]

Lovelace had taken Clarissa Harlowe to the playhouse, in hopes of breaking down her resistance, and it is interesting to note that the divine girl had found in the little library prepared for her at Mrs. Sinclair's house of ill fame the plays of Steele, Rowe, and Shakespeare.

One is not to believe, however, that, because the playhouse was to some a resort for amorous frivolity, the serious-minded and respectable abstained from theatrical recreation. In the rare *Memoirs of Sir Thomas Hughson and Mr. Joseph Williams, with the Remarkable History, Travels, and Distresses of Telemachus Lovet* (1757), when Telemachus Lovet returns from an expedition abroad, he meets at his lodgings a clergyman and his wife, in town for diversion. They are sociable folk, and the parson is no Jeremy Collier.

This Acquaintance led him [Telemachus] first to public diversions. At DRURY LANE *Theatre* was to be presented the Tragedy of ROMEO AND JULIET; *Mrs* —— was distractedly fond of that Play, and the *Doctor* prevail'd on TELEMACHUS to be of their Party. *Mr* LOVET had but one objection; he was afraid the Doctor's character, would oblige him to retire into the Gallery, which was a confinement he was never able to endure: The Doctor soon set him right in this; he said it was a play so much run after, and *Mr* GARRICK's attitudes so much admir'd, that there

[1] I, 241–245.
[2] II, 174.

was hardly such a thing as getting into the House, unless seats were pre-
viously procured: which he said he had done early that Morning, and had
got a Row in one of the front Boxes that would with pleasure accommodate them all. One Coach held the four; and they proceeded to the Theatre,
Mr LOVET, in their way, not a little admiring the Good-sense of the People of ENGLAND, who deny not their Clergy those decent liberties they
themselves enjoy; and are not displeas'd to see them partake of those
recreating amusements, which tho' the laws permit, the narrow minded
would be apt to condemn. While they were on that topick, he beg'd the
Ladies excuse, but would be informed whether Clergymen went also as
publicly to see Comedies. Being answer'd in the Affirmative; he said he was
sorry they did: he was afraid they would not always make a becoming
choice: and as many of our Comedies were notoriously unworthy of the
Ear of our Mob; they certainly did not deserve to be encouraged by the
countenance of our Clergy— He heartily wish'd no Piece could get access
to the Stage, without the Licence of an *Arch* Bishop as well as a *Chamber-
lain;* Churchmen then might not only enjoy the diversion, but be eas'd of
a burthen: Moral Duties might be inculcate from a Stage; and the Pulpet
be no longer debauch'd with the dull insipid harangues of a Moral Philosopher, but be fill'd as it ought with Ministers of the Gospel of Christ.
The *Doctor* could not help assenting to Mr LOVET's opinions in the
whole; he confess'd that preaching was become too much a mere ha-
ranguing; and he hoped one day to see it take another turn: But he was
afraid tho' Plays were ever so well conducted, People would still go thither
to be diverted. The Ladies here partly gave it against the Doctor. People
they said as seldom went to Church as to Play to be edifyed: Custom;
often worse, led most people to Church: a good Play or to spend a few
hours agreeably take 'em to the Theatre: and they did not see why a person might not fall in love with Virtue from the Behaviour of a BEVIL or
Lord TOWNLY, as take a dislike to Vice from the Deformities of the
Prodigal Son in a Sermon. The Doctor had preach'd a very elaborate discourse on that Subject the preceeding Sunday; and as his Sister said the
above, with a spice of drollr'y in the manner, the *Doctor* became warm:
which Mr. LOVET seeing, he interrupted. . . . "We must remember the
whole distress of to nights Entertainment arise from Family Quarrels;
which in all probability was first begun from a bare differing in opinion,
and perhaps of some matter much more trifling, than ours have been." . . .
    Thro' the rest of the Evening, Mr LOVET was silent and attentive. The
Doctor began to make some observations on the part of MERCUTIO, and
turn'd himself to TELEMACHUS; Mr LOVET told him he was sorry he
could not give attention to what he said; he beg'd to enjoy the Play. When
the 1st Act was over Mrs —— wanted to engage him in a little chat: He
begg'd her a thousand Pardons; he would listen to her with pleasure 'till
midnight, when the Play was over: but he was a lover of Musick; he had
not heard a tolerable consort for a long time past, and he hoped she would
permit him to give the Musick his Ear. Finding this the case, the Doctor
and the Ladies with a good deal of Good Nature, rather indulg'd than interrupted his silent Attention. The End of the Play took them home; the
Entertainment was some trifling affair which they had all of them often
seen. . . .
    The Discourse then turn'd to the Performers at the Theatre. Mr LOVET

being ask'd what he thought of *Mr* GARRICK— He said he was a surprising man.—

"But I am sorry to see the Public (said he continuing) give him such immoderate applause in what is not only turning *Tragedy* into *Harlequin* machinery, but what is most unnatural. I mean those attitudes you are all so fond of. I speak to you Doctor, as a Philosopher: and a little attention must convince you my remarks are just. In Surprizes, the Mind and of consequence the Body is variously affected— If any Object or Idea strange or shocking enter the Imagination or mind simply, that is, without any connexion with, or succession of other Objects or Ideas, to constitute the dread which siezeth the Mind; The Body then may be thrown into a sort of convulsions, which when well imitated in action may justly please. Of this kind we had an instance in the Character of JULIET a little before she drank the Mixture: Her distracted imagination brings her Cousin *Tibalt's* ghost to her view; The Idea, the Object is simple; nothing else at first succeeds in the fancy but the Apparition, and she is justly thrown into a beautiful attitude of horror in these words:

O look!

As Ideas grow upon the fancy she becomes a little milder—

Methinks I see my Cousin's Ghost
Seeking out ROMEO—

Need I ask any thinking person who has studied the subject, what a ridiculous piece of action it would be in the Actress to throw herself into the same attitude of horror, when she asks herself if the mixture may not be a poison. For it is evident, that tho' in the narration her reasons for so imagining follows the thought, they must have been previous in the Mind: The mind indeed must have had some small reasoning on the matter; and then, instead of an attitude of horror, a Just Actress will calmly after a sort of bewilder'd pause proceed in the Question,

What if it be a poison, which the Frier
Subtly hath ministred, to have me dead;
lest in this marriage he should be dishonoured
because he married me before to ROMEO?

And yet I do remember me somewhere to have seen an Actress, who because forsooth those attitudes strike the Galleries, did always throw herself into one of *them* in this passage."

"I already (said the *Doctor*) begin to find I have been unthinkingly led by the applause of the Mob."

"You shall be convinc'd of it immediately, (return'd TELEMACHUS). Now Sir, as touching ROMEO— I mean *Mr* GARRICK; for abstracting this error in Philosophy, he is the very character itself— When we see the monument op'ned; 'tis very nobly illuminated. But are we to suppose it was so in reality? was this the custom in VERONA? or did even SHAKESPEAR intend it so? So far to the contrary we find JULIET to Lady CAPULET says:

Delay this Marriage for a Month, a Week;
Or if you do not, make the bridal bed
In that DIM *Monument where* TIBALT *lies;*

Besides this, when JULIET is considering on what her situation in the
Tomb is like to be, she describes it in quite another form:

> *Shall I not then be stifled in the vault*
> *To whose foul mouth no healthsome air breaths in?*
>   *Is it not very like*
> *The horrible conceit of death and* NIGHT
> *Together with the terror of the place—et cætera—*

There are in all this no appearances of that lustre which in the representation takes off from the Gloomyness of the Scene. I have quoted these two
passages, because this is a principal thing to be settled; that tho' a Manager, the better to shew part of the fifth scene to the Audience, finds it
proper to have lights behind the Scene; The Actor ought to know no more
of them, than a spectator ought to know of a Prompter— He is to behave
himself in short as if all were dark and gloomy about him, seeing nothing,
but through the assistance of that light which the Author has put into the
hands of BALTHASAR. Now let us suppose him at the Monument;

> *A vault, an ancient receptacle*
> *Where for these many hundred years, the bones*
> *Of all my buried ancestors are pack'd—*

Would not one naturally expect a Gate decay'd through age; which rusty
hanging on its hinges would not admit a guest but with grumbling—
Having then with his wrenching iron enforced its

> *Rotten jaws to open—*

he with some force folds aside the leaves—with the calmness and resolution of a Hero, descends the dark abode; his light serves him to find out
where JULIET lies; Over whom, in silent agonies,—agonies which the
mind can only feel—indulging a solemn pause, the tears at last breaking
from him, forces from his mouth that tender, natural, calm observation,

> *O my love! My Wife!*
> *Death that suckt the honey of thy breath,*
> *Hath had no power yet upon thy beauty:*

In this speech he continues for some time; 'till having drank the poison,
taking his last embrace, he percieves she breaths and stirs— When a person awakes from a swoon, a fit or trance, it is always by slow degrees they
come to themselves: 'Tis so with JULIET, her short incoherent speeches,
and the great distance of time betwixt them, plainly show that SHAKE-
SPEAR intended his JULIET's first signs of life should be natural; should
be faint and small— Now in a place of darkness and drear conciet, the
eye may be much decieved; the Mind knows it—and no great Mind, as
ROMEO's must be, can possibly be thrown into any extream emotion,
upon an uncertainty— In his actions he is at first, Doubtfully serene; And
as he grows more assured of the thing, A surprize also naturally gains upon
him,

> *Soft—she breaths, and stirs!*

Still however something doubting—she speaks—doubts are all disspell'd,
and surprize is turn'd into raptures of Joy.

She speaks, she lives: and we shall still be bless'd!

Here is raptures—here is Joy: But thorough the whole, cannot I discover the smallest Thought, Idea or Expression, which by rushing unexpectedly and suddenly upon the Mind can throw the Body into extravagant attitudes.—

Instead of which the modern ROMEO, having broke the fastenings of the Door, is thrown into horror and surprize—what possibly can be the cause of such an emotion? had not CAPULET been painted o'er the door, I should have suppos'd the Scene shifters had been guilty of some mistake, or by design to fright the Actor, had brought from below, some of *Harlequin's* machinery.—How rediculous! an old rusty pair of Gates to fly open as by the assistance of Magick. However I soon saw it was the injudicious glare of light in the Monument, and the appearance of JULIET there— But this is not all: an attitude more of a like kind must surprize or please the Galleries. And when the Lady begins to shew signs of life; instead of a silent, doubtful, and attentive attitude, mix'd with an increasive surprize, following the word *Soft!*—He is instantly thrown into an attitude of extravagant extream, as if the Ghost of a BANCHO or a HAMLET, had fill'd him with Horror and Surprize— After all Sir I must confess *Mr* GARRICK has pleas'd me in his alterations on the play: and he is the only Gentleman ever charm'd me as an Actor."

"As an Actor then (said the *Doctor,* and was back'd by the Ladies) let us consider him; what have Players to do with Philosophy?"

"Pardon me Sir, (answer'd TELEMACHUS) no People have more; is it not their Art to Copy Nature? Nature is always best studied with the assistance of Philosophy."[1]

During the second half of the eighteenth century some picaresque novels of a curious type were published. Some of them have been noted already. They recount the adventures of lap dogs, cats, sedan chairs, stagecoaches, bank notes, guineas, black coats, and corkscrews. Unattractive as such stories by inanimate witnesses may seem, a number of them are not completely devoid of action or humor. In the very rare novel, *The Sedan* (1757), a sedan chair narrates episodes in the lives of its occupants. While undergoing repairs, it is placed near the door of the shop, where it can look out and speculate about humanity. From its observations we gain information about *Romeo and Juliet* from the point of view of the scullery and the top gallery:

Two servant-maids reading a play-bill pasted up against the door, said, My dear, I will explain the affair to you, for I have lived in town longer than you— This Romeo is Juliet's sweetheart, and the family are greatly against the match; and, I suppose, they never pay her any fortune (like parents in general on those occasions) so that I fancy their untimely end,—(for Oh! I once saw the play) is owing to their running in debt after the marriage, and not being able to support the expence, which I know by my last place

---

[1] IV, 224–233. Yale. The latter part of this passage refers to Garrick's additional scene. The last two quotations are of his composition.

must be very great; they give out other reasons in the play, as one does in common life, for the matter of that. . . . So that his banishment is little better than being a bankrupt, and afraid of his creditors. I can see thro' it all! for I was at a charity-school, and had a very good education afterwards, tho' now, indeed, I am down a little in the world, by the base usage of capt. ——; you know who I mean. The finest part is what they call the procession, and the burying;—there's all the singing folks attend, and such plenty of links and torches, that I never saw the like even when our dear Sir Watkin, the parliament-man died. Well! I have a friend there that can get an order, I believe, for the upper gallery; as among friends, I have granted him many a favour: but, if not, I'll treat you.[1]

In a novel of the same kind, Thomas Bridges' *Adventures of a Bank-Note,* the bank note alludes to Garrick's Romeo in its account of Captain Copper-phiz, who returns from sea to visit his cousin. Tricked out by a tailor in fantastic wise, his astonishment is so great that he does not recognize himself in the mirror. He sits down and breaks a guitar in a chair, knocks over a table with glasses, when his cousin's wife enters and sees the "strange wild looks of the salt-water animal."

Had Mr. Garrick himself been there, he would have frankly owned, that amazing fine attitude of his in Romeo and Juliet, which so much exceeds every thing the world ever saw before, or perhaps ever will again, is no more to be compared to the captain's astonished phiz, than a two-penny lobster to a Greenland whale.[2]

The popularity of *Romeo and Juliet* became somewhat dulled when Garrick, Spranger Barry, and Mrs. Cibber grew too old to impersonate young lovers. Barry's Romeo (or at least the decay of it) is noted in the anonymous *Edward. A Novel* (1774), when Louisa writes to her friend Lady Margaret in Dublin:

Our plays are but indifferently performed. Mrs. Barry, indeed, has met with that applause which those who can distinguish merit must always give her. Ah, alas! poor Barry, he is no more that Romeo, so universally admired; age has made sad ruin there.

And of Garrick's illness at that time:

No doubt the town would rejoice at Mr. Garrick's recovery, but he must go some time or other; they ought therefore to prepare themselves for a loss, which I fear never can be repaired.[3]

[1] II, 29–31. BM. With reference to the procession and the burying mentioned in this passage see the playbill for Covent Garden for September 28, 1750, reproduced in Tate Wilkinson's *Memoirs of His Own Life,* I, 37, which advertises "an additional scene . . . representing The Funeral Procession of Juliet, which will be accompanied with a solemn dirge, the Music composed by Mr. Arne." Wilkinson remarks that Rich's procession was very grand and adds that Garrick did not promise any procession or dirge in his bills.

[2] IV (1771), 12–13.

[3] I, 11, 22–23.

Although the older generation of actors was passing, the strollers carried on the torch, and it is not surprising that *Romeo and Juliet* should have maintained its appeal for provincial audiences. In Frances Brooke's very popular sentimental novel, *The History of Lady Julia Mandeville* (1763), the scene of which is, in the main, Lord Belmont's country house, Julia's friend, Anne Wilmot, writes to Colonel Belville about events in the country:

We are going to a strolling play to-night. My Lord encourages diversions on his estate, on the same principle that a wise Prince protects the fine arts, to keep his people at home.[1]

And later that night:

We have seen them enact Juliet and Romeo. Lady Julia seemed to sympathize with the heroine:

I'll not wed Paris; Romeo is my husband.[2]

That familiarity with Shakespeare's plays was considered part of the liberal education of young ladies is apparent in *The Picture. A Novel* (1766), by Margaret and Susannah Minifie. Emily Stanley's mother formulates an ideal system for educating her daughter. With the assistance of Mrs. Berkley, she devotes fourteen years to the pursuit of her scheme, which is fully described.[3] While Emily, her friend Louisa Orey, and Mrs. Stanley are visiting Mrs. Berkley in Derbyshire, their hostess proposes "going that Evening to a play at ——, a small town four miles from the lodge."

I am told, said she, Romeo and Juliet is to be acted for the benefit of the principal performers, some of whom are tolerable; that the house is not bad, and often honoured with many genteel families; so that on this occasion I may expect to see something of the neighbourhood in which I am to settle.—Besides, proceeded she, we have another inducement, the moon is full, and there can be no danger in our returning late.—The eyes of Emily and Louisa were instantly directed to Mrs. Stanley, seconding this proposal with their most insinuating eloquence.—That lady only held back her assent, to try if they would catch at pleasure with an unbecoming eagerness; when finding them quite silent, applied to these interpreters of their wishes, and immediately consented.—Her Intention in giving them a private education, was not to root from their minds the love of innocent amusements, only that they should consider them as the relaxations, not as the business of Life. . . .

They found the house so much crouded, that having got just within the door, it was impossible for them either to return or go forward.—A gentle-

[1] 4th ed., 1765, II, 34.
[2] II, 36.
[3] See chapter 24 of the first volume for the regimen of one day.

man who had seen our distressed damsels, came to their relief, but not without much elbowing and rhetoric, both which he was obliged to use in his passage through the multitude. . . . During the performance, the attention of every spectator seemed fixed on our heroines, who were entered so deeply into the representation of the two suffering lovers, as neither to see the glances, or hear the whispers, which they attracted from every quarter.—Amongst all who appeared to admire them, their conductor was the most conspicuous.—He gazed with transport,—he seized every interval to entertain, and when the play was concluded, requested the honour of leading them to their coach.[1]

In *Female Friendship; or, The Innocent Sufferer. A Moral Novel* (1770), a *valet de chambre* confesses that during his career with a strolling company notable for its performance of Young's *Revenge* and *Cymbeline,* he had swept the stage, snuffed candles, "and walked in a white sheet in Juliet's funeral procession."[2] A fuller account of a rural performance of *Romeo and Juliet* by actors of the same social level as the valet appears in Elizabeth Bonhote's *Rambles of Mr. Frankly* (1772–1776):

THE PLAY

The following evening we accompanied Sir John and lady Strother to see a company of strolling players perform Romeo and Juliet. Lady Strother had bespoken the play, merely to assist the needy actors. They were to exhibit in a barn,—and we found on our arrival a numerous audience assembled. The part of Romeo was acted—by a youth who had been apprentice to a barber, but who preferred the pomp of an imaginary hero to the drudgery of an useful mechanic. Juliet was some spruce Abigail, who, with a small smattering of reading, and a great deal of vanity and affectation, had been tempted to expose her weakness on the stage, by shewing that she could not speak her own language, and by murdering some of our favourite bard's unconfined excursions of fancy, noble and uncommon manner of expression. The Capulets were unmeaning beings—fitter for the flail and wash-tub than a stage. The Friar had once been master of an inn. Mercutio was the plague of the whole house—he almost deafened the audience. Nurse was the only good character amongst them—for infirmities and old age made her really feel the achs of which she vociferously complained, and truly did she enjoy the healing cordial they gave her.—Never were people more diverted at the most humourous comedy, than we were at this murdered murdering tragedy.

THE TOMB

When Romeo came to visit the tomb of his beloved Juliet, he, by some means or other, on his sudden entrance, fell against the scenes when lo, unfortunate disaster! down they dropt, and discovered the supposed departed Juliet in the arms even of the just-before murdered Mercutio. The scene was so truly ridiculous and comic, there was no standing it—and

[1] II, 35–36, 39–41.
[2] I, 217.

Juliet, with her paramour, fairly decamped, leaving the blundering Romeo to find some other Juliet, and get up again as well as he could,—cursing him heartily, no doubt, as the cause of all this bustle.—In the midst of the uproar we departed, perfectly satisfied with our evening's entertainment.[1]

In *The Younger Brother. A Tale* (1770–1772), the hero, Bob, having written a play which failed at Colman's theater, returns home with his sister and his friendly brother-in-law, Jack Rackett. The three arrive at Warwick:

Being informed that a company of strolling comedians would that night perform the play of *Romeo* and *Juliet,* my sister seemed desirous of seeing the exhibition; and therefore, after a dish of tea, we sallied to the theatre, under convoy of the landlord. The theatre was a barn; and the scenery and decorations were equal, at least, to those of the celebrated Cook and Flockton.

The music thrummed away upon Roast-Beef, Butter'd-Peas, Roger of Calverley, and many other good old tunes; and at length the curtain drew up. When Romeo and Mercutio appeared, I thought I knew something of their faces; and, on farther examination, I was firmly convinced that they were no other than my very worthy friends ORESTES and PYLADES, who had so civilly bilked me upon the road to London. I made some trifling excuse, stepped behind the scenes, and, as soon as they came off the stage, desired to speak with them. "Pray, Sir, (said I) is not your name ORESTES?" "Yes, honey, if you please, (quoth the fellow) I sometimes go by that name; or I am PATRICK MACLOCHLIN, which you will."—"And you, Sir, I think they call you PYLADES?"—"Oh yes, PYLADES, now and then; *alias* TERENCE O'CONNELL, joy. . . . We're of the kingdom of Ireland. PATRICK comes from Cork; and I was born in Dublin itself."

Bob reminds them of their debt, but Pylades and Orestes bid him not to interrupt the play.

I withdrew, took my seat again, and the play went on. The whole was highly ridiculous. Old Capulet, not being worth a pair of breeches, I suppose, appeared in the drawers usually worn in the character of Richard the Third; and instead of a bell, for the solemn dirge, the company had recourse to a neighbouring apothecary, for a large mortar and pestle.

But the last scene was inexpressibly great; Mr. MACLOCHLIN (who performed the part of Romeo) was very lusty; Juliet, a fine crumby pimple-faced lady; Paris, a half starved journeyman barber. Now they were all supposed to lie dead upon the stage; and when Prince Esculus comes on to tag the play, he, being unfortunately very regardless where he stepped, caused a little confusion.—"Zounds and fury! you tread upon my hand" (quoth Paris, loud enough to be heard all over the house). This recalled Romeo to life,—and lady Juliet, who was then lying upon his bosom, kept exact time with him in the up-and-down way, and put me in mind of something I will not name.

[1] IV (1776), 98–102.

My slippery friends, however, forgot their promise; for, as soon as the play was over, they stole slily out of the house by a private door.[1]

The fortunes of *Romeo and Juliet* in the strolling repertory assume a less farcical tone in Holcroft's *Alwyn*. Alwyn's courtship of Maria Stamford is temporarily obstructed by enemies who have forged a letter to her father in his name. Having joined the strollers, he writes to her brother that the company is preparing *Romeo and Juliet*.

We have not yet began to play, our theatre will not be ready before Friday. We are to open with Romeo and Juliet; and I, for my first appearance, am to be the hero of the night. A good mental physician would not, I believe, have prescribed so sweet a dose; the studying this character has not contributed to my recovery. But I have undertaken it, and must proceed. My feelings are so similar to those put into the mouth of the young Montague that it must be strange if I mistake my part. The company have formed great expectations of me, I am told, from hearing me rehearse; and the manager, who is a busy talkative person, is puffing his performers among the town's-people, and me among the rest.[2]

Alwyn does not describe the performance of the tragedy, for he interrupts his narrative to describe the makeup and government, the system of sharing, and the circuits of traveling companies. However, the evening was successful after the initial hissing, started by a former actor of Romeo, was quelled by a friendly young squire, who subsequently observes that Alwyn's voice was "sweetly plaintive and amorous," and that "it was impossible for any one who did not feel, or had not felt, the passion of love to have been so expressive."[3] Even strollers, under favorable direction, when seriously intent, could provide a dignified performance of the tragedy of the star-crossed young lovers.

3. *Julius Caesar*

OF LEGITIMATE performances of *Julius Caesar* there is little mention in fiction. Without serious alteration the tragedy had been popular

[1] II, 194–198. BM. Compare Goldsmith's account of a "straggling" performance of *Romeo and Juliet* in his "Adventures of a Strolling Player," in *Essays*, 1765, XXI, reprinted by J. W. M. Gibbs, ed., *The Works of Oliver Goldsmith*, I (1884), 295: "We had figures enough, but the difficulty was to dress them. The same coat that served Romeo, turned with the blue lining outwards, served for his friend Mercutio; a large piece of crape sufficed at once for Juliet's petticoat and pall; a pestle and mortar from a neighbouring apothecary's, answered all the purposes of a bell; and our landlord's own family, wrapped in white sheets, served to fill up the procession. In short, there were but three figures among us that might be said to be dressed with any propriety;—I mean the nurse, the starved apothecary, and myself. Our performance gave universal satisfaction: the whole audience were enchanted with our powers." This essay first appeared in *The British Magazine*, October, 1760.
[2] I, 129–130.
[3] II, 2.

during the Betterton and Cibber eras and could be seen regularly until 1750, after which its history was intermittent. Quin acted Brutus, one of his best roles, for the last time in 1750.[1] His great friend Lacy Ryan was memorable as both Cassius and Caesar. There was favorable remembrance in fiction of their performances. During the Garrick period, however, the play sank into desuetude: it was presented at Drury Lane in only one year from 1741 to 1776. In 1783 Thomas Davies observed that it was "laid aside and almost forgotten."[2] At Covent Garden it was presented in eleven different seasons from 1742 to 1758, and was revived in 1766, 1767, and 1773. Davies states that Garrick had once thought of acting Cassius and suggests that the actor refrained lest "he should only swell the consequence of his competitor Quin in Brutus."[3]

Quin's Brutus and Ryan's Cassius were lauded by an old parson in William Toldervy's scarce novel, *The History of Two Orphans* (1756). Of the title characters, Tom Heartley and George Richmond, George "had long had a taste for dramatic performances; and, when at school, expended much of his pocket-money in such entertainments. He read *Shakespear's* plays with more satisfaction than *Whitefield's* journals, and had got the *Distress'd Mother,* the *Conscious Lovers,* and Mr. *Addison's Cato* by heart."[4] While wandering about the country in search of fortune they meet Duroy, a sensible and well-behaved stroller, with whom they entertain some friends at a drinking party. Heartley and Duroy divert the company with part of the table scene between Brutus and Cassius in *Julius Caesar.*[5] The parson declares that he has never known it "so well done, excepting by *Quin* and *Ryan*":

"I remember to have heard a great judge in these matters say, that he would willingly bestow a guinea every month, for that exhibition by those persons, the former of these, continued he, the world has considered as a great actor, and I am told, that he has other merits: He has been known to deliver a few shrewd words in a blunt way; but two thirds of the sarcastical expressions, which are ascribed to him, he has no claim to at all. As to Mr. *Ryan,* he is a living and a striking instance, that the noble and

---

[1] For his performance see Thomas Davies, *Dramatic Miscellanies,* 1783, II, 248–250.

[2] *Dramatic Miscellanies,* II, 255.

[3] II, 212. For details of the stage history of *Caesar* see C. B. Young in the New Cambridge *Julius Caesar,* ed. J. D. Wilson, Cambridge, 1949, pp. xxxiv–xxxix.

[4] II, 79. Bodleian.

[5] *Julius Caesar,* IV, iii. "This scene between Brutus and Cassius was the admiration of the age in which the author lived, and has maintained its important character to this hour" (Davies, *Dramatic Miscellanies,* II, 250. See his full analysis of the quarrel and reconciliation, pp. 246–254).

manly virtues are not incompatible with the modern player; and it is generally allowed, as his action is the justest, so, if he had not met with two pieces of cruelty, from the hands of villains, we have all the reason in the world to suppose, that he would have been the first actor of his time." "Sir, replied *Duroy*, it is not the profession, to which I once belonged, that makes the coxcomb, or the knave, for in a great measure, 'tis the natural disposition of the people; they were so inclined, before their commencing actors; But, it must be owned, that many of the students in these schools are truly famous in furthering the bent of a licentious mind." [1]

A staunch defense of actors follows.

Neglected by the patent houses, *Julius Caesar* became the property of amateurs and the strolling actors. In George Smith Green's *Life of Mr. John Van, A Clergyman's Son* (*ca.* 1756), the hero as a youth of seventeen is apprenticed to a London cheesemonger. This position is, of course, humiliating to an ambitious boy, but John finds his way about town in his search for diversion.

As he mightily loved Plays, he engaged with a Company of Young Gentlemen, that used to perform once a Month for the Entertainment of their Friends. And as the Seeds of Glory were deeply sown in the Composition of our young Hero, he was wonderfully pleased to appear in one of those bloodless, fighting Parts that shine mechanically in many of our Plays. Plays, where Death is dealt about like a deck of Cards, and none but the Slaves,—who hav'n't the Hearts to die, left alive in the whole *Dramatis Personæ*. But Mr. *Van* was some Time in considering whether this kind of Diversion was any ways adequate to the Sentiments of Heroism, and stuck at several Stations called Scruples, 'till meeting with the Books of *Ben* the Bricklayer, he found that Kings and Queens, and some other Folks, as good as Cheesmongers, had done the same a hundred Years before. *Alexander* the Great, and *Julius Cæsar* were favourite Characters of his, upon some account or other. . . . Yet he was not so blindly fond of his Favourites, but he could see a Fault in them as soon as another Man: And has been heard to enveigh bitterly against the author of the last, for making a Clock strike, a thousand Years before such Things were invented: And for making *Cæsar* be killed in the Street, and afterwards saying it was at the Feet of *Pompey's* Image in the Senate-House. But this is a dangerous Subject, as *Shakespear* was the Writer thereof: So we shall break off abruptly.[2]

An elaborate production of the tragedy by amateurs is fully described in the rare and absorbing picaresque novel, of unknown authorship, *The Peregrinations of Jeremiah Grant, Esq., the West-Indian* (1763). Born in Jamaica, Jerry is sent to England to be educated. After running away from school and joining the army, he inherits his father's fortune, which he spends in riotous living. His house in fash-

[1] II, 179–180.
[2] I, 7–8. BM.

ionable Berkeley Square is managed by the meretricious Lyndamira. Having squandered eight thousand pounds during their first year together, the couple visit Bath, where they live on tick. Known as "Prince Grant," Jerry meets Horatio, a former actor, who is clearly intended to represent James Quin. Jerry establishes himself and his retinue at a magnificent seat in Gloucestershire, which he staffs lavishly. There he entertains his Lyndamira and his friend Horatio, whom he persuades to tell the particulars of his life. Horatio reveals his early admiration for the theater and confesses that "Shakespear was my favourite author, from the time I first could read him." Left destitute at the age of fifteen by his father's death, he enlisted in a troop of strollers at Coventry, from which he graduated to third-rate roles in London.

The first five years I could not get higher than the lieutenant of the Tower in Richard the third, or Rosincrans in Hamlet. But, as I paid great court to Booth, whose manner I imitated, . . . by steps I at last rose to the first class. When I arrived in this station, I became intimate with one of the first actresses, with whom I afterwards long cohabited, and shall ever think of her with reverence and esteem; when she died she left me a thousand pounds; the corner-stone upon which I have raised the comfortable pittance I am master of. . . . As I was now known to be a man of property, many of the actresses of the first class, laid all the snares they could, to draw me into matrimony; a trap which, I hope, to have discretion enough always to avoid; for I look upon that state as a civil death; . . . the famous Mrs. W—n, in particular, levelled her battery at me; but she was a bad canoneer, and not a shot took place. One evening, when I was playing with a spaniel, which formerly belonged to my defunct benefactress, the lady I am speaking of, came up to me: "I am glad, Sir, (said she), you love something in the world." "Yes Madam, I answered her, I love a dog, but I hate a bitch." This repartee so effectually cured the lady of her intentions upon my celibacy, that she seldom ever after troubled me with her coquetries.[1]

Horatio, older now and toothless, has retired to Bath, where he entertains the public with his wit. Lord Sparkle, one of Jerry's guests, suggests that the members of the party divert themselves by acting a play.

Sparkle now told me, that the scheme he had to propose, which would divert us for a considerable time during the summer, was the acting a play; he no sooner mentioned it, than the thought was applauded by the whole company, as a very bright one, and Horatio recommended the tragedy of Julius Cæsar; as we wanted a sufficient number of actors, I sent an express over to Bath, to Stephens and Jacobs [two old school friends], with so pressing an invitation, that . . . they . . . consented to be of the party.

[1] Pages 95–98. Mrs. W—n is Margaret Woffington.

Sparkle procured me the other members of the drama. Horatio, however, could not be prevailed upon to be of the number; alledging, that he would willingly act Brutus, to oblige Mr. Grant, but would whistle it for no man living; he promised to be a prompter, and give out the parts; accordingly he allotted me Brutus; Sparkle, Mark Anthony; Stephens, Cassius, which suited extremely well, as Stephens was of a consumptive habit of body, and gave a lively idea of the spare and hungry Cassius; Jacobs had Cæsar; Lyndamira, Portia; and Patty, Calphurnia.

We were now employed in getting our parts, rehearsing, and directing the workmen to fix up scenes and benches in the great hall. Sparkle undertook to get us dresses from a manager of one of the theatres, with whom he was intimately acquainted; but, in answer to a letter Sparkle wrote him for that purpose, he let him know it was not in his power to accommodate us; but if we chose to make new ones for the occasion, when our play was over, he would take them at half price; we were all fired with indignation at this proposal; and Horatio, who had been his rival upon the stage, could not forbear expressing his resentment: "I'll engage, said he, if Mr. Grant will but write to the manager of the other house, though he is unknown to him, he will obtain a promise of them immediately. I'll tell you this man's history in a few words: His father was a French officer in our service, who, when he was upon half-pay, lived at Litchfield; and this gentleman is so much ashamed of the country, from which he is so nearly sprung, that, in order to anglicise his name, he has tacked a letter to the tail of it, which is not to be found in the French alphabet; he went young to his uncle, a merchant at Lisbon, to whom he was bound apprentice; but, instead of attending to book-keeping, he used to divert the ladies of the factory, with speeches out of plays, that he had got by heart; so that his uncle, finding him incapable of minding his concerns, sent him back to England; his uncle soon after died, and left him a thousand pounds, with which, in partnership with his brother, he went into the wine trade; but thinking that it did not answer, he came to the resolution of studying the law; and flattered himself, that he should at least one day fill the Chancellor's seat; he boarded with an attorney, whose practice he was to have the liberty of inspecting. The intricacies of lord Coke had as few charms for him as merchandise in London, or at Lisbon; he therefore resolved to give way to his natural bent, and made his first appearance upon the stage at Goodman's-fields, in the character of Richard the third, in which he succeeded beyond his own wishes and expectations."

According to Horatio's hint, a letter was forthwith dispatched to the manager of the other house; who immediately granted our request without fee or reward.—The day after our theatrical exhibition was ended, the following paragraph, written by Horatio, was inserted in the Gloucester-journal:

"On Monday the 18th, Friday the 22d, and Monday the 25th past, was acted at Ingerford-park, the seat of Jeremiah Grant, Esq; the tragedy of Julius Cæsar, as written by Shakespear. The hall at Ingerford, which is a cube of thirty feet, was, upon the occasion, converted into a theatre, with scenes in front, and at the sides; the seats, which were all in front of the stage, held completely one hundred spectators, and were filled each night with persons of fashion, as well as of the neighbouring counties, as our own, to whom Mr. Grant sent cards of invitation; among others were the duke and duchess of ——, the marquis of ——, the earl and countess of ——, lord and lady ——, . . . Sir John ——, and lady ——, lady Mary ——, lady Betty ——, lady ——, the honourable Mr. Edward ——, and the miss ——. . . . There was a fine band of music, in which the principal parts were performed by the celebrated Mr. Burton, Mr. Gordon, and Seignor Franchisa, from London. The play was opened with a prologue, written upon the occasion, which was spoken, with great propriety, by Mr. Grant; the characters of the play were represented by gentlemen and ladies, whose rank in life made an easy elegance of deportment habitual to them.

"The calm, steady dignity of Brutus was nobly sustained by Mr. Grant, and excellently contrasted with the rash, vehement impetuosity of Cassius, by Capt. Stephens, especially in the scene of their quarrel, in the fourth act. The part of Mark Anthony was performed by the earl of Sparkle, who looked, as well as acted, the character; his manner was remarkably natural and easy, and his gesture such and such only, as the sentiments he expressed upon the occasion would naturally produce. The part of Cæsar was performed by Mr. Jacobs, and with great propriety, particularly in the scene of the Ghost, whom his voice and manner made very shining. Caska was done by Mr. Bun, who entered into the character with so much art, that it had the strongest appearance of nature; the very temper of the man, as Shakespear has drawn it, was expressed, as well in the tone and manner of utterance, as in the words themselves.

"Calphurnia was performed by Mrs. Martha Cultrap, whose figure was equal to whatever the fancy might conceive of the wife of Cæsar; her voice and manner were soft and plaintive, perfectly suited to the tender expostulation, for which the poet has principally introduced the character; and which, short as it is, did not less contribute to interest the audience for Cæsar, than the innate dignity of his own character. The part of Portia, the wife of Brutus, was performed by Mrs. Lyndamira Cultrap, to whom we dare not do justice, lest we should incur the imputation of flattery, and offend that delicacy which is so difficult to please by commendation; let it suffice to say, that she never appeared without giving fresh pleasure to the audience, whose fixt attention, while she was present, gave the most indubitable token of thorough approbation. The rest of the characters, though of less moment, were sustained with equal propriety, so as to render the whole representation uniform, as well as agreeable and affecting.

"At the end of the third act, after Anthony's oration to the people over the corps of Cæsar, a procession of Vestals was introduced with a solemn dirge; the Vestals were personated by six ladies, who made a most beautiful pleasing appearance; one of whom sung the dirge with such power of voice, expression, and skill in music, as perhaps cannot be equalled by any other.

"After the tragedy, the farce of The devil to pay, was performed by some of the same company; in which two Italian songs were introduced, sung by the young lady who sung the dirge in the play; and, by those who are the best judges, they were said to exceed every thing of the kind, that had ever been heard in this kingdom. Upon the whole, it may justly be doubted, whether any such dramatic representation has been seen in England, since the performance of plays was a royal amusement, practised by sovereign princes with the nobility of their court."

The high encomiums bestowed by Horatio on our performance, savoured so strongly of irony, that several people took it for a burlesque, instead of a panegyric. How it was meant, I will not pretend to determine; but, upon a second reading, I was rather inclined to think, my friend had exercised his talent for ridicule.[1]

Julius Caesar provided the strollers with five good roles in the characters of Caesar, Brutus, Cassius, Antony, and Casca. Sometimes these were decently played. But how inadequately at times even major characters were cast need not be left to the imagination. The author of *The Life, Travels, and Adventures of Christopher Wagstaff, Gentleman* (1762), during the course of a plea for proper casting of minor roles at urban dramatic exhibitions, recalls a country performance of *Caesar.*

Managers ought to take all possible care . . . in the judicious *casting* of the parts in a play, as the gentlemen of the stage phrase it. It has been usual to measure the excellence of a character rather by the *length,* than the *dignity* of it: And indeed it is right to do so, provided that even *appearances* are saved at the same time, and that *no* character of eminence and quality, if I may say so, be disgraced by a contemptible representative. *Inferior* characters (considered as *parts*) should never be assigned at random; and a proper regard ought to be always had to the *figure* of theatrical personages. The part of *Othello,* or of *Iago,* requires the talents of a *Garrick;* but does it therefore follow, that the *Duke of Venice* may be decently represented by a *candle-snuffer?* I have myself, in my time, seen, at the *Theatres Royal,* many persons of great name, both in antient and modern history, creeping along the stage with their hands in their pockets, like taylors.—These improprieties call to my mind a glaring one I was once witness of in a country town, where *Julius Cæsar* was acted by a company of itinerant comedians. The principal parts, those of *Brutus, Cassius,* and *Antony,* were tolerably well performed; but it gave me a kind of comical disgust to see the noble conspirator, *Cassius,* upon his knees, and humbly making the following petition,

> Pardon, *Cæsar,* pardon;—
> As low as to thy foot doth *Cassius* fall, &c.

to a *one-ey'd fidler,* who, upon this occasion, unhappily represented the emperor of the world.—Great indulgencies are due to the necessities of such vagrant performers; and therefore I take leave to publish this anecdote only by way of *hint* to the *upper houses!*—I will finish with remarking, that as the players cannot be too careful on their side to engage and keep up the attention of their audiences, by all possible means and precautions; so, on the other hand, let *them* be ever so deficient, good sense, fine language, and noble sentiments, are worth hearing at *any* time, and from *any* speaker.[2]

[1] Pages 101–108. BPL. This novel is interesting to the historian of fiction for its three chapters parodying Fielding, Smollett, and Sterne. For information about private theaters see T. H. Vail Motter, "Garrick and the Private Theatres: with a List of Amateur Performances in the Eighteenth Century," *ELH,* XI (1944), 63–75.
[2] II, 171–174. BM.

How the strollers advertised their offerings we learn in the discursive imitation of Sterne by William Donaldson, *The Life and Adventures of Sir Bartholomew Sapskull, Baronet* (1768). Sir Bartholomew's grandson tells the story of the education of his father, Simon Sapskull. The episode occurred at Canterbury.

My father . . . was disturb'd from his profound reverie by the clangor of drums and trumpets at some little distance; he immediately hasten'd to the place from whence the sound proceeded, when a paper was put into his hands by one of those party-colour'd gentlemen, known in Scotland by the whimsical appellation of Merry Andrew, who by a particular knack of making wry faces, had engaged the attention of a gaping multitude of men, women, and children, who gazed with astonishment at his wonderful ingenuity, and even the haughty 'squire Sapskull suspended his anger, and deign'd to laugh with the crowd.

But so fickle and inconstant is human nature, that he at length grew weary of their grimace; so turning scornfully upon his heel, left them to proceed in their humour: he had not gone beyond the hearing of the crackling trumpet, which (with submission) resembled the posterior sound, that notwithstanding the most painful caution, crepitates from the squeez'd bum of some city prude after a city collation; but he recollected the paper which he (regardless of its consequence) was torturing betwixt his fore-finger and thumb; he open'd it with some eagerness and read

No secret, but what all the world may read, as follows:

With Authority.

By command of Captain Thunderbolt, this present evening will be perform'd, at the Blue Barn behind the Cat and Porridge-pot, The tragical, bloody, and inhuman tragedy of

JULIUS CAESAR,

Containing the assassination of that mighty conqueror in the senate house. The life and death of those two noble Romans, Brutus and Cassius: with a full and true account how Portia, the daughter of Cato, and wife to Brutus, swallowed live coals to preserve her chastity pure and inviolate. To which will be added a farce (written by 'squire Foote) call'd

THE KNIGHTS.

The scenes, cloaths, decorations, &c. entirely new. Boxes one shilling, pit six-pence, and gallery three-pence. *Vivant Rex et Regina.* N. B. Cynthia has given her parole to light the ladies home. . . .

My father revis'd the bill of fare with particular attention, and was very much satisfy'd with the contents; it seem'd to want not a single circumstance to recommend it more to the palate of a true-born Englishman! Suicide! assassination! fire and sword were extravagantly display'd. Pleasing barbarities!

Such cruel exordiums, publish'd at the corner of every street, was for-

merly a theatrical device, which never fail'd to answer the purpose design'd, for a crowded house was always the consequence of it.

Nothing betrays an unnatural disposition in the English more, than this
longing after inhumanities; it shews an enmity in the mind, and conveys
an idea very unfavourable to our animal operations.

The author, reflecting on the English love of blood and inhuman
murder, calls for humanitarian reform, and concludes with regret
that "a tragedy, wrote with every circumstance that can excite horror
or distress, is sure to command a crouded audience." [1]

4. Hamlet

A WISE man in our day should think twice, hesitate like the protagonist himself, and pray devoutly before approaching the Serbonian
bog of *Hamlet* criticism, a morass now so vast and so murky that no
human being can hope to encompass it during a long and unusually
healthy lifetime. Yet, since every man believes at some time that
Hamlet is no other than himself, and since Hamlet's tragedy is unparalleled in having offered the greatest challenge to heart throbs and
brain waves in the history of literature, each thinker about the tragedy
must "cleanse the stuft bosom of that perilous stuff which weighs
upon the heart" or be till the end a doleful and frustrated being. The
approach may be temperamental, historical, subjective, objective, realistic, idealistic, mystical, impressionistic, expressionistic, analytical,
psychoanalytical, symbolic, melancholy, ecstatic, or purely demented.
It has rarely been as simple, practical, and factual as it was in the
heyday of the realistic eighteenth-century novel, when judicial criticism was wedded to humor, before the advent of the esemplastic
imagination, the rebirth of romantic melancholy, and the spontaneous
overflow of powerful feeling. The novelists loved and admired the
play. They did not greatly worry about its problems. Many of them
knew it by heart, for productions were not then exceptional, as now.
The tragedy was performed in every season during Garrick's regime
as manager, and he acted Hamlet almost without a lapse from his
first trial of the role at Drury Lane in November, 1742, until his last
appearance as the prince on May 30, 1776. The play was constantly
acted at Covent Garden as well.[2]

---

[1] I, 146–177. BM.

[2] The stage history of *Hamlet* is comprehensively presented by Harold Child in
the New Cambridge *Hamlet,* ed. J. D. Wilson, Cambridge, 1934, pp. lix–xcvii.
The completest information about casts for the Garrick era is in Dougald MacMillan, ed., *Drury Lane Calendar,* pp. 253–256.

The text for the play till the last quarter-century was the so-called Hughs-Wilks version, based on that of Betterton. Printed in 1718, the alteration was so popular that it ran to nineteen editions before 1761. The changes consisted mainly of cuts dictated by Wilks, while Hughs restored the text on the basis of Rowe's edition. The tragedy was not mangled structurally.[1] After Wilks' death in 1732, the most notable Hamlets before Garrick were Lacy Ryan, William Mills, and William Milward. There is no evidence that they acted any other than the Hughs-Wilks text.

The Ghost was a popular role with the actors and with the public. One of the most memorable impersonators of the elder Hamlet was James Quin, who copied Barton Booth's interpretation as closely as possible when he assumed the part in 1731. As late as 1771 Quin's Ghost was recalled by Tabitha Bramble in Smollett's *Expedition of Humphry Clinker*. A "nice derangement of epitaphs" was to be expected when Miss Bramble directed her malapropisms towards dramatic criticism. At Bath, in awe of Quin's sarcastic humor, she found, we are happy to say, her caution "no match for her impertinence."

"Mr. Gwynn, (said she the other day), I was once vastly entertained with your playing the Ghost of Gimlet at Drury-lane, when you rose up through the stage, with a white face and red eyes, and spoke of *quails upon the frightful porcofine*— Do, pray, spout a little the Ghost of Gimlet." "Madam, (said Quin, with a glance of ineffable disdain), the Ghost of Gimlet is laid, never to rise again—" Insensible of this check, she proceeded: "Well, to be sure, you looked and talked so like a real ghost; and then the cock crowed so natural. I wonder how you could teach him to crow so exact, in the very nick of time; but, I suppose, he's game— An't he game, Mr. Gwynn?" "Dunghill, Madam." "Well, dunghill, or not dunghill, he has got such a clear counter-tenor, that I wish I had such another at Brambleton-hall, to wake the maids of a morning. Do you know where I could find one of his brood?" "Probably in the work-house of St. Giles's parish, madam; but I protest I know not his particular mew." My uncle, frying with vexation, cried, "Good God, sister, how you talk! I have told you twenty times, that this gentleman's name is not Gwynn.—" "Hoity toity, brother mine, (she replied), no offence, I hope— Gwynn is an honourable name, of true old British extraction— I thought the gentleman had been come of Mrs. Helen Gwynn, who was of his own profession; and if so be that were the case, he might be of king Charles's breed, and have royal blood in his veins—" "No, madam, (answered Quin, with great solemnity) my mother was not a whore of such distinction." [2]

[1] For details see G. W. Stone, Jr., "Garrick's Long Lost Alteration of *Hamlet*," *PMLA*, XLIX (1934), 890–921. For critical opinions about *Hamlet* see Paul S. Conklin, *A History of Hamlet Criticism, 1601–1821*, New York, 1947, and C. H. Gray, *Theatrical Criticism in London to 1795*, New York, 1931.

[2] Shakespeare Head edition, Oxford, 1925, I, 75–76. The passage quoted was included, without credit to Smollett, in a collection of anecdotes inscribed to Gar-

From 1742 to 1776 Hamlet was one of Garrick's most successful parts. He began as the Ghost at Goodman's Fields in December, 1741, a role, incidentally, which he played at his own theater for John Palmer's benefit on April 4, 1763. He first appeared as Hamlet in Ireland on August 12, 1742. During his first season at Drury Lane (1742–1743) he established himself in the role by appearing fifteen times, with Mrs. Clive as Ophelia and Mrs. Pritchard as the Queen. He used the Hughs-Wilks text, which he gradually revised until he finally created his own text.[1] By 1756 his repute was so great that Edward Kimber, author of eight minor novels, made him the hero of his *roman à clef*, *The Juvenile Adventures of David Ranger, Esq. From an Original Manuscript Found in the Collections of a Late Noble Lord*. The novel gives a diverting fictional account of the great actor's early career. David is born and brought up in Ireland. With a passion for acting from his earliest youth, he indulges in several amorous adventures, joins a company of strollers, and goes to England, where he becomes famous as an actor. In the most colorful passages we observe Ranger redeeming the theater, rescuing the profession of acting from disrepute, and introducing performers "whose natural abilities and talents were adapted to the parts they exhibited; . . . and who, in private life, were inoffensive and amiable. . . . Those dramatick productions, which do honour to our nation and language, were revived, and the immortal *Shakespear* shone with that lustre and fire that none but a *Ranger* could have given him." [2]

---

rick, *The Fashionable Tell-Tale*, 1778, pp. 11–14. There is an allusion to the Ghost in "Sir" John Hill's *Letters from the Inspector to a Lady, with Genuine Answers*, 1752, p. 3: "I remember a gentleman staring at me as I passed under the musick, much as I have seen a bad player do at the ghost in Hamlet." In the picaresque and bawdy *Life and Real Adventures of Hamilton Murray. Written by Himself*, 1759, I, 183, Hamilton meets a company of strollers in a stagecoach, one of whom is dressed like the Ghost in *Hamlet*. BM.

[1] Garrick seldom permitted his texts and revisions to be printed. But during his absence in France, George Colman as acting manager published his text for *Hamlet* in 1763. Upon returning from Paris in 1765, Garrick took Voltaire's attack on the tragedy seriously and prepared a new version, based on the 1747 edition of the Hughs-Wilks text. The new version was first presented at Drury Lane on December 18, 1772. The manuscript, now in the Folger Library, has been studied in detail by G. W. Stone, Jr., in "Garrick's Long Lost Alteration of *Hamlet*." Dr. Stone presents the entire fifth act (pp. 906–921), which Garrick cut drastically. For a summary of changes which make this version radically different from earlier versions see pp. 898–901. The alteration was successful: it held the stage for eight years and was acted thirty-seven times. From 1772 to 1776 Garrick received for this alteration alone £3426. 14. 10.

[2] 2nd ed., 1757, II, 217–218. See Frank G. Black, "Edward Kimber: Anonymous Novelist of the Mid-Eighteenth Century," *Harvard Studies and Notes in Philology and Literature*, XVII (1935), 27–42.

As a lad this prodigy found encouragement from his mother.

One effect of his mamma's bent of mind, it was not possible to guard him against; she had not only read plays before him, but had initiated her son into the tragick stile and manner. Already he pronounced the word *farewell* in the accent and with the emphasis of the stage, could soliloquy with *Hamlet,* and stab himself with *Cato,* and what the good gentlewoman seem'd only to suffer him to be diverted with, soon became the passion of his soul. In dying agonies he had already measured every carpet in the house, and young as he was, was become a finish'd lover, which his innocent sister had often experienced in a tender embrace, and every glass had witness'd *attitudes* that were surprizingly perfect for his years; if he call'd for a servant, it was, *who waits without there!* If his father or mother requested his attendance, it was, *I wait your commands, Madam; I attend your call, Sir,* and, *I fly to obey you.* When his sister accosted him, he cry'd out, . . . *My charming fair I burn to greet thy wishes.* Mr. *Ranger* imagin'd that these forms of speech would soon be banish'd, when he came under school discipline, and mingled with boys of his own age, in their learning, and in their sports, and therefore only smil'd at these little theatric sallies; whilst his lady hugg'd herself in the thought of his early proficiency in a language, which she verily look'd upon as the most polite and finish'd in the world. Often had he woed his sister, *Monimia,* with all the melting softness of *Castalio,* as often transform'd himself into the enamour'd *Juba,* and had out axalla'd *Axalla* himself.[1]

At the Reverend Mr. Birch's school Davy falls in love with Birch's daughter Sophia:

and whenever *Davy* diverted his mamma, with the softness of *Romeo, Sophia* was now the *Juliet* to whom he address'd his amorous tale; she was his *Monimia,* his *Marcia,* his *Calista,* and had so profited by the instructions of Mrs. *Ranger,* that she even top'd her parts in all those characters.[2]

At sixteen Davy "was a perfect idolizer of *Shakespear,* many of whose productions he had seen exhibited, also, by a company of no mean performers, who frequently came from *Dublin* to divert the inhabitants of his native city." [3] For them the boy, who possessed a poetical genius, wrote many occasional prologues and epilogues, in reward for which the actors "let him into all the mysteries of the drama."

After the death of his mother, his sister, and Sophia, his father sends the bereft youth to his grandfather's, where he meets Captain Dennis Mackenzie, a stroller who admires Davy's judgment in theatrical

---

[1] I, 15–16. Monimia and Castalio are in Otway's *Orphan,* Juba in Addison's *Cato,* and Axalla in Rowe's *Tamerlane,* all very popular plays on the eighteenth-century stage.

[2] I, 18. Marcia is in *Cato;* Calista is in Rowe's *Fair Penitent.*

[3] I, 47–48.

representations and his ability to discourse learnedly about poetic justice and the theory of comedy and tragedy. Davy prefers the latter. The captain observes that Shakespeare had clearly studied the ancient dramatists.

Davy was lavish in his eulogies on his favourite poet, and said he principally admir'd that terror he was able to excite in many of his scenes, and particularly instanced in his *Macbeth* and *Hamlet,* many parts of which he repeated, with so just an action and accent, that the captain was quite transported and in perfect raptures.[1]

The strollers arrive in town:

[Davy] had not yet got into bed, when a medley of sounds assail'd his ears, made up of oaths, cries of joy, salutations, the rumbling of wheels, and confusion of bustle and hurry, underneath his apartment. Immediately, suspecting the cause, he opened the casement, and perceiv'd three men and two women alighting from the top of a well fill'd cart, and another as heavily laden, waiting for room to draw in, and by the light of the tapers . . . [he] could discover the canvas representation of woods, groves, palaces, halls and bedchambers, and a confus'd huddle of swords, pikes, truncheons, guns, masks, and other such like implements of mimic state and dignity, or comic fancy. The women were muffled up in cloaks and handkerchiefs, and as to their apparel, bespoke very little of the high characters they were destin'd to fill, and the men were not distinguishable from the carters, but by their speech, which bore a tincture of their profession, for, my host offering to salute one of the tragedy queens, one of them bellow'd out—death and dam—n, what is't I behold! perjur'd *Statira*—ah! thou fickle B—*h!* Upon which *Statira* answer'd— *Beware of jealousy that green-ey'd monster.*[2]

Captain Mackenzie, certain that Davy will "equal a *Roscius, a Betterton* or a *Booth,*" persuades him to join the company. Davy, nothing loath, agrees "to spout forth heroics for a fortnight, or three weeks" without reward. The company are delighted, and the captain assigns him the roles of Osmyn in *The Mourning Bride,* Othello, Castalio, and others. An excellent barn is prepared for the debut of the gifted tyro, who enraptures the audience as Osmyn. Moving on, the strollers hire a handsome room for their exhibitions, "which, by dint of *Davy's* genius, was decorated like a real theatre, and afforded commodious seats for persons of all ranks." Here Davy becomes a full-fledged actor in *Hamlet.*

The company were getting up the tragedy of *Hamlet,* in which Mr. *Ranger* was to personate that prince, in preparing for which he made such judi-

---

[1] I, 90.
[2] I, 91–92. Statira is in Lee's *Rival Queens.* For her quotation here see *Othello,* III. iii. 165–166.

cious observations upon the several parts, to the captain, that he lifted up his hands in admiration of those perfections, of which he observ'd no end in his associate. . . . The others, both men and women, were merely spouters, and had not good sense or discernment sufficient to enter into the characters they assum'd. . . . The whole town . . . waited in earnest expectation of having the new theatre opened with this celebrated play.

The audience was brilliant. Crowds were turned away, and the receipt of the house was nearly seventy pounds.

No words can describe the pleas'd surprize, the joy and rapture, that sat upon every countenance, when *Hamlet* made his appearance, in all the majestic blooming graces of that character. Astonishment, for some moments, kept the whole audience upon a pause, every one consulting the eyes of his neighbour, to see if he felt in the same manner with himself. At length a roar of applause broke out, like the explosion of a blast of wind that had been pent up in some subterraneous cavern, which continued to echo out every speech to the end of the play. . . . Thus every one sat 'till near the conclusion, when *Hamlet* is kill'd, at which catastrophe, a shrill schriek was heard from one of the middle seats, which proceeded from a young lady, very gaily dress'd, and who really fainted in the arms of her friends, and was carried out into the air, it being suppos'd that the heat of the room, which was indeed very great, might have overcome her.[1]

The audience visit Davy after the play, treat him like a little divinity, present him with a gold snuffbox, and hand Mackenzie ten pieces, upon his promise "to let *Hamlet* rule the roast for the whole week." More than this, the lovely Mary McCarthy sends him a letter of assignation and subsequently becomes his mistress.

Later, when he has decided to embrace the stage professionally, a manager overhears him displaying his dramatic ability in a coffeehouse.

Struck with hearing him, and knowing most of the company, [he] broke into the coffee-room, with G—d—n me, gentlemen, what have you got a *Powel* or a *Booth* amongst you, or has *Betterton* once more revisited these earthly mansions? These words rais'd a loud laugh of applause, in those who heard it, and drew blushes from poor *Ranger*.[2]

But the manager means what he says:

If, my worthy friend, I could persuade you to exhibit upon our stage, I am certain you would gain more applause than any actor has done for these twenty years.

He offers Davy six guineas a week and top roles. Davy is afraid of his uncle's disapproval of a stage career, and his fears are well grounded, for "the old gentleman was all in a foam, talk'd of disgrace to the family, vagabonds, stage-players, goals, debts, extravagancies,

[1] I, 154–157.
[2] I, 282.

&c. and, finally, told his nephew, that, since his mind had taken so low a turn, he desir'd him to quit his house." [1] However, Davy makes his professional appearance with enormous success, earning so much that his uncle becomes reconciled. Such, at least in fiction, was the beginning of Garrick's brilliant career. [2]

Garrick's Hamlet quickly attracted the novelists' attention. In the anonymous *Travels and Adventures of Mademoiselle de Richelieu* (1744), Mademoiselle in masculine disguise visits the London theater:

We went to *Drury-Lane* Play House in the Count's Coach, and as it had been advertised in the publick Papers that a new Actor was to make his first Appearance, from whom a great deal was expected, the House happened to be very full, and we saw abundance of pretty Women. The Amphitheatre is mostly filled with Ladies, and as the Box we were in was not far from it, I could observe that their Eyes were mostly turned towards us. The Play, as the Count told us, was *Hamlet* Prince of *Denmark,* which drew Tears from many a fair Lady there. The Count who understood every Word the Actors said, told us so much of it, that we had more Pleasure in the Action, than if we had known nothing of the Plot or the different Characters. After the Play we returned to the Count's Lodgings, where we supped in Company with some *English* Gentlemen. [3]

The heroine of *The History of Lavinia Rawlins* (1756), the poor daughter of a clergyman, receives letters dated 1740 from two of her friends, Sarah Morris and Gatty Coningsby, who describe their round of delights in London. Gatty has met a young man who courts her, an episode which Sarah describes to her country friend.

He begged her Company to the Play with him. She was never more driven to a Non-plus in all her Life, she says, than on this Demand; neither knowing where it was, or what it was, or how she was to behave there. She was ashamed to declare her Ignorance, but charged her Disapprobation of it, to her being but just arrived from the Country, and the Want of proper Habiliments to appear in.

This Put off, could by no Means be complied with; the Clothes she then had on, he said, were most agreeable to the Pit, and such only, as the very best of Lady's appeared in, when they mobbed it. This last Word, struck her all of a Heap, and she then, more vehemently than ever, desired to be excused: For that a Mob, was so terrifying a Thing to her, as to be absolutely her Aversion.

She says, that thereby discovering her Ignorance, he caught her in his Arms, and almost pressing her to Death; my dear little Innocent! said he, I can perceive you have not long been acquainted with this Town. Why? Child! what we Persons of Fashion of both Sexes call Mobbing, is only

---

[1] I, 285.
[2] The second volume contains several long interpolated narratives, together with an account of Ranger's career on the London stage.
[3] III, 315.

David Garrick as Hamlet

going into public Places in a Dishabille, or Incog, not to be known, or at least, taken Notice of.

This Salvo, she says, reinstating her Tranquillity, she consented; and sending for a Coach, away they went to the Play-house; but surely, to hear her Description of it, my dear *Lavy,* would think herself in a little Heaven; for she says, that every Thing was so fine and the Lights so numerous and dazling, it is impossible to describe it; and then there was such ravishing Music, and such Dancing, as she could have attended to for the whole Night; so that she was never more heartily sorry than when it was over.[1]

Gatty writes Lavy about her conquest:

May I die, my Dear, if I believe there is such another pretty Fellow in the whole Military, as now pays his Addresses to me. Bless me! that I should not have known *London* before! Never tarry in *Yorkshire,* my Dear, whilst there is such a Place as this to resort to. I was at the old Playhouse last Night, to see *Hamlet;* when that dear little Fellow *Garrick!* O! how delightfully mad was he! And, my Dear, there were several of the Royal Family there, I know them all by Sight; and so elegantly were we Ladies drest, in the Front-Boxes, as would have done your Heart good to have seen us; but possibly I may be talking Gibberish all this while, to you, who are a solid Country Lady, and whose only Scenes are bleak Hills, and dreary Valleys. Alas! my Dear, thou knowest not what Life means! [2]

Garrick's wonderful portrayal of Hamlet, one of the histrionic marvels of the age, inspired in 1749 the finest scene about the theater to be found in any eighteenth-century novel. Every schoolboy knows the masterly episode of Tom Jones and Partridge at one of Garrick's consummate performances of the most coveted of all dramatic roles. The passage is a distillation of the art of the great ironist, Henry Fielding. Familiar though it be, no account of the drama and the novel which omitted it would be worth a tinker's dam.

As soon as the play, which was Hamlet, Prince of Denmark, began, Partridge was all attention, nor did he break silence till the entrance of the ghost; upon which he asked Jones, 'What man that was in the strange dress; something,' said he, 'like what I have seen in a picture. Sure it is not armour, is it?'—Jones answered, 'That is the ghost.'—To which Partridge replied with a smile, 'Persuade me to that, sir, if you can. Though I can't say I ever actually saw a ghost in my life, yet I am certain I should know one, if I saw him, better than that comes to. No, no, sir, ghosts don't appear in such dresses as that, neither.' In this mistake, which caused much laughter in the neighbourhood of Partridge, he was suffered to continue, till the scene between the ghost and Hamlet, when Partridge gave that credit to Mr. Garrick which he had denied to Jones, and fell into so violent a trembling, that his knees knocked against each other. Jones asked him what was the matter, and whether he was afraid of the warrior upon the stage? 'O la! sir,' said he, 'I perceive now it is what you told me. I am

[1] I, 68–70.
[2] I, 77. The novelist has erred in dating the letters 1740, for Garrick had not appeared as Hamlet so early.

not afraid of anything; for I know it is but a play. And if it was really a ghost, it could do one no harm at such a distance, and in so much company; and yet if I was frightened, I am not the only person.'—'Why, who,' cries Jones, 'dost thou take to be such a coward here besides thyself?'—'Nay, you may call me coward if you will; but if that little man there upon the stage is not frightened, I never saw any man frightened in my life. Ay, ay: go along with you: ay, to be sure! Who's fool then? Will you? Lud have mercy upon such fool-hardiness!—Whatever happens, it is good enough for you.—Follow you? I'd follow the devil as soon. Nay, perhaps it is the devil—for they say he can put on what likeness he pleases.—Oh! here he is again.—No farther! No, you have gone far enough already; farther than I'd have gone for all the king's dominions.' Jones offered to speak, but Partridge cried, 'Hush, hush! dear sir, don't you hear him?' And during the whole speech of the ghost, he sat with his eyes fixed partly on the ghost and partly on Hamlet, and with his mouth open; the same passions which succeeded each other in Hamlet succeeding likewise in him.

When the scene was over Jones said, 'Why, Partridge, you exceed my expectations. You enjoy the play more than I conceived possible.'—'Nay, sir,' answered Partridge, 'if you are not afraid of the devil, I can't help it; but, to be sure, it is natural to be surprised at such things, though I know there is nothing in them: not that it was the ghost that surprised me, neither; for I should have known that to have been only a man in a strange dress; but when I saw the little man so frightened himself, it was that which took hold of me.'—'And dost thou imagine, then, Partridge,' cries Jones, 'that he was really frightened?'—'Nay, sir,' said Partridge, 'did not you yourself observe afterwards, when he found it was his own father's spirit, and how he was murdered in the garden, how his fear forsook him by degrees, and he was struck dumb with sorrow, as it were, just as I should have been, had it been my own case?—But hush! O la! what noise is that? There he is again.—Well, to be certain, though I know there is nothing at all in it, I am glad I am not down yonder, where those men are.' Then turning his eyes again upon Hamlet, 'Ay, you may draw your sword; what signifies a sword against the power of the devil?'

During the second act, Partridge made very few remarks. He greatly admired the fineness of the dresses; nor could he help observing upon the king's countenance. 'Well,' said he, 'how people may be deceived by faces! *Nulla fides fronti* is, I find, a true saying. Who would think, by looking in the king's face, that he had ever committed murder?' He then inquired after the ghost; but Jones, who intended he should be surprised, gave him no other satisfaction than 'that he might possibly see him again soon, and in a flash of fire.'

Partridge sat in a fearful expectation of this; and now, when the ghost made his next appearance, Partridge cried out, 'There, sir, now; what say you now? is he frightened now or no? As much frightened as you think me, and, to be sure, nobody can help some fears. I would not be in so bad a condition as what's his name, squire Hamlet, is there, for all the world. Bless me! what's become of the spirit? As I am a living soul, I thought I saw him sink into the earth!—'Indeed, you saw right,' answered Jones.—'Well, well,' cries Partridge, 'I know it is only a play; and besides, if there was anything in all this, Madam Miller would not laugh so; for, as to you, sir, you would not be afraid, I believe, if the devil was here in person.—There, there— Ay, no wonder you are in such a passion; shake the vile wicked wretch to pieces. If she was my own mother, I would serve her so. To be sure, all duty to a mother is forfeited by such wicked doings.—Ay, go about your business, I hate the sight of you.'

Our critic was now pretty silent till the play which Hamlet introduces before the king. This he did not at first understand, till Jones explained it to him; but he no sooner entered into the spirit of it than he began to bless himself that he had never committed murder. Then turning to Mrs. Miller, he asked her, 'If she did not imagine the king looked as if he was touched; though he is,' said he, 'a good actor, and doth all he can to hide it. Well, I would not have so much to answer for as that wicked man there hath, to sit upon a much higher chair than he sits upon. No wonder he run away; for your sake I'll never trust an innocent face again.'

The grave-digging scene next engaged the attention of Partridge, who expressed much surprise at the number of skulls thrown upon the stage. To which Jones answered, 'That it was one of the most famous burial-places about town.'—'No wonder, then,' cries Partridge, 'that the place is haunted. But I never saw in my life a worse gravedigger. I had a sexton, when I was clerk, that should have dug three graves while he is digging one. The fellow handles a spade as if it was the first time he had ever had one in his hand. Ay, ay, you may sing. You had rather sing than work, I believe.'—Upon Hamlet's taking up the skull, he cried out, 'Well! it is strange to see how fearless some men are: I never could bring myself to touch anything belonging to a dead man, on any account.—He seemed frightened enough too at the ghost, I thought. *Nemo omnibus horis sapit.*'

Little more worth remembering occurred during the play, at the end of which Jones asked him, 'Which of the players he had liked best?' To this he answered, with some appearance of indignation at the question, 'The king, without doubt.'—'Indeed, Mr. Partridge,' says Mrs. Miller. 'You are not of the same opinion with the town; for they are all agreed that Hamlet is acted by the best player who ever was on the stage.'—'He the best player!' cries Partridge, with a contemptuous sneer; 'why, I could act as well as he myself. I am sure, if I had seen a ghost, I should have looked in the very same manner, and done just as he did. And then, to be sure, in that scene, as you called it, between him and his mother, where you told me he acted so fine, why, Lord help me, any man, that is, any good man, that had such a mother, would have done exactly the same. I know you are only joking with me; but indeed, madam, though I was never at a play in London, yet I have seen acting before in the country: and the king for my money; he speaks all his words distinctly, half as loud again as the other.—Any body may see he is an actor.'. . .

Thus ended the adventure at the playhouse; where Partridge had afforded great mirth, not only to Jones and Mrs. Miller, but to all who sat within hearing, who were more attentive to what he said than to anything that passed on the stage.

He durst not go to bed that night, for fear of the ghost; and for many nights after sweated two or three hours before he went to sleep, with the same apprehensions, and waked several times in great horrors, crying out, 'Lord have mercy upon us! there it is.'[1]

---

[1] *The History of Tom Jones, a Foundling,* Book 16, chapter 5. The Ghost at this time was played by Dennis Delane and Edward Berry, and the King by Luke Sparks and Mr. Bridges. The Queen was played by Mrs. Bennet and Mrs. Pritchard, and

Much in Partridge's vein, an old woman and a barber in *The Sedan* (1757) comment on the Ghost as acted by Edward Berry and the King as acted by Richard Winstone. Some playbills are posted near the door where the sedan chair is undergoing repairs.

The play bills . . . being pasted up pretty near where I was planted, I had perpetual amusement. An old woman this morning, with great exactness put on her spectacles, and looking over the characters of some tragedy, when she came to the part of the Ghost to be done by Mr. *Berry,* said, then He will be damn'd eternally, as he deserves, a wicked profane sinner:— Why, what an abominable world we live in! they'll all be damn'd that are in that paper, but particularly himself. When so many sermons have been wrote against profaneness, and folly, and luxury, and immorality, 'tis very amazing to me that they still will follow it. I should not be surprized, if the devil was to fly away with the roof of the house, and particularly Covent-Garden, when they are shewing the devils and hell-fire, as cousin Edward has told me; and as I live, here is a dance by a devil; Madam Cap-devil too,—so there are she-devils then; I believe they will find old Satan alone enough to manage them, or I am mistaken greatly, and have heard homilies and prayers to no purpose. Away she pac'd, or rather hobbled.
A pert barber and his brother shaver next read them over; and when he saw the part of the *King* to be perform'd by Mr. ——, he said, I know him well! and a great man he is; for you generally see he does the king, while your famous Garrick seldom does any thing better than a tobacco-man or gamester, or some such low thing. Lord! it is not the number of lines they speak (you understand me) that makes the part, but the cloaths and the attendants. Why now you shall see that Garrick, whom his particular friends puff so mightily, coming in, as I say, like a beggar, and the moment this man appears, all the drums beat, and the trumpets sound, and the scene all drawn back, and such numbers of fine attendants on him, so that the whole house applaud before they see his face, which is a compliment due to majesty, and then he appears as fine as a lord, and is a king indeed: —then sneaks in your Garrick again, without even a lac'd hat, or a sword on;—no, no, talk of your Garrick's, and your Quin's, Winston for my money.[1]

It seems probable that Fielding's matchless praise of Garrick's Hamlet discouraged other novelists from attempting an extended episode about performances of the tragedy at the legitimate houses. They chose rather productions at a less awe-inspiring level, where they could write within their range about *Hamlet* at the mercy of amateurs and strollers. The play received, however, passing allusions in a number of

---

the First Gravedigger by Macklin and Richard Yates. Fielding's placing of the closet-scene before the play-scene must be due to inadvertence.

[1] II, 46–48. BM. The tobacco-man was Abel Drugger in Jonson's *Alchemist,* one of Garrick's most famous roles. The gamester was Beverley in Edward Moore's *Gamester,* 1753. Thomas Davies notes that "Winstone, who was tolerated in other parts, in Downright [*Every Man in his Humour*] was highly applauded" (*Dramatic Miscellanies,* 1783, II, 66).

novels and was especially popular with the ladies. In the notorious John Cleland's *The Surprises of Love* (1765), Felicia Norgrove, visiting her aunt in London, is eager to be introduced to its delights:

Soon after . . . tea was served in, Felicia, taking up the General Adver- tiser for the day, as it lay on one of the window-seats, happened to remark in it one of the playbills, specifying the Tragedy of Hamlet to be acted that night at Covent-Garden; and spoke of it as a piece, the reading of which had ever given her great pleasure; and spoke of it without so much as dreaming of the consequence. But her aunt . . . readily . . . snatched this opportunity of sacrificing . . . her own . . . indifference, to the pleasure she imagined it would be to her niece, to see a play, that she pro- fessed to like, and to see one too, for the first time, at least in London.[1]

Unfortunately, we do not learn about Felicia's evening at "the other house," where she might have seen Spranger Barry, Garrick's most formidable rival, or William Smith as Hamlet.

In *The History of Alicia Montague* (1768), Lord L——is attracted by a pretty woman at the theater:

Let not my fair readers altogether despise his lordship for his insensibil- ity to their charms. Think not that love had rendered him so stupid as not to distinguish a woman of beauty and merit from a mere picture. As an instance of the contrary, one evening at the play-house, he observed lady *Charlotte R——* from an opposite box. The justly admired tragedy of *Hamlet, prince of Denmark,* was performing. Her ladyship seemed so deeply interested in every scene, and all her features were so finely ani- mated, that lord L—— naturally distinguished her from the many flutter- ing and insipid beauties, which generally are seen in a crouded audience.[2]

When Miss Petworth's guardian took her to see Garrick's Hamlet, in *'Twas Right to Marry Him* (1774), she sat in the greenboxes and was "never more entertained in [her] life."[3] And Adeline Belville found similar pleasure in Charlotte Palmer's *Female Stability; or, The History of Miss Belville* (1780), when she went to the playhouse with Lord William and Mr. Grenville:

We went, and saw Garrick in Hamlet, the first time I had ever beheld him in that noble character. He surpassed even the high idea I had formed of him, and by his admirable performance did ample justice to the inimitable language of that justly admired play.[4]

Young aspirants to the stage always hope one day to act Hamlet. There is a spirited account of the education and trials of one of these hopeful youths in *The Adventures of an Author. Written by Himself*

---

[1] Page 95. Bodleian.
[2] Dublin, II, 227. Pickering and Chatto.
[3] I, 183–184. BM.
[4] III, 24.

and a Friend (1767). John Atall, the hero, began his career by studying law:

But let it not be imagined he confined his ideas intirely to law: no, he would now and then relax from the fatigue of business, take a slice of George Barnwell, or a shilling touch at Jane Shore. Jack had read some comedies, and more tragedies; and he thought, he entered into the wit of Congreve, and the flights of Shakespear: this is almost enough for a young fellow to have an itch for spouting; but this was not all: he fancied he had a good voice, and an agreeable figure—that he was graceful in his action, and happy in his pronunciation. Upon these principles he studied the soliloquy in Hamlet, the balcony scene in Romeo, and the smoothering scene in Othello. He was informed there was a spouting-club in Fetter-lane, and he soon had the honour of becoming a member. This inclination for acting increased with his success at the club, and from the applause he met with from his fellow-members—

To be, or not to be—

was now no question with him; he had already resolved upon dedicating his future studies to Melpomene and Thalia—leaving blind justice to courts of law and inns of court.[1]

In preparation for winning the approval of a theatrical manager, Jack "read Shakespear with admiration, and spoke him with enthusiasm."

His knowledge of the dead languages enabled him to throw many lights upon this sublime bard, which he thought had hitherto escaped all his commentators; and this surprising depth of criticism and erudition gained him more applause amongst his competitors in acting, than all his spouting powers. The loquacious barber was greatly astonished at his quotations from Aristotle, having never in his life once thought about the unity of time or place: the voiceferous cheesemonger was still more astonished to hear him distinguish episodes, protasis, epitasis, catastasis, catastrophe; and the journeyman taylor, who was reckoned the best performer of them all in tragedy, but who did not know an *alpha* from an *omega,* swore by Jasus he could not tell what the devil he was talking about with his dactyls and spondees.[2]

Jack is growing up: at seventeen, under the spell of Otway and Rowe, he walks out of a Sunday in the Park with Sophy, a cheesemonger's daughter, to whom he pours out his soul in quotations from *The Orphan.* "She would tell him he was the very picture of Garrick —that their eyes and complexion were exactly alike; and that he every day the more resembled him."

This last observation would sting him to the soul, and stop the full career of all his tragedy heroism. What, he would say to himself, can my resemblance of that great man fail in, but in point of beard? This he thought

[1] I, 30–31.
[2] I, 32–33.

the rub, and, therefore, in the full resolution of being Garrick himself, the powdered charcoal was the next day most amply applied.

Sophy, . . . when she saw him, could not help smiling, and jocosely asked him if he had washed his face? Yes, he would say, but I have not been shaved today.—No; she would reply, nor yesterday neither. Such an attack upon a man's virility might have disconcerted a hero of more effrontery than Jack, especially when his rival was present, with a genuine long beard.[1]

Giving up hope of winning Sophia, Jack "read tragedy deeper than ever—mouthed all the dagger scenes with more than foaming anger," and becomes a misogynist. He feels better "upon the virtuous Sophia's being brought to bed of a young *blacksmith*, the miniature representative of his bristly rival, whom her father compelled to join hands in lawful wedlock." [2]

He haunts the Robin Hood and other disputing clubs, where he acquires repute as an orator, and after six months he believes himself ready to be introduced to a manager. A lucky opportunity provides a conference "with one of the theatrical monarchs." Mr. Hyper, a genius and a critic, conducts him to Southampton Street and Covent Garden. An interview with Garrick follows. Jack's knees knock together, and he can scarcely walk into the parlor.

Atall's thoughts were, during this period, solely occupied with the manner in which he should address the theatrical monarch, upon his entrance, and what kind of a reception he should meet with.

At length the parlour door opened; the manager entered; and now we will commence a short dialogue.

Man. Gentlemen, your servant— How do you do, Mr. Hyper?

Hyp. Sir, much at your service— I have brought you a young gentleman of my acquaintance, who has some thoughts of coming upon the stage, and is desirous, Sir, of the honour of your protection.

Man. He does me great honour— You know, Mr. Hyper, any thing in my power you may command.

[*A couple of bows now took place, and Jack's spirits were, by this declaration, much recruited.*]

Hyp. You are very polite, Sir—I believe you will find Mr. Atall to be possessed of some theatrical talents, which, when properly cultivated, with a little of your instruction, will, I doubt not, shoot forth to the satisfaction and amusement of the town.

Man. Very prettily expressed, Mr. Hyper— You were always happy at an extemporary allegory.—Pray, Sir, did you ever appear in public? [*To Mr. Atall*].

[1] I, 36–37.
[2] I, 38–39.

At. Never, Sir.

Man. I presume, Sir, you have made some experiments in private.

At. Yes, Sir.

Man. Pray, Sir, what *walk* may you have chosen?

At. Tragedy, principally, Sir.

Man. It is a pity that young performers would not endeavour more at comedy—we have fifty tragedians for one good comedian: but this error does not seem confined to acting only: the writers of the present age are all the votaries of Melpomene, and leave poor Thalia, with great impropriety, to bemoan her fate.—We have not had a decent comedy, since the Suspicious Husband, except—but, Sir, what parts have you particularly studied?

At. Castalio, Othello, Jaffier, Hamlet, Richard—

Man. But pray, are you perfect in any of these?

At. Yes, Sir, I believe I can repeat many passages pretty correctly in either—

Man. You'll excuse me, Sir,—but, pray have you learnt to dance and fence?

At. No, Sir, neither—

Man. Why, Sir, these accomplishments are absolutely necessary in an actor; a man cannot present himself decently without having acquired the first; and the second, you are sensible, is very essential in the last act of every tragedy.

At. I propose going for a month to Mr. ——, who teaches grown gentlemen.

Man. That will be scarce a sufficient period to learn to make a bow— But pray, Sir, with submission, do not you perceive that you have some impediment in your speech?

At. Sir, I was told, when a child, that I was tongue-tied; but I thought I had got the better of it, since I had spoke so many famous speeches, with applause, at the spouting club in Fetter-lane.

Man. You must inevitably have a chirurgical operation performed before you can come upon the stage.—I observed as soon as you began to speak, that you was tongue-tied.

At. Very well, Sir.

Hyp. Oh—there is nothing in it—there is no more pain in the operation than in a cut finger.

Man. And then, Sir, I would advise you to apply yourself assiduously to dancing and fencing—

At. Very well, Sir.

Man. And then after that, when you have made some progress, if you will come to me the beginning of next season—

At. Next season, Sir!

Man. Yes, *next season*—I am quite full this— I have engaged more hands than I have occasion for already— I say next season—we'll see what can be done— I am a little busy at present— I've a gentleman waiting for me in my library—and so, gentlemen, your servant.[1]

Poor Jack undergoes the operation and studies acting and fencing. But when at the end of six months he shows no improvement, he abandons hope of shining as an actor and turns to other occupations.

Although they did not aspire to the professional stage, devotees of spouting clubs might carry into maturity their passion for orating Shakespeare. In the same year as *The Adventures of an Author,* there appeared a novel by John Robinson of Norwich, *The History of Mr. Charles Chance and Miss Clara Vellum,* whose hero works as copyist for the heroine's uncle, Mr. Vellum, a lawyer.

Mr. Vellum, who was not yet thirty years of age, still belonged to a spouting club, of which he had commenced member during his clerkship. . . . A great part of Mr. Vellum's time being employed in preparations for his evening's exhibitions at the club, . . . I had a very considerable deal of leisure. . . . Mr. Vellum having accidentally found out that I had a smattering of literature, had curiosity to make trial of my taste; and accordingly taking me with him into a backward room, acquainted me with his intention, and did me the honour to let me hear him speak half a dozen of Hamlet's speeches. I cannot say that he really merited the commendation I bestowed on him, but I praised his performance with so good a grace, that he declared he had seldom met with so judicious a critic on theatrical elocution as I was. I had from this time very frequent occasions to exercise my critical faculty, for whenever a new character or a new scene tempted Mr. Vellum to study, I was very sure to be consulted on his manner of speaking, and as sure to commend him.[2]

With the strollers *Hamlet* long enjoyed a lusty career. Many a rafter in country barns reechoed to the soliloquies orated by old and young troupers. The raucous Grubstreet journalist, John Shebbeare, devoted many pleasant pages of his best novel, now unfortunately very rare, to the adventures of actors in traveling companies. In *Lydia; or, Filial Piety* (1755),[3] Mr. Cook joins Mr. Archer's company. Cook,

---

[1] I, 53–58.

[2] Pages 25–28. The copy of this novel in my possession seems to be unique.

[3] For a summary and critical analysis of *Lydia* see J. R. Foster, *History of the Pre-Romantic Novel in England,* pp. 91–94; and for Shebbeare the same writer's "Smollett's Pamphleteering Foe Shebbeare," *PMLA,* LVII (1942), 1053–1100. I quote from the first edition of *Lydia* in the Bodleian, but the novel was reprinted in *The Novelist's Magazine,* XXII (1786).

"who had begun his first Struttings on the Stage as an Actor at *Barnstaple* in *Devonshire*," had been bred a wigmaker, "but from dressing the Perriwigs of a Company of Strollers, and being free of the House, he had conceived such an ardent Desire of appearing in the first Characters as a Player," that Archer permitted him to appear as Othello. Cook has the not unique talent of "transposing an Author's Intention, by making the Audience weep at Comedy, and laugh at Tragedy," and, of course, he aspires to the London stage. During his travels with a Welsh friend, Mr. Popkins, he recites the "To be or not to be" soliloquy. An interview is arranged with John Rich. When asked about his roles, Cook lists Othello, Hamlet, Jaffeir, and Polydore, "which I have play'd in the Country."

'Well, then, says the Patentee, 'give me the Soliloquy in *Hamlet*.' At these Words Mr. *Cook* began, 'To be, or not to be'; beginning and ending with an extremely low Bow to Mr. *R—h;* which Bows were well received, and added weight to the speaking. 'Why this may do, Mr. *Cook;* I thi—nk your Name is *C-o-o-k,*' taking Snuff thro' the Words *think* and *Cook—* 'You have a Genius for the Stage, you copy nobody, you are an Original, yet there must be much Pains to instruct you; therefore, hark you, Sir: If you will confine yourself to my Instruction, I shall give you two Hundred a Year, and a Benefit; you may not play these two Years, but your Salary begins this Day; but on Condition only, that you are instructed by me alone; and ha-rk-ee, remark my Attitudes in Harlequin, carry them into Tragedy, and you'll succeed.' 'Yes, Sir,' replied *Cook.*[1]

Later on, Parson Pugh, a relative of Lydia, having read in the papers that she has married Lord Liberal and has become the mother of a son and heir, decides to leave Wales to visit her. In his travels he stops at Bideford.

At this Town . . . there was at that Time a Company of strolling Players; this Troop had most judiciously pitched upon a large Slaughter-house for their Theatre, the Place being the best adapted in the World for the executing Comedies and Tragedies in their Manner.

The Troop indeed was small, consisting of five Men and three Women; but then it made amends in Goodness for what was wanting in Number, all of them being Geniuses in the dramatic Way, not one of the whole Set, Male or Female, but what was universal in his Profession; they were not like your *London* Players confined to a few particular Parts only, each performed every Character with equal Perfections; the Men from King *Lear, Hamlet*, and *Othello*, to the Grave-digger, Lictor, or Executioner in Tragedy; and, in Comedy, either Lord *Foppington*, Sir *John Falstaff*, or *Abel Drugger*, made no Difference: the Ladies also in Tragedy and Comedy dropt from *Belvidera* to *Nell*, from the Fair Penitent to Mistress *Abigail* in the *Drummer;* and all this in so excellent a Way, that the nicest Judge could not decide which Part was best play'd; a Circumstance very rarely to be found on any Stage.

[1] II, 21–22, 39, 83–84.

Delivering playbills in the country

Their Wardrobe indeed was but slender, the Fate of Merit, yet showy for the Quantity; the Suits of Mens Apparel extremely well laced with gilt Leather, which being disposed with Taste and Utility, a Union so rarely to be met with in the same Person, at once by most excellent Contrivance cover'd Holes, and display'd Finery; one Coat besides, which had been formerly black, and was still mistaken for that Colour by night, together with Tye-wigs and Bags, Daggers made of Oyster-knives, Swords whose Rage no Scabbard could contain, together with an old Blanket died blue, to be spread for Information to the Audience that some Death was approaching, and to receive the falling Lover, made the Play-house Stock, besides one Set of Scenes adapted to all Plays; the Ladies Dress indeed should claim a separate Description, but as it answered in full Justice to that of the Gentlemen, we shall omit them. Their Dressing-room may be seen in Mr. *Hogarth's* Print of that Subject, better than I can describe it.

These Deficiencies in outward Appearances, were amply supplied by the Goodwill of the young Gentlemen of the Town; *Juba* never wanted a Banyan to make him an *African* Prince, nor *Cato* and his Senate good Night-gowns befitting the Dignity of *Roman* Senators; besides clean Shirts, which were frequently of no little Advantage when the idle Laundress had forgotten to bring home in the Evening the Linnen, which was delivered in the Morning; so that the Stock of Shirts being large, almost every Man having one at the Washing, and the other on, it could not be for want of Linnen, but clean Linnen, that sometimes these Heroes, like *Harry* the Fourth of *France,* were distrest for a clean Shirt.

The Ladies were all born of very good Families, render'd unhappy by Love, turn'd out to the World by some cruel Parents or Guardian, left Orphans without Support, or by some other blameless Misfortune, which had forced them, contrary to their natural Inclinations, upon the Stage; for being bred Gentlewomen, they knew not how to work, yet still of most severe Chastity.

This was a Life, however, they were most heartily tired of, as appeared from their Conversation in every Town they play'd, particularly towards the Approach of a Benefit-night; for which Reason they never failed most humbly to intreat the Favour of the Town, on this particular Occasion, to honour them with their Company, and enable them to quit that wretched Life, and return to some distant Relation who had promised to receive them; thus moving the Compassion of all kind Hearts, and unhackney'd Heads.[1]

In William Toldervy's *History of Two Orphans* (1756), Tom Heartley and George Richmond, already displayed as ardent devotees of Shakespeare, volunteer to help a poor company of strollers at a little town on the border of Oxfordshire. Heartley is to appear as Hamlet, Richmond as Laertes, and their friend Mr. Duroy as the Ghost. Duroy, himself a practiced stroller, conceives that "the novelty of gentlemen playing for their diversion may probably bring half of the inhabitants: when the poor players, tho' perhaps better performers,

[1] IV, 62–65. Belvidera, in Otway's *Venice Preserved; The Drummer,* by Joseph Addison; Nell, in Charles Coffey's ballad-opera, *The Devil to Pay.*

might exhibit to empty benches, and with stomachs in the same lamentable condition." The company was in pitiful circumstances,

for, as they had been accustomed weekly to see a justice of the peace, besides franking all his relations; their receipts becoming short, the tribute was omitted, and they were now threatened by the said magistrate, with the punishment of a bridewell, and all its terrors.[1]

The three gentlemen will perform on condition that their real names be concealed.

The next day at noon, these words were proclaimed throughout the town by the beat of drum and sound of trumpet:

'This present evening will be presented that celebrated play, written by your countryman *Shakespear,* called *Hamlet Prince of Denmark.* The parts of *Hamlet, Laertes,* and the *Ghost,* to be performed by gentlemen of *distinction* for their own amusement. With singing and dancing between the acts. The whole to be concluded with an epilogue written, and to be spoken, by the gentleman who will appear in the character of *Hamlet.*

To begin exactly at six o'clock.
God Save the King, and *Justice* Joram.'

It so happened, that poverty had considerably thinned this company of comedians, that, though they had received our potent reinforcement, one character yet remained to be filled up; when *Duroy* observed 'that *Copper* [their servant] might supply that defect, for that he had heard him speak many things in tragedy, but not any part of this play; however, gentlemen, continued he, *Humphrey* may appear in the character of *Guildenstern,* which you know is very short.' *Richmond* then called *Copper,* who was swigging ale in the kitchen with one of the comedians, whose name was *Finny Roach.*[2]

The play is performed. The orphan Heartley wears his own mourning suit, purchased at the time of his mother's death, for it is better than anything in the company's wardrobe.

Humphrey Copper, together with his friend, who was to personate *Rosincrans,* had been so very busy with a barrel of humming ale, that when they came upon the stage, neither of them could repeat a word. Indeed, *Roach* had prudently placed his part in the crown of his hat, and read it tolerably well: but *Copper* continued to be as silent as the dumb alderman in *Richard* the third.[3]

At the end, Tom Heartley "came upon the stage, in his common coat, and spoke the following short Epilogue":

'Such is the tale which Stratford's bard has told.
(How great the lesson both to young and old!)

[1] III, 51–52. Bodleian.
[2] III, 53–54.
[3] III, 54–55.

A bard, the deepest skill'd in nature's laws,
Gives guilt its payment, and explodes the cause.
O! may each breast be mov'd with such a deed!
And all such villains thus unpitied bleed!
To you, for others, let me here express
Their gratitude, for you've remov'd distress.
So may your hearts and hands for ever be
Bless'd with intention, and ability.
For us, we neither ask, or merit praise,
Kind health and peace, enliven all our days,
But let not calumny our fame abuse,
For all the candid will our faults excuse.' [1]

So warm is the reception of this impromptu presentation that the four travelers give two more performances. Later, their charity towards impoverished strollers, not to mention their own lack of cash, impels them to join a company managed by Mr. Shulee, who offers them "the preference in all his best plays; such as the characters of *Hamlet, Orestes, Oroonoko, Othello, Anthony, Jaffier, Chamont,* and *Bevil.*" [2]

His company, it must be confessed, was found to be indifferent, but his scenes and machinery were considerably worse: for though *Duroy* knew him, in other respects, to be a man of integrity, yet a propensity for gaming always intervened when he had fortune in possession, which generally kept this itinerant *Roscius* very poor. . . . The sum received by *Heartley* and *Richmond,* for appearing in the best characters, and by *Humphrey Copper* for drum-beating, trumpet-blowing, fiddle-scraping, and candle-snuffing amounted in the whole three weeks to one pound seventeen shillings and sixpence only.[3]

In 1769 John Potter, professional dramatic critic and author of *The Theatrical Review* (1772), in *The History of the Adventures of Arthur O'Bradley,* devoted some vigorous passages to a chronicle of barnstormers. Arthur, a young Englishman sent by his father into the world to seek his fortune, meets an old acquaintance and schoolfellow, Mr. Caleb, who relates his history. Some years since, he was engaged by the manager of a company of players in Wales, in which he served as "Footman, Scene-shifter, Candle-snuffer, and I know not how many Capacities besides. . . . But I lived well." [4] When he grew older, he was instructed in the art of acting, "in which I soon made some Figure; was taken notice of, and applauded." For a time, as the manager's favorite, he progressed, "but, as I grew older, I found I was linked with

---

[1] III, 55–56.
[2] IV, 102. Orestes, in Ambrose Philips' *The Distrest Mother;* Oroonoko, in Southerne's *Oroonoko;* Jaffeir, in Otway's *Venice Preserved;* Chamont, in Otway's *The Orphan;* Bevil, in Steele's *The Conscious Lovers.*
[3] III, 102–113.
[4] I, 129. BM.

a Set of Men, of dissolute, licentious Principles; whose Lives, were a
Scene of Dissipation and Distress." [1]

The Manager was a Tyrant, preying upon the Exigencies of his People,
and starving them to enrich himself. His Shares, for having the Direction
of the Company, Cloaths, Scenes &c which were his Property, and acting
himself; engross'd the greatest Part of what we got, so that we were a set
of Beggars, rul'd with a high Hand by an avaricious, despotic Monarch.[2]

With no alternative but to submit, Caleb is still with the same manager, although his "Situation [is] so deplorable, as to be beneath the
notice of Envy." However, his performance is so pleasing that his
benefits generally exceed the rest in point of profit. He is presently
selling tickets to the gentry. When Arthur asks why he does not quit
this company, Caleb replies:

"I have of late been considering of various Methods to accomplish it, but
the Prospect before me, seems difficult to approach. I have several times
determined to visit the Capital, and try my Fortune there; but have been
dissuaded from it by an Assurance, that I should fail in the Attempt;
notwithstanding, I have been told, many worse Performers than myself,
have, and do succeed. The Difficulty of getting on either of the London
Stages, is beyond Description, for I am informed, that, at one of the
Theatres in particular, the principal Manager is a great Actor himself, and
therefore, does not chuse to encourage Merit or Genius, for fear they
should eclipse his own Glory."
        "You are misinformed, be assured, said Arthur, I have been a great
Frequenter of the Theatres, and know the Genius and Disposition of our
modern *Roscius* too well, to suppose him capable of such mean Artifice.
He is the Patron of Merit, and the Nurse of Genius, whenever he meets
with them, however disguised they may appear at the first View. To him,
the British Theatre, is indebted for most of its Improvements; and to him,
the present Generation of Actors owe all their Knowledge and Excellence.
Yet all this, has not been sufficient to secure him from the Slander and
Malevolence of envious Persons; who traduce his Character, because they
are incapable of equalling his Perfections.
        "The Science of acting (for I think it should be considered as one) is
not easily attained; Genius is the Gift of few;—scarcely one Garrick is
born in a Century; and it requires great Knowledge and some Degree of
Excellence to form even a secondary Actor.—Nineteen out of twenty, who
attempt the Stage, fail of Success, for want of the essential Qualifications;
and whenever this is the Case, they are unwilling to suppose, that the
Defect is in themselves, and hence ascribe it to Causes, that are neither
just, or generous. However, let not these Things damp your Resolution,
go and offer yourself; but with this Resolution, to stand or fall, as this
great Master pronounces his Opinion. If he rejects you, be wise, and rest
satisfied; nor foolishly, as I have known many do, persist in Impossibilities:
And condemn not his Judgment, but attribute it to your own Imper-

[1] I, 130.
[2] I, 130.

fections; for be assured, his Knowledge is too extensive, to render him liable to be mistaken. The vain Fool, and the undiscerning Idiot, frequently meet with his Disapprobation, and hence take Occasion to rail, which may have furnished Slander with Materials for Defamation; but these Things will have little Weight with the discerning few, who know his Worth and Excellencies.—If he should find you are deserving, and to have Abilities, he will promote and protect you: And notwithstanding, the Public know good acting, and the Merits of a Performer, better in this Age, than in former Times, yet, such is their Generosity of Temper and desire to encourage even the humblest Attempt of Genius, that they are indulgent beyond Expectation; slow to Censure, but eager to applaud. Such is the Disposition of a British Audience." [1]

Somewhat later, Arthur meets his friend again in Devonshire, where Caleb is trying to obtain permission to act from a provincial mayor. The mayor is obdurate: "he would not suffer *Strolhers* in his Town, because the *Lau* said they were Waggabones. . . . Get out of Town immediately, or I shall *reprehend* you, for I'll not *remit Waggabones* in my *Juredickson*." [2] When Arthur pleads with the mayor, permission is granted. The mayor has "no *Dejection* to it, provided it will not *degrate* the Dignity of my *Sofrain Hauthority;* but you know Sir, I must *desarve* and *retain* that, or I shall not support my *Carractur.* So look you, d'ye see, if so be as how the *Townclark* thinks it will hold good in *Lau,* I have no *Dejection* to it, since you *bequest* it." [3]

When his predecessor is run out of town for immoral behavior with one of the actresses, Caleb becomes manager. He will produce *Hamlet.*

Caleb played the Part of Hamlet with great Correctness and Judgment; and gave evident Proofs, that, he had carefully studied the intention of the Poet, respecting the Connection and Dependance of Hamlet's Character, with the General Design of the Piece. This kind of Attention, is too often neglected by many of our Actors, though essentially necessary for the Support of that Propriety in theatrical Representations, on which alone true Excellence depends. He who plays a principal Character in any dramatic Performance, ought to make himself acquainted not only with the rest of the Characters, but the general Plan and Business of the whole Piece; for by this Knowledge, his Ideas will be enlarged and perfected; which will undoubtedly give Ease and Freedom to the Powers of Speech and Action.—The inimitable *Shakespeare,* in *Hamlet's* Remarks to the Players, has given every young Actor an admirable Lesson; which if properly attended to, is alone sufficient to inform the Understanding, and correct those Incongruities, committed by young Performers in their Attempts to please and excel; who for Want of real Excellencies, vainly fly to imaginary ones, and as *Hamlet* says, '*Tear a Passion to Tatters, to very Rags, to split the Ears of the Groundlings,*' &c.[4]

[1] I, 133–137.
[2] II, 93.
[3] II, 94.
[4] II, 167–169.

During the performance of the scene in the third act between Hamlet and Ophelia, a gentleman in the audience fainted and had to be carried out.

George Keate, in his popular imitation of Sterne, *Sketches from Nature; Taken and Coloured in a Journey to Margate* (1779), narrates in detail the vicissitudes of *Hamlet* at a seaside resort.

THE THEATRE

All the crowned heads of the MARGATE drama would, unquestionably, take it amiss, should they be passed over in silence.—Though it is my wish to *please* all,—I possess a desire equally strong to *offend* none,—and least of all, those who exert their abilities for the entertainment of others. —Though the Kings,—Lords,—and Commons,—in their theatrical barn assembled, convey such confused ideas of the personages they represent, that they become caricatures instead of characters;—nor do they probably, in general aim at any thing more,—for there is usually such a poverty, and laughable distress, running through the whole performance, as renders Comedy extremely ridiculous, and Tragedy truly comical.—

Some ladies of AMELIA's acquaintance, having, through humanity, patronized one of the poor players, bespoke HAMLET,—and exerted their interest to fill the house—it being for the *benefit* of the GHOST, and his wife.

CLERMONT and I were solicited to be of the party;—but the Theatre being much crowded, I found myself unable to sustain the heat of it.—My friend and I, therefore, before the curtain drew up, retired behind the scenes;—and indeed, when we were got there, perceived but little probability, that it would draw up the whole evening,—for surely never was beheld such a scene of confusion, as then appeared, in what served both for their general dressing-room and green-room.—

The centinels, who were to mount guard before the palace of the *Royal* DANE, for want of having any uniform in the wardrobe, had borrowed a couple of sailors jackets.—HORATIO was striding about in a monstrous rage,—declaring he would not act, because his own benefit had been unjustly put back.—The manager, who was corpulent enough to have personated FALSTAFF, even almost without stuffing,—apparelled as young HAMLET, was in no less a passion too,—damning the GHOST's *blood* for being in liquor,—who, as well as his wife, had, on the credit of the many tickets which were taken, given way, through excess of joy, at dinner, to an indulgence they should more prudently have postponed till night.— The GHOST had little to say in his defence,—but his lady, now the *Queen Mother,*—sat royally robed on a joint-stool,—and whilst she was dabbing the last colouring on her cheeks, hickupped, with much brevity, their mutual apology.—Nor did the distress end here—a smith was sent for to break open OPHELIA's *coffin,*—which serving as a travelling trunk to this itinerant company, the GHOST's *helmet,* POLONIUS's *wig,* together with some of the DANISH *regalia,* were lodged within it;—and the manager, having also deposited with them a half anchor of *run spirits,* had so carefully put away the key, that in the hurry it could not be found,—so that the music kept playing *roast beef,* and every popular tune they could think on, to amuse the impatient audience, who knew nothing of the woeful disorder that reigned behind.

The performance was such as might naturally be supposed from the situation and temper of the *Dramatis Personæ.*—The GHOST composed himself far better than I expected,—except, that in the closet scene, he exerted more violence than became his character,—and rushing in, too eagerly, dropped his coat of mail which was accidentally untied.—However, as his shirt happened to be clean, he might pass in it full as well for an inhabitant of the other world, as he did in his old leathern armour.

OPHELIA's dirty silk gown, had been destined for a woman far more slender than herself,—on which account, the robings pinned almost at her hips, and left her in great difficulties to form a convenient stomacher.— Neither she, nor the QUEEN could raise a pair of gloves,—and the latter having scalded her arm, by taking off a pot from the fire, was compelled to appear with it bound round with old linen,—which, in truth but *ill became the majesty of* DENMARK.—The play was received with great indulgence, and excited much more mirth, than it did either terror or pity.—

I have often considered myself, when behind the scenes of more respectable theatres, to be in the situation of those who are in reality about such elevated characters in life, as on the stage are only personated.—They stand in a very different point of view to those who observe them near, when they are not acting their parts,—and who see what poor, flimsy materials contribute to deck them out, as objects for the public eye!

It is of much moment, on which side of the curtain we contemplate either men, or things!—

It were next to impossible to see such noble scenes, as are interspersed in this whimsical tragedy, blundered through, and converted to farce, without their exciting a hearty laugh;—and yet, on the best regulated theatres, how few are there who can support a fine drawn character *chastly* and admirably throughout?—The dignified scenes of the *Tragic Muse,* besides an harmonious voice and ear, superadded to very many personal accomplishments in the player, demand strong judgment, and delicate feelings,—and such who possess this assemblage of endowments (a few exceptions allowed) rarely choose to expose their talents in a situation of this nature.—Should any future fashion render the profession eligible, there would be found, with such advantages, no mystery in it,—nor would the stage feel the want of as great ornaments, as it hath hitherto ever boasted.—The same argument must inevitably appear just, with respect to the *lighter scenes* of the drama;—it being difficult for an actor, without the aid of a very superior genius, to delineate, with ease, and propriety, manners which he is not *familiarized* to himself.—Hence it is, that the characters of genteel comedy, are those which in general suffer the most in representation,—while the strong-marked features of common life, rarely fail of receiving their due colouring.—

As CLERMONT and I, between the play and the farce, were debating these matters, on an old form, which ten minutes before had constituted the *Throne* of DENMARK— Our neighbors, says my friend, understand this business better. . . . I know not whether a long absence from the ENGLISH theatre, and a frequent attendance on the FRENCH one, hath vitiated my judgment,—but I confess, I love a tragedy that ends happily, and where the struggles of virtue are crowned with triumph.—*Pity* is a more pleasing exercise of the human mind, than *terror!*—Scenes of this kind, I have ever observed, are honoured with the most tears;—and tears are the plaudits of unerring nature!—A judicious writer will deeply interest the passions—awaken sensibility,—and penetrate every avenue to the heart, without the aid of either murder, or of death;—which, by being made too familiar to our sight, soon lose the effect they should inspire.— To speak plainly, I think we have dealt rather too largely in daggers, and poison, on this side of the water.—I hate a fifth act, which, as this of to-night, makes the stage like the shop of a *carcase butcher.*—If we had our eye a little more on the FRENCH theatre, I can never believe we should write the worse for it.—

For Heaven's sake, my good friend, cried I, forbear any parallel!—Ever live *well* with those you must live *with;*—people do not always give up opinion with good-humour.—The great scenes of SHAKESPEARE,— which no pen hath hitherto either *rivalled,* or *approached,*—will, I hope, ever live on our stage, in spite of some few absurd ones with which they are intermixed.—You must consider this PRODIGY of NATURE, as born in an age, when the rules of dramatic writing were but little studied, even in the most polished nations.—Many of his successors, who copied his faults, though unable to imitate his beauties, may in truth, afford you an ample field for criticism— However, to pacify your spirit, allow me to say, that since the period when you left ENGLAND, we have had our obligations to the FRENCH theatre,—and very many pieces, whose gross *Absurdities* did not shock our wise grand-fathers,—nor whose great *Immodesty* put our virtuous grand-mothers out of countenance,—would not, I assure you, now be allowed an audience.—

Step by step, we shall draw nearer to truth,—and it is no small advance toward *Taste* and *Nature,* to have got rid of *Indecency,* and *Improbability.*[1]

Hamlet continued as a favorite with strollers into the decade after Garrick's death. The fullest and one of the most rollicking descriptions of its performance, illustrative of the picaresque "punch-bag" technique, was written by Charles Johnstone in *The Adventures of Anthony Varnish; or, A Peep at the Manners of Society. By an Adept* (1786).[2] The novel offers a wealth of detailed and vivid sketches. After his parents die, Anthony sets out on his travels through Ireland and England. At Coventry he visits a theater constructed out of an

[1] II, 165–176. See K. G. Dapp, *George Keate, Esq., Eighteenth Century English Gentleman,* Philadelphia, 1939, pp. 104–114. This novel is interestingly reviewed as a "legitimate offspring" of Sterne's *Sentimental Journey* in *The Monthly Review,* LXI (1780), 111–117. Keate, for his praise of Shakespeare in *Ferney: An Epistle to Mons*r *De Voltaire,* 1768, was honored by the Stratford corporation with an inkstand made from Shakespeare's mulberry tree. The Shakespearean excerpt from *Ferney* was reprinted in *The Poetical Works of David Garrick, Esq.,* 1785, I, xxxvii. The music for the popular tune "The Roast Beef of Old England" is printed in William Chappell, *Popular Music of the Olden Time* [1855–1859], II, 636.

[2] This novel is ascribed to Johnstone by Halkett and Laing, Andrew Block, and the British Museum, whose copy I have used. It is excessively rare. For a brief account see Miss J. M. S. Tompkins, *The Popular Novel in England, 1770–1800,* 1932, p. 48.

old stable. The only distinction between boxes, pit, and galleries consist of a board nailed across to separate them.

As the audience, which was composed of a motley assemblage of different characters and ages, became riotous, an old man, with one eye, came into the orchestra, which was made out of a large box, with the lid taken off. After he had bowed respectfully to the company, he pulled from under his coat the instrument of harmony, and played, with excellent discretion, the well-known and celebrated tune of *Buttered Peas;* but the audience growing particularly clamorous for *Roast Beef,* this half-sighted musician complied with their request. . . .

But the bell ringing from within indicated to the company that the play was going to begin; and, agreeably to the summons, the curtain was drawn, and discovered Francisco and Bernardo in close conversation. It was soon noticed, by the noisy part of the audience, that Bernardo's nose was of an uncommon size; and indeed it resembled more a protuberance of mulberries, which hung in rich clusters, than a human feature. I soon found that this gentleman was the most conspicuous personage of the drama; for he received more distinction, on account of that amazing ornament, than all the rest of the actors put together.

When the ghost made his appearance, it had a visible effect on the majority of my neighbors in the gallery, some of whom were almost petrified with awe at the dreadful solemnity of the object; but, as our admiration is built upon comparison of one thing with another, so did the ghastly appearance of the royal Dane operate to make the succeeding scene more captivating;—the reader will easily conceive that I can mean no other than the brilliant court of Denmark, which burst upon our sight with as much grandeur as the wardrobe could furnish, assisted by all the credit that the company could procure in the town for tinsel, tie-wigs, clean linen, and potlids.

As soon as young Hamlet came forward, all eyes were centered upon him, for he had long been considered as the Roscius of Warwickshire. I observed he made three solemn strides, then enfolded his arms and stood still; for which uncommon excellence he received the loud applause of the audience.—I was going to inquire of a person, who sat next to me, into the reason of their applauding him so much above the rest, when my notice was riveted upon a comical fellow, who sat near me, roaring out, "Here comes Nosey!" which appellation I soon found to belong to my friend Polonius, who was the identical being that had five minutes before personated Bernardo with so much honour.

The unexpected salute of my friend in the gallery so discomposed the muscles of the whole court of Copenhagen, that, in spite of their best efforts to appear grave, a simper became universal, and it was some time before her Danish majesty could recover herself sufficiently to reprove the young prince for his unseemly melancholy: however, every thing went on very smoothly until Hamlet began his first soliloquy; but he had scarce uttered his wish, that

'His too, too, solid flesh would melt!'

than a countryman, who sat in the pit, bawled out, 'Noa, noa, friend, you needn't wish any more of thy flesh to melt; why, mon, you're as thin as a whipping-post already:' and, indeed, though the observation was rather *mal-à-propos* in point of time, it was strictly justifiable on the score of truth; for the poor fellow, who played the character, had not flesh enough, upon his whole carcass, to give a cat a breakfast. However, this interruption was warmly resented by the friends of the performer, and a battle would have taken place in the pit, had it not been for the interposition of the manager, who had condescended to perform the King himself: he came round from the stage among the combatants; and, whether it was by the persuasion of his tongue, or the influence of his dignity, I will not determine; but he certainly restored peace to the theatre, and the players were ordered to proceed.

Every thing now went on in the proper *routine* of business, except in the scene between Laertes and Ophelia, when it was very palpable that the young lady had been imprudent enough to drink too much that afternoon; indeed she had hurt her memory so much by the sacrifices she had been making to Bacchus, that she scarcely remembered a single word of her part, and, in one particular passage, when the prompter neglected to assist the fallibility of her memory, she forgot her dignity so far as to damn him for a lazy son of a b—ch; however, the indecorum was committed by a lady, and, consequently, permitted to pass without censure.

But shortly she was relieved from that temporary embarrassment by the entrance of old Polonius, the purple majesty of whose nose was a never-failing source of mirth whenever he came forward. Three times did he attempt to give the celebrated instructions to his son Laertes, and was as often obliged to desist, from the roars of laughter that issued whenever he opened his mouth. At last they were fairly obliged to conclude the scene without it, and poor Laertes was dismissed to France without the benefit of those solid apothegms of wisdom and experience.

At the commencement of the second act, attention seemed to have resumed her throne, and every thing jogged on tolerably quiet till the closet-scene between Hamlet and his mother, when the Ghost made his *entré* with prodigious majesty. I should have before observed, that the wardrobe of this company being rather scanty, it was absolutely necessary to make a coat of mail for the spirit in question, there being no suit in their cabinet of wearables. To effect this in a hurry, they were obliged to sew a few pieces of pasteboard together, which, when covered with old play-bills, made a very tolerable *succedaneum* for the want of something more resembling the supposed habit of the departed Dane; and, considering every thing, the poor Ghost acquitted himself tolerably well until the moment he was preparing to take his leave, when, unluckily, in facing about to the queen, to enforce the directions to the young prince to persevere in his conduct towards his mother, he was under the necessity of standing with his breech to the audience. Now the point of good manners which might have been invaded by this manoeuvre would have been over-looked with great good-humour, but the infringement on decency, that it occasioned, could not; for it must be observed, that the ghastly shade wore a black pair of breeches, under his coat of mail, which were rendered something the worse by the depredations of time; indeed so much so, that, between the legs, there was a rent of most capacious magnitude, out of which a remnant of the spirit's shirt hung in a most ungraceful manner.

This breach in the galligaskins of the Ghost was no sooner perceived by the motley audience than an universal uproar ensued, accompanied by incessant roars of laughter.—The poor fellow felt himself embarrassed; and, finding that his person was the center of the joke, turned himself to the right and to the left, but without the desired effect. At last, mustering up an unusual degree of courage, he stepped forward, and attempted to address the audience, but was most violently repelled with groans and hisses. At length, finding all his endeavors ineffectual to learn the state of their wishes, he was preparing to walk off; but had not got above a yard from the side-scene, when an unlucky spark, who occupied one of the side-boxes, set a large pointer, which he had with him, at the miserable remains of departed majesty, whom he caught hold of, just as he was slipping off the stage, by the shirt, which hung out behind, and which he shook, to the unspeakable diversion of the company, fairly dragging the unfortunate spirit to the center of the stage before he quitted his hold. Irritated to a degree of madness at this insult to his dignity, which was more than flesh and blood could endure, and eager for revenge, he tore off his paper armour in a twinkling (which, indeed, was tantamount to his stripping in buff, for, the little shirt that he had left, and which composed the whole stock of linen that belonged to this calamitous son of Thespis, had been completely torn away by the fangs of the animal that had annoyed him,) and, coming to the point of the stage, offered to box the best man in the company for a gallon of beer: but the Ghost's challenge not being readily accepted, he misinterpreted their forebearance into a spirit of cowardice in the audience, and began to abuse them in terms which sufficiently proved, that his godfathers and godmothers had completely taught him the vulgar tongue, in the most extensive sense of the phrase.

Before he had proceeded far in his passionate address to the spectators, he was stopped by a domestic enemy, who, by her great zeal in endeavoring to regulate his behaviour, put a period to the dramatic entertainments of the evening. This heroine was no other than the unfortunate Ghost's wife, who personated her majesty of Denmark for that night; and, hearing of the misbehaviour of her spouse, hurried to the scene of action, with a full determination to punish her yoke-fellow for this breach of decency, which, she wisely apprehended, would be the ruin of her benefit, which was to have taken place the next evening. The furious lady, totally regardless of the dignity of the character she had assumed in the play, rushed on her ill-fated husband, and, by a well-directed blow, which, unhappily alighting on his eye, levelled the vaunting spirit with the stage. But, though it was evident that the salutation had disconcerted, it by no means subdued, him; for, springing immediately from the boards with great facility, he returned the compliment with such address as made the blood royal of Denmark flow most copiously through the apertures of her majesty's nose. Now the audience, beginning to interfere warmly in the dispute leaped upon the stage, and, dividing into different factions, each supported the object they thought most aggrieved; but, the majority turning eventually in favour of the lady, she gave her miserable husband such a drubbing as almost deprived him of existence, for he lay extended upon the scene of action sightless and forlorn, like one who was shortly to pay a long visit to the Stygian shore.

But it was ordered, by the inflexible destinies, that the perils of that evening should not end here; for, while the Amazonian queen was panting with her victories, and receiving the applause of her surrounding admirers, the manager of the company entered with two constables, and charged her majesty with a breach of the peace, and instantly ordered her to the county-jail, to remain there until time, chance, or circumstance, should enable her to satisfy him for the robes of royalty she had utterly destroyed in the engagement, and other properties, which he estimated at a very consider-able amount.

It was at this instant that the misguided heroine began to perceive that she had been acting a very unprofitable part:—it was in vain for her to hope for relief; for, those very persons, who had been most instrumental in extolling her prowess as a bruiser, were now most forward in ridiculing her distress.

As the husband, in the awful eye of the law, is considered as forming a material part of his wife, the wretched Ghost was lifted from the ground to accompany his lady to prison, as being responsible for her errors; to which place they were conveyed amid the shouts of an unfeeling multitude, who inevitably desert the objects that have delighted them, when their power to amuse exists no more.—The poor Queen, as she was hurried away, turned about, and surveyed the scene of slaughter with such a piteous look as brought the following lines to my recollection:

> 'The tempest o'er, and the wild waves allay'd,
> The calm sea wonders at the wrecks it made.'[1]

Analytical and psychological study of Shakespeare's imagery has been one of the special concerns of scholarship in the twentieth century.[2] Modern criticism calls psychology to its aid in studying the sleeping images in the poet's "deep well of unconscious cerebration," which emerge in his verse as metaphors and similes. Psychologizing about Shakespeare's characters began in the last quarter of the eighteenth century before the romantic critics habitually probed them as though they were living beings, but psychoanalysis was an unknown approach to the poetic process in the work of such critics as William Richardson and Maurice Morgann. The eighteenth century exploited little more than analysis of ruling passions and Locke's doctrine of the association of ideas.[3] However, in an age when young men were still familiar with the principles of formal rhetoric, it is not startling to discover interest in Shakespeare's power of transmuting into poetry

---

[1] II, 156–172.

[2] Caroline F. E. Spurgeon, *Shakespeare's Imagery and What It Tells Us,* New York, 1936. For *Hamlet* see especially pp. 316–320.

[3] See T. M. Raysor, "The Study of Shakespeare's Characters in the Eighteenth Century," *MLN,* XLII (1927), 495–500; R. W. Babcock, *The Genesis of Shake-speare Idolatry,* Chapel Hill, 1931, chapter 12, "The Psychologizing of Shake-speare"; David Lovett, *Shakespeare's Characters in Eighteenth Century Criticism,* Baltimore, 1935; and the thorough analysis of the development of psychological criticism by Gordon McKenzie, *Critical Responsiveness: A Study of the Psychologi-cal Current in Later Eighteenth-Century Criticism, University of California Publi-cations in English,* Berkeley, XX (1949), particularly chapter 5, "Association and Emotion," and chapter 8, "Words, Images, and Figures."

what he had learned from observation of life and from his reading. Hamlet's "To be or not to be" soliloquy (III. i), with its flow of images drawn from diverse sources, was subjected to captious analysis by the author of "An Essay on Metaphors" which has been questionably attributed to Oliver Goldsmith.[1] The author dissected the soliloquy academically as a confusion of mixed metaphors and "a strange rhapsody of broken images."

Neither can any figure be more ridiculously absurd than that of a man taking arms against a sea, exclusive of the incongruous medley of slings, arrows, and seas, justled within the compass of one reflection.[2]

From long experience in the art of the stage, Garrick wrote several years later a more intelligent account of the great soliloquy in his *Oration in Honor of Shakespeare's Jubilee:*

Shakespeare's terms rather than his sentences are metaphorical; he calls an endless multitude a sea, by a happy allusion to the perpetual succession of wave on wave; and he immediately expresses opposition by 'taking up arms,' which, being fit in itself, he was not solicitous to accommodate to his first image. This is the language in which a figurative and rapid conception will always be expressed.[3]

This interpretation has come to be accepted, and nobody today is greatly concerned when a genius' extravagant metaphors arise from the hot fire and rapidity of his imagination, and the fury of his fancy carries him beyond the bounds of judgment. Metaphors, on the contrary, which are mixed because of ignorance, illiteracy, and paucity of imagination move the sophisticated critic merely to laughter.

Hamlet's soliloquy was analyzed by the author of the educational novel, *Genuine Letters from a Gentleman to a Young Lady His Pupil* (1772), attributed to John Preston. In a letter to Nancy Blisset, dated in Oxford, December 18, 1743, the writer presents an imaginative rather than a literal point of view.

Allegory is said to be a String of Metaphors; but I think this Description defective; for unless that Series of Metaphors depends on some one particular Point, it is either a faulty Allegory, or, rather, no Allegory at

[1] Peter Cunningham, ed., *The Works of Oliver Goldsmith*, Boston, 1854, III, 314–324; J. W. M. Gibbs, ed., *The Works of Oliver Goldsmith*, I (1884), 361–377. The essays in which this criticism appeared were published in *The British Magazine* in 1761, 1762, and 1763. H. H. Furness, in the New Variorum *Hamlet*, 4th ed., Philadelphia, 1877, I, 204–207, doubted Goldsmith's authorship. Gibbs, in *Works*, I, 406–408, presents arguments *pro* and *con* for Goldsmith's authorship, favoring the view that "Goldsmith wrote the first essay only, though perhaps he had also some hand in the succeeding essays."
[2] Goldsmith's *Works*, ed. Gibbs, I, 370.
[3] Quoted in Furness' New Variorum edition, I, 207.

all. To explain what I mean, I will quote a Passage from *Shakespeare's Hamlet.*

> *Whether 'tis nobler in the Mind to suffer*
> *The Slings and Arrows of outrageous Fortune,*
> *Or to take Arms against a Sea of Troubles,*
> *And, by opposing, end them.*

This has been much censured as a faulty Allegory, because the Writer flies from one Allusion to another, from *Slings* to *taking up of Arms*— against what?—*a Sea*—and then *opposing a Sea*, &c. Now if *Shakespeare* meant this for an Allegory, it is doubtless very faulty; but I verily believe that was not his Meaning. I am of Opinion that he only took the first strong Metaphor which came into his Head, to express himself forcibly and pathetically, and then another, and another, as the Subject rose upon them, but had no Idea of making them connected with, or dependent on each other. I will not venture to affirm I am right.[1]

5. *Othello*

F R O M the Restoration on, *Othello* was one of the most continuously performed of Shakespeare's tragedies. It appears to have been almost as popular as *Hamlet*. Perhaps because it is the most nearly classical of the four great tragedies, it enjoyed the rare distinction of being presented in a version which was cut but not substantially adapted or "improved." [2] From Betterton's death in 1710 to the first London season of Garrick (1741–1742) there were only two seasons when it failed to be advertised at Drury Lane. During the latter's regime, however, it was permitted to lapse for ten of the thirty-four seasons, because he failed to place the public under his spell as either Othello or Iago.[3] He stopped playing Othello partly because of his slight stature and partly, no doubt, because of Quin's sarcasm about his performance. When asked by a lady how she liked Garrick as Othello,

---

[1] Letter CXXII, II, 297–298. The review of this novel in *The Monthly Review*, XLVII (1772), 218–222, quotes the *Hamlet* passage as an example of the general merit of this educational novel, in which the letters "breathe a strain of the purest morality; . . . they open the understanding, and improve the taste." For present-day analysis of the images in the passage quoted see Mikhail M. Morozov, "The Individualization of Shakespeare's Characters through Imagery," in *Shakespeare Survey*, ed. Allardyce Nicoll, Cambridge, II (1949), 99–100.

[2] The version, which Odell believes to be the exact acting text, is in Bell's *Shakespeare*, 2nd ed., 1774, I, 211–293. It is analyzed by Odell in *Shakespeare from Betterton to Irving*, II, 33–35, who notes: "This edition is a landmark . . . in showing how the work had come through from Betterton's time to Garrick's." Desdemona's death was apparently hastened by a dagger. On this point see Sprague, *Shakespeare and the Actors*, pp. 214–216.

[3] Garrick acted Othello only three times in England, from March 7, 1745 to June 20, 1746. He played Iago to Spranger Barry's Othello in 1749, but not after April, 1753.

the wit replied: "Othello! Madam. . . . Psha! no such thing!—
There was a little black boy, like Pompey attending with a tea-kettle,
fretting and fuming about the stage; but I saw no Othello." [1]

At Lincoln's Inn Fields and Covent Garden from 1720 to 1741–
1742 the tragedy appeared with considerable regularity, and from
1742 to 1776 it missed only seven seasons. There Quin and Spranger
Barry were highly valued as Othello. Indeed, Barry was the great
Othello of the age.

There is an amusingly ironic thrust at the license of conjecture
practised by contemporary Shakespearean editors and commentators
in Henry Fielding's Lucianic journey to Hades, *A Journey from This
World to the Next* (1743). In the realm of Minos the author observes
Virgil, Addison, Dick Steele, and Shakespeare.

I then observed *Shakespeare* standing between *Betterton* and *Booth,* and
deciding a Difference between those two great Actors, concerning the
placing an Accent in one of his Lines: this was disputed on both sides
with a Warmth which surprized me in *Elysium,* till I discovered by In-
tuition, that every Soul retained its principal Characteristic, being, indeed,
its very Essence. The Line was that celebrated one in *Othello;*

Put out the Light, and then put out the Light,

according to *Betterton.* Mr. *Booth* contended to have it thus;

Put out the Light, and then put out the *Light.*

I could not help offering my Conjecture on this Occasion, and suggested it
might perhaps be,

Put out the Light, and then put out thy *Light.*

Another hinted a Reading very *sophisticated* in my Opinion,

Put out the Light, and then put out thee, Light;

making Light to be the vocative Case. Another would have altered the last
Word, and read,

Put out thy Light, and then put out thy Sight.

But *Betterton* said, if the Text was to be *disturbed,* he saw no reason why
a Word might not be changed as well as a Letter, and instead of *put out
thy* Light, you might read *put out thy* Eyes. At last it was agreed on all
sides, to refer the matter to the Decision of *Shakespeare* himself, who delivered his Sentiments as follows: 'Faith, Gentlemen, it is so long since I
wrote the Line, I have forgot my Meaning. This I know, could I have
dreamt so much Nonsense would have been talked & writ about it, I
would have blotted it out of my Works: for I am sure, if any of these be
my Meaning, it doth me very little Honour.'

---

[1] [William Cooke], *Memoirs of Charles Macklin,* 1804, p. 113.

He was then interrogated concerning some other ambiguous Passages in his Works; but he declined any satisfactory Answer: Saying, if Mr. *Theobald* had not *writ about it* sufficiently, there were three or four more new Editions of his Plays coming out, which he hoped would satisfy every one: Concluding, 'I marvel nothing so much as that Men will gird themselves at discovering obscure Beauties in an Author. Certes the greatest and most pregnant Beauties are ever the plainest and most evidently striking; and when two Meanings of a Passage can in the least ballance our Judgements which to prefer, I hold it matter of unquestionable Certainty, that neither of them are worth a farthing.' [1]

Dispute about Othello's famous line led to most tragic consequences in Eliza Haywood's novel *The Husband. In Answer to the Wife* (1756). This work of fiction has no regular plot. It is, indeed, a courtesy book embellished with *exempla* to enliven discourses on such subjects as family finance and lyings-in. Mrs. Haywood, in the section entitled "Giving way to rage," observes that terrible events have often resulted from indulgence in this deadly sin by fiery "Iracundians." Listen to this happy marriage which came to a "melancholy catastrophe." A husband and wife loved each other and lived happily together for four years. But alas!

He was . . . of that unhappy disposition which is the subject of this section:—the lady had a brother who was exactly of the same, yet had these jarring spirits never happen'd to clash till one dreadful night; just after they had all three supp'd together, a dispute arose between the two gentlemen concerning the true pronunciation of this line in Shakespear's Moor of Venice:

'Put out the light,—and then,—put out the light.'

Each of them would have it their own way,—both were equally positive, and some hasty words being dropp'd, either on the one side or the other, their swords were immediately out:—the wife, who a little before had stepp'd into the next room on some occasion, on hearing the bustle return'd, but too late for any endeavours she could use to hinder the sad event;—the moment she enter'd her brother fell,—crying out,—'Oh! I am kill'd!'—The husband ran to him, and fearing it was indeed as he had said, spoke nothing but went directly to his closet, and having taken out of his buroe what bills and money he had there, quitted the house that instant; but just as he was doing so, call'd to the servants, who being all in the kitchen had heard nothing of what pass'd above,—'Go, said he to his man, fly with all the speed you can for a surgeon,—my brother has hurt himself.'
In the mean time horror and astonishment had froze up all the faculties of the wretched wife;—she saw her brother lie weltering in his blood, a pale and breathless corpse;—the person who had reduced him to this condition was her husband,—a husband most dear to her, and whom all laws,

[1] Golden Cockerel edition, Waltham Saint Lawrence, 1930, chapter 8. The line is in V. ii. 7. For commentaries see H. H. Furness, ed., *Othello* (New Variorum edition), 2nd ed., Philadelphia, 1886, pp. 294–296.

both human and divine, oblig'd her to protect:—no words can paint the misery of such a situation;—but long it was not that she endur'd the pain of thought,—sense was too weak to bear it, and she sunk beneath the weight.

The hapless wife suffered repeated fits of convulsions. The servants summoned a surgeon, who found the brother dead and temporarily revived the lady, although "her fits continued the whole night." Her terrible disorder "had seiz'd on her brain, and depriv'd her of what alone can make life a blessing,—her Reason—which she never more recover'd the right use of." When the husband, who had escaped to Holland, heard of his wife's condition, he was thrown into melancholy and developed a "languishing disease," which "took him from the world" in a few months.[1] Such dire misfortunes from controversy over Shakespeare's meaning!

Sarah Fielding pursued her brother's satirical vein in *The Adventures of David Simple* (1744). David, in search of a true friend, observes various walks of life in London. Together with the abusive Mr. Spatter, who, like Matthew Bramble, actually practices universal benevolence, David calls on a witty lady who is holding a kind of salon, composed of a large company of ladies and two or three gentlemen, all busy in discourse.

First Lady. Indeed, Madam, I think you are quite in the right, as to your Opinion of *Othello;* for nothing provokes me so much, as to see Fools *pity a Fellow,* who could *murder his Wife.* For my part, I cannot help having some Compassion for *her,* though she does not deserve it, because she was such a Fool as to marry a *filthy Black.* Pray, did you ever hear any thing like what my Lady *True-wit* said the other Night, that the Part of the Play which chiefly affected her, was, that which inspired an Apprehension of what that *odious Wretch* must feel, when he found out that *Desdemona* was innocent; as if he could suffer too much, after being guilty of so barbarous an Action.

Second Lady. Indeed, I am not at all surprized at any thing that Lady *True-wit* says; for I have heard her assert the most preposterous things in the World: Nay, she affirms, a Man may be very fond of a Woman, notwithstanding he is jealous of her, and *dares suspect her Virtue.*[2]

Miss Fielding compares the chatter of these pretenders to learning to the cackling of geese. David and his friend are happy to escape from their irresponsible bandying of great names.

A farcical summary of the plot of the tragedy was one of the additions made by Francis Coventry in his revision of *The History of Pompey the Little; or, The Life and Adventures of a Lap-Dog,* the

[1] Pages 142–145.
[2] 2nd ed., 1744, I, 149–150.

first edition of which, published in 1751, he considered "very hasty and unfinished." The improved version was dedicated to Henry Fielding. Little Pompey has fallen into the possession of a milliner, who treats him kindly.

Three or four days after he was settled in these apartments, as he was frisking and sporting one morning about the shop, a young lady, who lodged in the house, came down stairs, and accosted his mistress in the following terms: 'I want to see some ribbands if you please, madam, to match my blue gown; for lady *Bab Frightful* is to call upon mamma this evening, to carry us to the play, to see *Othellor whore of Venus,* which they say is one of the finest plays that ever was acted.' 'Yes really, mem, 'tis a very engaging play to be sure,' replied the milliner; 'indeed I think it one of the master-pieces of the *English* stage—but you mistake a little, I fancy miss, in the naming of it, for Shakespear I believe wrote it *Othello moor of Venice. Venice,* mem, is a famous town or city somewhere or other, where *Othello* runs away with a rich heiress in the night-time, and marries her privately at the fleet. By very odd luck he was created lord high-admiral that very night, and goes out to fight the *Turks,* and takes his wife along with him to the wars; and there, mem, he grows jealous of her, only because she happens to have lost a handkerchief, which he gave her when he came a courting to her. It was a muslin handkerchief, mem, spotted with strawberries; and because she can't find it, he beats her in the most unmerciful manner, and at last smothers her between two featherbeds.' 'Does he indeed,' cries the young lady; 'well, I hate a jealous man of all things in nature; a jealous man is my particular aversion—but however, no matter what the play is, you know, ma'am, so we do but see it; for the pleasure of a play is to shew one's self in the boxes, and see the company, and all that— Yes, ma'am, this here is the sort of ribbands I want, only if you please to let me see some of a paler blue.' [1]

A more serious consideration of *Othello* was presented to the English public in 1755. Representative of the tendency of critics in the second half of the eighteenth century to study Shakespeare's characters psychologically, John Shebbeare included in that year a long and sympathetic analysis of Othello's jealousy in his *Letters on the English Nation.* Shebbeare stands forth as one of the pioneers in the new method of interpreting Shakespeare's great comic and tragic figures. His Jesuit, having asserted that the exalted Englishman was of superior genius, ventures to "point out such characters as have never been conceived by any French tragic writer, conducted and sustained in a manner which no other nation has ever seen, ancient or modern."

In the tragedy of Othello, the Moor all artless, open, and brave, is seduced by the wiles and subtilty of the hypocritic Jago. The seeming simplicity of an honest heart is so exquisitely supported, and practised by him on the unsuspecting disposition of a virtuous, valiant, and ingenuous mind,

[1] 3rd ed., 1752, pp. xi, 197–200.

that no instance is to be produced of any thing parallel in any theatrical production.

In each of these characters there is not one mistaken deviation; every spectator excuses the Moor in his being deceived, and pities with sincerest sorrow the fate of open honesty, seduced by artifice and wiles.

The difficulty is not easily imagined, which attends the preservation of these two characters. The Moor must be supported as brave, sensible, and honest; the skill lay in preserving all these from the imputation of weakness in Othello, thro' the conducting the imposition which was to be play'd upon him.

The simple, plain, and seemingly artless cunning of Jago, was attended with no less difficulty; to preserve the separate characteristics of this personage, without deviating into one instance, which might betray his design to a man of sense, is of all the things the most difficult.

Yet, thro' the whole conduct of both characters, there appears no one violation of the intended and original design of the poet.

In this consistency of character, the superiority of the English poet appears above all others, unless the critics devoted to the Greek, and antiquity, should contest it in favour of Homer; you, madam, will allow, that the great Corneille affords no instance of this nature, comparable to the English author.

His management of Cassio, and Roderigo, is in the same simple, natural, and apparent honest strain; we see that the deceit must be invisible to such men. The scene in the third act, between Othello and Jago, where the latter first insinuates the idea of jealousy into the mind of the Moor, that timidity of accusing the innocent, that regard for the reputation of Desdemona, with the insinuation against her fidelity, are so artfully mixt, that it is impossible, but that Othello must have been insnared by his manner of conducting the conversation; how inimitable is his pretended love for Othello, his conjuring up the Moor's resolution to know his sentiments, by distant hints and suggestions, and when Othello breaks out,

> I'll know thy thoughts,

he answers,

> You cannot, if my heart were in your hand;
> Nor shall not, whilst 'tis in my custody.

At this seemingly determined secrecy, the Moor pronouncing "ha!" Jago with all possible art cries out,

> Oh! beware my lord, of jealousy;
> It is a green-eyed monster, which doth mock
> The meat it feeds on. That cuckold lives in bliss
> Who, certain of his fate, loves not his wronger:
> But oh! what damned minutes tells he o'er
> Who doats yet doubts, suspects yet strongly loves?

This speech necessarily turns the thoughts of Othello on the idea of jealousy, with all the appearance of nature, and refined art; and then by proceeding in the same manner, he leads him to examine the conduct of Desdemona, and creates a suspicion of her infidelity to the Moor, from her having chosen him, and refused those

Of her own clime, complexion, and degree.

From this he draws an inference which reflects on the character of Desdemona; this almost convinces the Moor of her being false to his bed, and he desires Jago to set his wife to watch Desdemona. In answer to this, the subtle villain pretends to intreat Othello to think no more of what he had told him, to attempt discovering Desdemona's true disposition, by the vehemence of her suit to him for restoring Cassio, and to believe his fears for his honour had been too importunate in the affair; with this he leaves him. In all this scene there appears nothing which can discover the Moor weaker than an honest, plain, brave man may be allowed to be; not one step carried beyond the truth in nature, by Jago.

The knowledge of the promptness of jealousy in the bosom of man, which the author shews in the character of Jago, is beyond all comparison; when he has possest the handkerchief which Desdemona drops, he says,

> I will in Cassio's lodgings lose this napkin,
> And let him find it. Trifles light as air
> Are to the jealous confirmations strong
> As proofs of holy writ. This may do something.
> The Moor already changes with my poisons:
> Dangerous conceits are in their nature poisons,
> Which at the first are scarce found to distaste;
> But, with a little act upon the blood,
> Burn like the mines of sulphur.

At seeing Othello, he continues:

> Look where he comes! not poppy nor mandragora,
> Nor all the drowsy syrups of the world,
> Shall ever medicine thee to that sweet sleep
> Which thou hadst yesterday.

The operations which the jealous mind undergoes, were never so truly described by any author; the trifles light as air, the tasteless poison of a hint becoming mines of burning sulphur to the soul, and the irrevocable power of sweet slumber to a mind haunted with jealousy, are beyond all conception just, great and sublime, and I think to be found in no other author.

The Moor enters with a conviction of the truth of what Jago had said in the above soliloquy; his mind now burning with suspicion, lighted up from those sparks which Jago had thrown upon it, without seeing him, he says,

> Ha! false to me.

to which Jago replies,

> Why, how now, general? no more of that,

Oth.   Avant! begone! thou'st set me on the rack,
> I swear 'tis better to be much abused
> Than but to know a little.

This answer shews that the revealing this infidelity of Desdemona, had made Jago insufferable to his eyes; the combat between the violation of

his bed, and the love of Desdemona, working strongly in him, he therefore swears 'tis better to be much abused in secret, than not to know what
may be avowed to be sufficient to vindicate the vengeance which an in-
jured man should take upon the author of his dishonour. At this Jago,
fearing lest he should retreat from the degree to which he had brought him,
delay the pursuit, and relapse to love, cries

> How, my lord!

Othello answers,

> What sense had I of her stol'n hours of lust?
> I saw't not, thought it not, it harm'd not me;
> I slept the next night well; was free and merry:
> I found not Cassio's kisses on her lips:
> He that is robb'd, not wanting what is stol'n,
> Let him not know't, and he's not robb'd at all.

In this speech, the whole bent of his mind is turned on the mischief and
disquiet which Jago's discovery had brought upon his soul; without his
revealing it he had been happy, untouched by pangs of injury. Jago's answer is,

> I am sorry to hear this.

Othello proceeds still in the same sentiment, exclaiming

> I had been happy if the general camp
> (Pioneers and all) had tasted her sweet body,
> So I had nothing known. Oh now, for ever
> Farewell the tranquil mind! farewell content;
> Farewell the plumed troops, and the big war,
> That make ambition virtue! Oh! farewell,
> Farewell the neighing steed, and the shrill trump,
> The spirit-stirring drum, th' ear-piercing fife,
> The royal banner, and all quality,
> Pride, pomp, and circumstance of glorious war.
> And oh! you mortal engines, whose rude throats
> Th' immortal Jove's dread clamours counterfeit,
> Farewell! Othello's occupation's gone!

These reflections bring back on his soul, like the returning tide, the
wretched change of situation which Jago's discovery had produced in him;
upon which Jago asks,

> Is't possible, my Lord?

Othello, still improving the former sentiment, and feeling his fallen
state with infinite sensibility, flies impetuously into rage, and seizing Jago,
cries,

> Villain, be sure thou prove my love a whore;
> Be sure of it; give me the ocular proof;
> Or, by the worth of mine eternal soul,

> Thou hadst been better have been born a dog
> Than answer my wak'd wrath.

When proceeding in the same passionate manner, Jago answers,

> Oh grace! oh heaven defend me!
> Are you a man? have you a soul? or sense?
> God be w' you; take mine office. O wretched fool,
> That liv'st to make thine honesty a vice!
> Oh monstrous world! take note, take note, oh world!
> To be direct and honest is not safe.
> I thank you for this profit; and from hence
> I'll love no friend, sith love breeds such offence.

This speech contains as much art as ever entered into the conception of human nature. He first appeals to Othello's humanity and understanding; then at that instant, as intending to leave him, he says "God be with you," and throws up his commission; he then exclaims at his own folly that has thus converted his honesty into vice; when throwing a sarcastic reflexion on the world, and thanking Othello for this information of what is to be expected from man, he determines to renounce all love for human nature. What ideas are there to be imagined, which can be thrown together with more judgment, and propriety, to reclaim Othello from that outrage which he has committed?

It has its proper effect; the mind of man, strongly agitated between two passions, suddenly veers from one to the other, like the uncertain blowings of a storm; in consequence of which, Othello comes about to believe that Jago is honest, and says,

> Nay stay—thou should'st be honest.

Jago, who perceives this approaching change, answers,

> I should be wise; for honesty's a fool,
> And loses what it works for.

After this, Othello, reduced to the æquipoise between the love of his Desdemona, and the truth of Jago's story, cries out,

> By the world,
> I think my wife is honest, and think she is not:
> I think that thou art just, and think thou art not.
> I'll have some proof.

This suspence Jago seizes, to fix him in the firm opinion of her being false to his bed; when Othello says,

> Give me a living reason she's disloyal.

At this Jago recounts what Cassio said in a dream, and wins upon the mind of the Moor entirely; at which he cries,

> I'll tear her all to pieces—

Jago, not content with this, most artfully mentions to him the handkerchief in the hands of Cassio, which he had formerly given to Desdemona: this rivets him in the belief of his being dishonored by Cassio; at which he exclaims,

> Oh that the slave had forty thousand lives!
> One is too poor, too weak for my revenge.
> Now do I see 'tis true.—Look here, Jago,
> All my fond love thus do I blow to heaven.
> 'Tis gone—
> Arise black vengeance from the hollow hell;
> Yield up, oh love! thy crown and hearted throne
> To tyrannous heat! swell bosom, with thy fraught,
> For 'tis of Aspic's tongues.

Jag.   Yet be content.

Oth.   Oh blood, blood, blood!

Jag.   Patience, I say; your mind perhaps may change.

Oth.   Never, Jago. Like to the Pontic sea,
> Whose icy current and compulsive course
> Ne'er feels retiring ebb, but keeps due on
> To the Propontic and the Hellespont;
> Even so my bloody thoughts with violent pace
> Shall ne'er look back, ne'er ebb to humble love,
> Till that a capable and wide revenge
> Swallow them up.—Now by yonder marble heaven,
> In the due reverence of a sacred vow,
> I here engage my words.

Having thus wrought him up to his purpose, Jago swears that he will give himself up entirely to the service and revenge of Othello's injury.

In these last quotations it is easy to see, that figurative expressions, when they arise from the subject, unforced, and unsought after, are the most naturally expressive of passion; the mind, dilated and carried on by the desire of revenge, rises into metaphor and simile, with the utmost propriety; the occasion is equal to the conception and ideas, and not the least colour of bombast or false expression, appears thro' the whole.

In all the French theatre I know of no play, in which equal knowledge of human nature is manifested, where two characters so justly drawn, so nicely contrasted, and so well sustained, are to be found; a common genius would have erred a thousand times in writing such parts, Othello would have manifested a thousand marks of being a fool, in not seeing Jago's designs, and Jago betrayed himself by too bare-faced a conduct of his intention: as it is managed by Shakespeare, there is no one slip or deviation of character in either, in one single instance.[1]

Admiration for Othello's passionate character is apparent in Sir Herbert Croft's *roman à clef* based on the murder of Martha Ray by the Reverend James Hackman, *Love and Madness: A Story Too True, in a Series of Letters* (1780). Miss Ray, Lord Sandwich's mistress, was

---

[1] II, 233–246.

shot by Hackman as she was leaving Covent Garden theater in that year. The man's letters represent the epitome of sensibility: "I have no head; you have made me all heart, from top to bottom. . . . I am out of my senses."

The element, out of which I am formed, is fire. Swift had water in his brain: I have a burning coal of fire: your hand can light it up to rapture, rage, or madness. Men, real men, have never been wild enough for my admiration: it has wandered into the ideal world of fancy. Othello (but he should have put *himself* to death in his wife's sight, *not* his wife), Zanga, are *my* heroes. Milk-and-water passions are like sentimental comedy. Give me . . . give *me*, I say, tragedy, affecting tragedy, in the world, as well as in the theatre. . . . While I am ranting thus about tragedy, blood, and murder—behold, I am as weak as a woman. My tears flow at but the idea of losing you. Yes, they don't drop only; they pour; I sob, like a child. Is this Othello, is this Zanga? [1]

The impress of Iago on youthful minds is apparent in another *roman à clef,* the anonymous *Life, Adventures, Intrigues, and Amours of the Celebrated Jemmy Twitcher* [?1770], which reveals the indiscretions of John Montagu, Earl of Sandwich. Twitcher's parents endeavor to interest their son in the theater, "flattering themselves with the hope, that the great and Virtuous characters of the Stage would catch his attention and inspire him with worthy and elevated sentiments."

But they had the mortification to find their generous cares wholly fruitless, or rather productive of ill-consequences than otherwise. It was their custom, on the morning succeeding any theatrical representation, to ask him his opinion of the principal characters of the play:—they found that he had talents to distinguish, but that he always judged wrong; evermore preferring the trifling, the mischievous, or the infernally wicked characters, to the great, the good, the respectable. With him, *Syphax* was a character superior to *Cato;* and *Iago* and *Shylock* were two of his greatest favourites. The stage, therefore, was tried in vain, to operate on the mind of this wayward youth. [2]

The novelists made little reference to the performance of legitimate actors in *Othello.* Quin's interpretation of the title role was described by an admiring member of the college of authors in *Peregrine Pickle* (1751) as "excellent," but Smollett's hostility to Quin at that time is reflected in Peregrine's contemptuous comments which follow. [3] Of Barry's admired conception there is no mention in fiction.

[1] Pages 26–27. Zanga is the villain, derived from Iago, in Edward Young's *Revenge,* 1721.

[2] Pages 35–36. BM. Syphax is the villain in Addison's *Cato,* 1713.

[3] *The Adventures of Peregrine Pickle,* Shakespeare Head edition, Oxford, 1925, IV, 100–104.

Othello in the provinces is the subject of an episode in *Memoirs of a Demi-Rep of Fashion; or, The Private History of Miss Amelia Gunnersbury* (1776). Marianne, a school friend of Amelia, tells of her life with her lover Beaumont, a comedian. Beaumont's alluring description of the life of an actor persuades Marianne that she has a penchant for the stage, in which her lover encourages her, for he "found in her all the requisites of a complete actress. In this presumption she learned several speeches, as well in tragedy as comedy."

"You do not know," continued he, "all the advantages of a theatrical life; the paths are all strewed with flowers; it is a continual succession of pleasures; the different countries one travels through, afford a variety of adventures upon the road, whilst we are ever free, ever unconstrained; and then upon your return to the capital, where your fame, no doubt, will long have reached, the rival managers will each exert their utmost endeavors to get you, and you may command your own terms. This done, your fortune's made. No woman ever arrived at any pitch upon the stage, but the men were all mad after her; and if you should think a handsome settlement, with a good round sum down, unworthy your acceptance, you may strike up a match with a nobleman, and be a lady for the rest of your days." [1]

Though warned by a Methodist preacher, formerly an actor, that the playhouse is "a universal seraglio, or reservoir of lust for the whole town," Marianne accompanies Beaumont to Liverpool.

Marianne's first appearance in Desdemona obtained her so much applause, and particularly from the person that performed Othello, who was younger and handsomer than Beaumont when his face was washed, that the latter became quite jealous of his mistress.

Not surprisingly, perhaps, Marianne runs off to Lancaster with her leading man, but ultimately, forsaking the stage, she marries an old lover.[2]

In the country *Othello* provided lusty barnstorming bands with many an opportunity to split the ears of the groundlings. The company in Mozeen's *Young Scarron* (1752), whose mishaps in *Richard III* have been recounted, followed their performances of Lee's *Rival Queens* and Congreve's *Old Bachelor* with *Othello*, "where Mr. *Spruce* was so violently fond of his *Desdemona,* in the second Act, and embrac'd her so close, that, to the amazing Mirth of the Audience, she grew *black in the Face;* which so surpriz'd him, that he grew *white,* 'till it was imagin'd they had chang'd Complexions." [3]

[1] Dublin, I, 28–29. BM.
[2] I, 33–34.
[3] Page 133.

Mr. Cook, the stroller in Shebbeare's *Lydia* (1755), having made his first appearance as Othello in Mr. Archer's company ("the Part of *Othello* by a Gentleman who never appeared on any Stage before"), is assured by his colleagues "that they had never seen any young Gentleman come off so well the first Time . . . since they were upon the Stage." [1] This acclaim establishes Othello as Cook's favorite medium in tragedy. On the road to London with his friend Mr. Popkins he is invited by Snap, a companion at dinner, to recite his favorite part.

Mr. *Cook* said, *Othello* was his first and most favourite Part, and if he pleased he would give him a Speech or two from that Play.

With all my Heart, says *Snap;* but give me leave to tell you, Sir, that unless your Face is blackened, I would not give Sixpence for what you can play; it is impossible for me to judge of what a man can say in a black *Face,* from what he may deliver in a white; Sir I only mention this for your sake, that I may the more effectually recommend you to Mr. *R—h* from my own Judgment.

This the Landlord and Mr. *Popkins* agreed was right, from two very different Reasons; one for the sake of more Laughing and the other seduced by the false reasoning.

Mr. Cook applies wagon grease to his face.

Cook repeated a Speech or two, bounding in his Voice, now high, now low, now one Hand up and then the other, now the right Foot foremost, and then the Left, splitting Sentences, and annihilating the Sense. . . . He ended by striking his Breast and tumbling back over the Tables which held the Wine.[2]

Cook's subsequent interview with Rich has already been described.

By all odds the best recreation of a performance of *Othello* in the country is in Herbert Lawrence's pleasant novel, *The Contemplative Man; or, The History of Christopher Crab, Esq.; of North-Wales* (1771). Lawrence took Henry Fielding as the model for his characters and comic situations. Mr. and Mrs. Crab, *en route* to Oxford to visit their son, encounter a troupe of strollers at the Red Lion Inn. The actors have just finished a performance of *King Lear,* when Mr. Crab's attention is engaged by the sight of a man walking back and forth with his arms crossed, clearly in a state of disorder.

Without any Sings of Provocation, he flew like a Madman, upon the poor Ostler, who was cleaning some Coach-Harness at the Stable-Door, and seizing him by the Collar with both his Hands, he cried out as loud as his Voice would let him,

[1] II, 22.
[2] II, 51–52.

THE PLAYS: THE TRAGEDIES

Villain, be sure thou prove my Wife a Whore;
Be sure of it: Give me the occular Proof,
Or by the Worth of mine eternal Soul,
Thou hadst better have been born a Dog,
Than answer my wak'd Wrath.

When Mr. *Crab* had heard and seen this, he hastened back to the House, saying to himself as he went along, the Devil may part you both for me. And as he came into the Room to Mrs. *Crab* and the Captain, here, says he, we have got a Madman in the Yard: I wish we were well out of this Town. I'm afraid this Fellow will drive in here and do us a Mischief. I'll bolt the Door. Pray, says the Captain, how does the Man behave? Behave! says Mr. *Crab*, why he run like a Fury at the Ostler, and collar'd him; and then he roared out, *Villain be sure thou prove my Wife a Whore*, and such stuff as that. Ha! ha! ha! I'll be hang'd, says the Captain, if this same Madman be not my Friend *James Maccloud*, rehearsing the Part of *Othello*.

Upon Enquiry it turned out just so. And as the Captain could not stir out of his Chair for Want of his Leg, he begged Mr. and Mrs. *Crab* would permit *James* to be brought into the Room; which being complied with, *Othello* entered and bowed in the same Manner he would have done, if the Senate of *Venice* had been present.

James, says the Captain, I find you have been rehearsing *Othello* with the Ostler in the Stable yard. I desire you will now give us the Speech in that Play, which has this line in it,

Farewell the plumed Troops and the big War, &c.

I forget how it begins. I'll give it your Honour directly, says *James*; so without any more Ceremony, he turned himself round and composed his Countenance to express the united Passions of Rage and Sorrow, and then whipping out a half-dirty Neckcloth from his Coat-Pocket, which was to do the Office of a white Handkerchief, he began with these Words,

I had been happy if the general Camp,
Pioneers and all, &c.

And went thro' the Speech with *universal Applause;* that is to say, Mr. *Crab*, having never before seen any Thing above a Puppet-Shew, was quite Thunder-struck. Mrs. *Crab* was astonished to see the Captain so agitated, and the Captain himself was as much affected as if *Garrick* had spoken it; which may be asserted without any Disparagement to the Captain's Judgment, or Flattery to *James's* theatrical Merit; for it was *Othello's* pompous Farewell to the Army, that struck the Captain, being somewhat similar to his own Thoughts, when he was wounded and carried off the Field of Battle; and the Reader knows it is common enough for an Audience to applaud the Author, when they would, if it was possible to make the Distinction, have hiss'd the Actor, whose Vanity generally prompts him to believe the Approbation was given intirely to his Performance.

James Maccloud was however encored three Times; and at the Conclusion, when he says, *Othello's Occupation's gone*, the Captain threw himself back in his Chair, and kept his Eyes fixt for a Minute at least, on his

wooden Stump; then looking up, says he, When do you perform this Play?
To Night, Sir, says *James*.[1]

6. *King Lear*

IN VIEW of the continuous and distinguished stage record of *King
Lear* it is singular that novelists mentioned the tragedy infrequently.
The role of Lear descended to Garrick through Betterton, Booth, and
Quin, and came to be considered his greatest part. The tragedy missed
only five seasons at Drury Lane from 1742 to 1776, and only fourteen at Covent Garden. After "the little dog made it a *chef d'oeuvre*,"
as Macklin said, the records indicate twice as many performances up
to the time of his retirement as the public had seen from 1702 to 1740.
"A *chef d'oeuvre* it continued to the end of his life." [2]

The version presented was the abominable contrivance of Nahum
Tate perpetrated in 1681, which, with some tinkering, held the stage
for a century and a half, until William Macready scrapped it in 1838.
Almost everyone is familiar with Tate's manipulations: he cut Shakespeare's text by a third, provided a love-affair and a marriage between
Cordelia and Edgar, restored the aged king to his throne, poisoned
Goneril and Regan, and omitted the Fool. It is true that he accom-
plished a more closely integrated action, without, however, observing
the unities, but despite Dr. Johnson's defense of the changes in a play
which for him was too terrible to bear, Tate sacrificed more at the
altar of poetic justice than any other "improver" of any other English tragedy.[3]

In 1756 Garrick produced his revision of Tate, which he presented
henceforth, and which was printed in Bell's *Shakespeare* in 1773.[4] In
this blend of Tate and Shakespeare, Garrick retained but abridged the

[1] Dublin, 1772, I, 69–72. For the collaring scene in *Othello* see Sprague, *Shakespeare and the Actors*, pp. 197–199. At "Villain be sure thou prove my love a
whore! . . . give me the ocular proof," "Othello has suddenly rushed upon the
villain, collared him, throttled him, flung him down, or across the stage, threatened
his very life" (p. 198). This business was in all probability as old as the play itself. Tate Wilkinson in his *Memoirs*, 1790, II, 87, acted Othello in London: "In
the collaring scene, . . . I not only received repeated plaudits, but even a huzza!"
Barry's collaring of Iago is mentioned in *The Theatrical Review of 1757*, p. 24.
Arthur Murphy, in *The Apprentice*, 1756, II. i, used the scene farcically.

[2] [William Cooke], *Memoirs of Charles Macklin*, 1804, p. 107.

[3] For the alteration see Hazelton Spencer, *Shakespeare Improved*, pp. 241–252;
Odell, *Shakespeare from Betterton to Irving*, I, 53–56; G. W. Stone, Jr., "Garrick's
Production of *King Lear*: A Study in the Temper of the Eighteenth-Century Mind,"
SP, XLV (1948), 89–103, *passim*. For Samuel Richardson's objection to poetic jus-
tice in Tate's *Lear* see the Postscript to *Clarissa* as printed in the first edition, VII
(1748), 428. He was eager for Garrick to produce the original text.

[4] 2nd ed., 1774, II, 1–80.

love-scenes between Cordelia and Edgar, and preserved the "happy ending" with Lear restored to the throne. Although the Fool does not appear, Garrick replaced many of Tate's lines with the original speeches of Shakespeare.[1]

For alleged lack of decorum *Lear* received adverse criticism from a stupid woman in Sarah Fielding's *Adventures of David Simple* (1744). When David attends a salon of pretentious female wits, who display their ignorance every time they open their mouths, their conversation turns to Shakespeare. The opinions of the intelligent Lady True-wit, who is absent, are repeated with disapproval.

> *Third Lady.* That Lady once said, that one of the most beautiful Incidents in all *King Lear,* was, that the Impertinence of his Daughter's Servant, was the first Thing that made him uneasy; and after that, I think one can wonder at nothing: For certainly it was a great Oversight in the Poet, when he was writing the Character of a King, to take notice of the Behaviour of such *vulgar Wretches;* as if what they did was any thing to the purpose. But some People are very fond of turning the greatest Faults into Beauties, that they may be thought to have found out something extraordinary: And then they must admire every thing in *Shakespear,* as they think, to prove their own Judgment: But for my part, I am not afraid to give *my Opinion* freely of the greatest Men that ever wrote.[2]

Three years later Miss Fielding made use of the tragedy to express an unfavorable opinion of Shakespearean commentators so common in the eighteenth century. In *Familiar Letters between the Characters in David Simple* (1747), Lysimachus writes to Cratander from Cambridge, describing a dinner with a gentleman-bachelor, Minutius:

> The Conversation turned mostly on Learning. After we had run through a Criticism on the Surface of all the best Authors amongst the Classics, it was natural for *Shakespear* not to escape coming under our Observation. The Play that was chiefly talked on, was King *Lear.* You know I am so great an Admirer of that Play, I cannot help being pleased whenever it is mentioned; as I think it is impossible ever to read or consider of it, without finding new Beauties unobserved before. I hoped to hear something new on that Head, therefore hearkened at first with the strictest Attention; but I soon perceived the Characters, the Moral, the nice Touches of the Passions, were not the Points to be considered; but in their stead, the finding out the Meaning of some obsolete Words, and obscure Expressions made use of by *Edgar,* when he was personating a Madman, and by the Fool, when he was rattling on, to divert his poor distressed Master, seemed to be the only thing worthy Attention. *Minutius* has a very good Library in

---

[1] For further details see Stone's article. Of George Colman the Elder's version of 1768 no account is necessary, for the production was a failure; see Odell, I, 379–381.

[2] 2nd ed., 1744, I, 150.

the next Room to that in which we sat, and in a quarter of an Hour all the several Editions of *Shakespear,* and all the old Dictionaries that could be thought on, overspread the Table. Each Man took one, and was very busy in looking over it. But now I soon found, that the finding out the Meaning was not the Design neither; but the Point chiefly aimed at by every Person, was to prove his own Conjectures right; and, as soon as any one mentioned a Hint, that he thought he had discovered the Author's Meaning, all the rest, without considering of it, set themselves immediately to prove him in the wrong with so eager an Emulation, that they would hardly give one another Leave to speak.

When I was convinced this was the Case, I left them, alternatively disputing and poring over their Books; and yet I will answer for it, if they sat all Night, they were never the nearer concurring in their Opinions. I could not forbear smiling, to see them so long neglect what was really valuable, to employ themselves with such Earnestness about a Trifle; not that I have any Fault to find with this Branch of Criticism; for the busy, restless Mind of Man is well employed, when it is innocently amused: But I should be sorry to see the Farmer, altho' Straw and Stubble may be useful properly applied, take a fancy that he could make them into Bread, whilst he litter'd the Stable, and fed his Hogs with Wheat and Oats.

True Wisdom consists in making the right Use of every thing, even what is most trifling, but always so as to keep the Power of distinguishing what is estimable in itself, from that which at best can only be said not to be hurtful. But the Reflection on this, has since become a melancholy Consideration to me, by observing that the Eagerness for this Sort of Criticism in those Gentlemen, really arises from a Motive which spoils their Characters, hardens their Hearts, and makes them secret Enemies to each other: for, altho' a Delight in the same Subject of Conversation brings them often together, yet they rather meet like Prize-Fighters, in hopes of gaining a Victory, than like Friends to instruct and please each other: and, like Prize-Fighters, they shake Hands at meeting, tho' each knows in his Heart, he comes there to slash and cut his Antagonist without Mercy, deep enough to draw the Blood, only to shew his own Strength and Skill.[1]

That the Dover cliff scene was admired for its magnificent description is apparent in a novel attributed to Francis Fleming, a violinist at the Pump-Room at Bath, *The Life and Extraordinary Adventures . . . of Timothy Ginnadrake, That Child of Chequer'd Fortune* [1771]. Tim and his French wife make an excursion to Paris in 1752:

When Tim arrived at Dover, his curiosity led him to enquire for the Cliff which Shakespeare has so beautifully pictured in his tragedy of Lear; but the persons of whom he enquired, did not know what he meant.[2]

So far as the acting of *Lear* on the legitimate stage is concerned, there is commendation of Garrick's distinguished predecessor, Barton Booth, in *Memoirs of Sir Charles Goodville* (1753). The author of the forty-eighth letter, dated August 1, 1743, recalls the great actors

[1] II, 6–9.
[2] II, 157. Yale.

of the age of "the famous Triumvirate, who had the Direction of the Theatre in *Drury-Lane*— I mean *Booth, Wilks,* and *Cibber.* . . . I cannot help conceiving, it was not in Nature to go beyond what I have seen executed in various Characters, by the three Gentlemen I have named— What was *before* them, I cannot indeed determine upon— what has followed them I will venture to pronounce, has not by many Paces reached them." This theatrical conservative has recently been conversing with a competent judge about the requisites for a good tragedian.

The Requisites necessary to form a perfect *Tragedian,* are Memory, a manly Person, a round, strong, melodious Voice— If Melody be wanting, Art, and judicious Modulation, may, in a tolerable Degree, supply the Defect— He must by Nature be graceful and easy; for Action learned, will be perpetually stiff and forced— His *natural* Understanding must be good— and some Learning is absolutely necessary— And though all these happy Requisites should center in the same Man, he may yet be quite unqualified for the Profession of a Player—for unless *strong Genius,* blended with *sound Judgment,* attend them, they will be totally useless for that Purpose. *Genius,* indeed, with the Requisites I have named, may tolerably support him, though his *Judgment* should prove a little defective— But the Man, in whom Nature has bountifully united all, she proposed as the *Standard* of Tragic Acting—and such was the late Mr. *Booth*—with an additional Merit, I ought to have mentioned, in speaking of the *Person* of the *Man,* properly adapted to form a Tragedian— I mean that of the most pleasing, as well as the most *commanding* Eye, and Countenance, I ever beheld. . . .

A Gentleman who was present at this Conversation, but too young to remember Mr. *Booth,* said, he had been told, he was frequently apt to be indolent, and unspirited— If Sir, returned Mr. ——, the Persons who gave you this Information, meant, that he was not always writhing his Body, making a Number of absurd Starts, falling into trifling minute Action, distorting his Visage, and wringing his Limbs and Features, into antic Positions, he gave you a just Account of him— But if he did not tell you—the Majesty of *Lear, Pyrrhus, Tamerlane,* &c. was supported in the utmost Conception, or Idea that can be held of it—that the Rage, Madness, and Grief, of the first of those Characters, were such as became a *King*— That the Fire of *Othello,* and *Hotspur,* was not that of Mr. *Booth,* but blazed as differently, as *Shakespear* intended they should— If he did not tell you, the stern Rigour of *Cato,* and affable Complacency of *Brutus,* so distinguished with unequalled Art in this Gentleman's Performance, yet made it evidently appear, both had the same Impressions from *Philosophy,* but widely different from *Nature*—. . . . If Sir, your Friend did not give this Account of Mr. *Booth's* Appearance in these Characters, and in many others, with equal Propriety—you'll pardon me, if I tell you the Gentleman was not a little defective in his Judgment of Nature, and the Theatre.[1]

An extended eulogy of Garrick's interpretation of Lear by his sincere admirer, John Shebbeare, was included in *Letters on the English*

---

[1] II, 259–265. Pyrrhus is in Dryden and Lee's *Oedipus.*

Nation in 1755, the year before Garrick appeared in his own alteration of the tragedy. Although the text cited is Tate's, Shebbeare, by
emphasizing the psychology of the characters and by commenting on
precise passages, anticipates the impressionistic criticism so characteristic of the later eighteenth-century and of the romantic generation,
Shebbeare (or his spokesman Angeloni) maintains that only production can bring the written text to life: a good actor gives the true idea
of the author of a great dramatic character. A rapturous poet writing
about Lear may be "infinitely inferior" in genius to an actor who "fills
up this character with all that fire and majesty which becomes the
personage, as Shakespeare has completed it. This, a player on the English stage perfectly accomplishes: his name is Garrick." [1]

In the action of all other men I have imagined something yet farther than
has been exprest by them; in this player, and in this part, this man has exceeded all my imagination; and as Poussin is considered the painter of men
of taste, so in like manner Mr. Garrick is the player.

He is the only man on any stage where I have been, who speaks tragedy
truly and natural: the French tragedians mouth it too much, and to appear
something more than men, they lose the resemblance of humanity: a hero
on that stage, in dress and expression is a complete exotic of all nations,
and seems a creature just arrived from some distant planet.

It must be allowed however, that the passion of anger is the easiest to be
imitated of all those which the human mind is subject to; but to be angry
with superior sovereignty is as difficult to attain as any part, to be executed
with that dignity which this English actor imparts to it.

In the first act of the tragedy of Lear, when Cordelia has displeased him
by that which ought to have had a contrary effect, his anger is shewn by
very great expression, very just tone of voice, and propriety of action; yet
it still augments, and becomes more energic, as the rising occasions require
it, till at length when Goneril refuses him his hundred followers, and says,

> Be then advised by her, that else will take
> That which she begs, to lessen your attendance:
> Take half away, and see that the remainder
> Be such as may befit your age, and know
> Themselves and you.

After these words of insolence, Lear replies,

> Darkness and devils!
> Saddle my horses, call my train together.
> Degenerate viper, I'll not stay with thee:
> I yet have left a daughter— Serpent, monster!
> Lessen my train, and call them riotous!
> All men approved of choice and rarest parts,
> That each particular of duty know—
> How small, Cordelia, was thy fault? Oh Lear!

[1] II, 284.

> Beat at that gate which let thy folly in,
> And thy dear judgment out; go, go, my people.

This all other actors speak with that kind of rage, with which a drunken shoemaker curses his daughter that has secretly taken his money from him, and prevented his going to the alehouse; it is indeed a sheer scolding. In Mr. Garrick it is a prince in anger, and every accompaniment expresses it thro' the whole passage. "How small Cordelia," &c. This reflection, so natural to human minds, and parents in particular, to compare what they think a less fault in one child, whilst they are suffering under the influence of a greater in another, is as truly exprest by the actor, as imagined by the poet; and then reverting on himself at the words which follow, "Oh Lear," he absolutely imparts a power to them, which cannot be conceived but with much difficulty by those who have never beheld him: the whole bitter tide of resentment pours back on himself, and is as fully exprest from the fingers to the toes, thro' the flashing eye and keen feature, as Raphael has exprest the being possest, in his demoniac, in his picture of the transfiguration; and in these words, the soul of every hearer shivers as he pronounces them,

> Blasts upon thee;
> Th' untainted woundings of a father's curse
> Pierce ev'ry sense about thee.

Indeed, I could not avoid expecting a paralytic stroke would wither every limb of Goneril; the power of expression seemed as if of necessity it must prevail over heaven.

Then follows that which is so natural to the soul of man in excessive anger, when it suffers equally from the faults of others and itself, turning back with threats upon this weakness, which had made him weep, he utters with the utmost internal sensibility, and yet weeps in opposition to his own resolution,

> Old fond eyes,
> Lament this cause again, I'll pluck ye out,
> And cast you with the waters that ye lose
> To temper clay.

It is not possible to decide which is superior in the knowledge of nature, the poet who wrote, or the player who animates these passages. Afterwards when he begins

> Hear, nature,

And passes on to that most beautiful of all expressions,

> How sharper than a serpent's tooth it is,
> To have a thankless child!

All is so forcibly and interestingly exprest, with attitude and action so becoming the occasion, that, forgetting where I am, astonishment seizes me that Goneril has power to go off the stage unblasted at this imprecation: so perfectly the character is realized by every part of the player.[1]

The analysis continues with praise of Garrick's action in the second act, where, in his scene with Gloster ("Vengeance, death, plague,

[1] II, 284–289.

confusion!") the passages appear like flashes of lightning. And in the storm scene in the third act ("Rumble thy fill . . . oh, oh, 'tis foul"):

This speech is spoken at first with defiance; then, as the scene changes, the player falls into an acquiescence with this suffering; till coming to the last part, he feels with much contempt, that coward cruelty of basely joining with the perpetrators of filial disobedience; this is performed with such natural and easy transition, as if his soul conceived originally every sensation, as they follow one another in the poet.

As the madness advances in the character of Lear, it increases in the action and expression of the player; you scarce see where he first begins, and yet find he is mad before Kent says,

I fear'd 'twould come to this; his wits are gone.

It steals so gradually and imperceptibly, the difference grows like a colour which runs on from the lightest to the darkest tint without perceiving the shades, but by comparing them at different parts of the whole: when he enters mad in the fourth act, with the mock ensigns of majesty on him, thro' this whole scene, that which the poet has marked so strongly, the player has also preserved; that satyric turn, which accompanies madness arising from wrongs, is inimitably conceived by the poet, and sustained by the player; that vague and fugitive manner of pronouncing, mixt with the sarcastic touches of expression, is truly exhibited; and as in the poet's writings, so in the player's behaviour, the king is never one moment forgotten; it is royalty in lunacy: to quote every passage, would make a letter a whole play.[1]

Shebbeare observes that Garrick represented the restoration of Lear's sanity as a gradual process; the scenes with Cordelia in the fourth act possessed great pathos and simplicity. "The unornamented simplicity of Lear's words . . . has more sublimity and pathos, than all the powers of figure and metaphor could impart to them; and as it was imagined by Shakespeare, it is spoken by Mr. Garrick: my tears have ever testified this approbation."[2]

With regard to the final act, with its notorious happy ending, Shebbeare writes:

This play terminates happily, as it is acted different from the manner in which Shakespeare wrote it; Cordelia is made Queen, and Lear retires to pass away his life in quietness and devotion: many of the passages are transposed from the order they stand in the original; for that reason I have sent you the alteration, that you may see it as it is played: the words which express the joy at the thoughts of Cordelia's being a queen, are spoken with an emphasis and energy, which is peculiar to Mr. Garrick only; and tho' the poet is no longer visible in this place, the player sustains his character in this also.[3]

[1] II, 291–292.
[2] II, 294.
[3] II, 295.

David Garrick in the character of King Lear

The author's conclusion is that Garrick as an actor is on a level with great painters and musicians like Raphael and Corelli.[1]

At the mercy of the strollers *King Lear* underwent what must have been one of the world's unique productions in Herbert Lawrence's *Contemplative Man; or, The History of Christopher Crab, Esq.* (1771). The Crabs, as already noted, are staying at the Red Lion Inn with their friend the Captain, when they hear trumpet and drums and the following announcement by the scarlet-clad trumpeter:

Gentlemen and Ladies, this present Evening will be performed, at the Great Room in the White Talbot Yard, the Tragical History of King LEAR and his three Daughters, by a Company of Comedians, who have had the Honour to perform with great Applause, before the King and all the Royal Family. The Characters are all new dress'd; and the Part of *Cordelia* to be performed *by a Gentlewoman being her first Appearance*. To which *by Desire*, will be added, *The Devil to Pay*. The part of *Nell* by the Lady who plays *Cordelia*.

The announcer is James MacCloud.

Well, *James,* says the Captain, but who is this Gentlewoman that never performed before? God bless your Honour, I did not say she never performed before, I said *Being her first Appearance*, meaning here. It is a common Thing at the Theatres-Royal in *London*, to say in their Play-Bills, *The Part of* —— *to be performed by a Gentlewoman, or Gentleman, being their first Appearance*, tho' perhaps they have play'd in most of the stroling Companies in *England*. You know, your Honour, we cannot do better than follow the Example of the Commanders in Chief, the Managers of the King's Theatres. As to the Gentlewoman that is to play *Cordelia* to Night, it is my Wife, and a very good Hand she is, only the poor woman's very big with Child at present, or else she would have danc'd a Hornpipe between the Play and the Farce. This is the first Night of our performing in

---

[1] With regard to Tate's and Garrick's versions of *Lear* at this time, it is interesting to read in *The Old Maid, by Mary Singleton, Spinster,* a periodical conducted by the novelist Mrs. Frances Brooke, a review of Spranger Barry's performance as Lear. In No. XVIII, for Saturday, March 13, 1756, Mrs. Brooke concludes her review with the following comment: "It has always been matter of great astonishment to me, that both the houses have given *Tate's* wretched alteration of *King Lear,* the preference to *Shakespear's* excellent original; which Mr. *Addison,* the most candid, as well as judicious of critics, thinks so infinitely preferable, as to bear no degree of comparison; and one cannot help remarking particularly, and with some surprize, that Mr. *Garrick,* who professes himself so warm an idolater of this inimitable poet, and who is determined, if I may use his own words, in the prologue to the *Winter's Tale,* 'To lose no drop of this immortal man,' should yet prefer the vile adulterated cup of *Tate,* to the pure genuine draught, offered him by the master he avows to serve with such fervency of devotion. As to Mr. *Barry,* I think he was perfectly right to take the *Lear* which is commonly play'd, that the competition between him and Mr. *Garrick* in this trying part, may be exhibited to the public upon a fair footing; I have not yet been so fortunate as to see the latter in it, whose performance, I doubt not, is no less justly, than generally, celebrated and admired."

this Town. I hope we shall have your Honour's Company? Why look you, Friend *James,* says the Captain, I should have had no Objection, if it had happened to have been a Comedy, but these Tragedies affect me Spirits too much, and make me unhappy; if it had been the Recruiting Officer, (placeing his Cane upon his left Shoulder like a Firelock) I would have said something to you.

The Recruiting Officer, answered *James* eagerly, your Honour shall have it. It makes no Difference to us. We intend to play it o' *Wednesday* next; and we are ready dressed for either. I am obliged to thee, *James,* says the Captain for thy Offer, but as you have given out King *Lear,* it would be a Disappointment to your Audience; so (giving him a Crown) I wish thee Success, *James,* with all my Heart.[1]

The two servants of the Captain and Mr. Crab, Cork and Thomas, gain their masters' permission to attend the performance. Untutored, neither had ever seen a play.

Well, *Cork,* says the Captain, how did you like the Play? I lik'd it hugely, Sir, says *Cork,* the Shew-Folks were all mortal finely dress'd, except one, and he was cover'd with Rags: I verily believe he was a downright Madman; but they seem'd to be main proud, for they spoke to no Soul but one another. Well, *Cork,* says the Captain, but what is the Play about? Why, you must know, Sir, says *Cork,* there's a King, and he has three Daughters, and he has a Mind to leave off being a King, so he divides all he has amongst his three Daughters, only he does not give the youngest any Thing; and in my Mind he was quite wrong, for she had done nothing at that Time to disoblige him; but he was rightly serv'd, for when the two eldest Daughters got into their Father's House, they turn'd him out of Doors in one of the bitterest Nights that ever was known. And what became of the youngest Daughter, says the Captain? Why, poor Soul, she was almost distracted, so she went and took on with the ragged Madman that I told your Honour of; but to be sure she must have kept him Company long before, because she was taken in Labour soon afterwards. How, *Cork,* says the Captain, was the youngest Princess *Cordelia* taken in Labour? I fancy you must mistake. As I have a Soul to be sav'd, says *Cork,* it's as true as I stand here. Ask *Thomas* else, if the Gentleman Trumpeter, that talked with your Honour this Afternoon, did not come from behind the Blanket and tell us so; nay, for that Matter, we could hear her plain enough. And so the Play ended. Ay, ay, says the Captain, laughing, now I recollect, *James* told me the Princess was very near her Time. But there was something after the Play, was there not? No, Sir, says *Cork.* They told us if this Accident had not happened, they would have shewed us the Devil and all his Works. Here the Captain laughed again, and at the same Time gave a Signal which *Cork* understood, and he withdrew to the Kitchen, where he told his Tale again, with many more wonderful Circumstances.[2]

7. *Macbeth*

SHAKESPEARE'S shortest, and in some respects most uneven

[1] Dublin, 1772, I, 58–60. *The Devil to Pay* was a popular afterpiece by Charles Coffey.
[2] I, 61–62.

tragedy, *Macbeth,* has held the stage persistently since the Restoration.[1] In the forty-one years preceding Garrick's appearance there were over two hundred performances. Indeed, during the first half of the eighteenth century, of the great tragedies, *Hamlet* alone surpassed *Macbeth's* stage record. Before 1744 it was always given in the execrable version by Sir William Davenant, printed in 1674, whose operatic embellishments and flying witches gave the public an entirely corrupt notion of Shakespeare's structure and poetry. On January 7, 1744, Garrick, with his concern for guiding the taste of his age toward the genuine Shakespeare after the distortions of the Philistines, restored most of the original text, when at the age of twenty-seven he made his first appearance as the Scottish king.[2] He had already acted Richard III, Lear, and Hamlet in the altered versions of his predecessors. He advertised his *Macbeth* "as Shakespeare wrote it." Basing his text on Theobald's, he succeeded in presenting in a little over two thousand lines "the most accurate stage version of a Shakespearian play which had appeared since 1671."[3] He continued the ejection of the drunken Porter and the omission of Lady Macbeth from the general conference after Duncan's murder; he cut heavily Lady Macduff's scene with her small son, as well as the murder of the boy; and he abridged Macduff's persuasion of Malcolm to lead an army against the tyrant. The cavorting witches, impersonated, as traditionally, by men, were retained.

From 1742 to 1776 *Macbeth* was presented during every season but four at Drury Lane. At Covent Garden it missed ten seasons. From 1748 to her death in 1768 Mrs. Hannah Pritchard was Garrick's distinguished Lady Macbeth. In that year he relinquished his role to Spranger Barry, Samuel Reddish, and "Gentleman" Smith. At Covent Garden, Macbeth was played by Barry, William Powell, and Thomas Sheridan; the best-known Lady Macbeths there were Mrs. Barry, Peg Woffington, and Mrs. Yates.

The "great Nestor of the stage," Charles Macklin, was responsible for dressing the tragedy with historical accuracy at Covent Garden in

---

[1] For a comprehensive stage history see C. B. Young in the New Cambridge *Macbeth,* ed. J. D. Wilson, Cambridge, 1947, pp. lxix–lxxxii.

[2] See Hazelton Spencer, *Shakespeare Improved,* pp. 152–174, for a full account of Davenant's alteration; for a short summary see Odell, *Shakespeare from Betterton to Irving,* I, 28–30. G. W. Stone, Jr., "Garrick's Handling of *Macbeth,*" *SP,* XXXVIII (1941), 609–628, analyzes in detail Garrick's version in comparison with Davenant's. Davenant's text is reprinted in the New Variorum edition of *Macbeth,* ed. H. H. Furness, Philadelphia, 1873, II, 303–355. The text in Bell's *Shakespeare,* 2nd ed., 1774, I, 61–131, is a faithful Drury Lane version.

[3] Stone, p. 622.

1773, an innovation which was adopted at Drury Lane three years later. Garrick always costumed Macbeth in an officer's red coat and a tie-wig, while his Lady Macbeth wore the latest eighteenth-century confection of pleats, tucks, and ruffles.

The earliest view of Garrick's Macbeth in fiction was hostile. Consumed with personal ire at the manager of Drury Lane, Smollett poured forth his Caledonian venom in the first edition of *Peregrine Pickle* (1751), with a sideswipe for good measure at the actor's Hamlet.

I have observed the same person, in the character of Hamlet, shake his fist at his mistress, for no evident cause, and behave like a ruffian to his own mother. Shocked at such a want of dignity and decorum in a prince, who seemed the favourite of the people, I condemned the genius that produced him, but, upon a second perusal of the play, transferred my censure to the actor, who, in my opinion, had egregiously mistaken the meaning of the poet. At a juncture, when his whole soul ought to be alarmed with terror and amazement, and all his attention engrossed by the dreadful object in view, I mean that of his friend whom he had murthered; he expresses no passion but that of indignation against a drinking glass, which he violently dashes in pieces on the floor, as if he had perceived a spider in his wine; nay, while his eyes are fixed upon the ground, he starts at the image of a dagger, which he pretends to see above his head, as if the pavement was a looking-glass that represented it by reflexion and at one time I saw him walk across the stage, and lend an inferior character a box on the ear, after he had with great wrath pronounced "Take thou that," or some equivalent exclamation, at the end of the scene. He represents the grief of an hero, by the tears and manner of a whining school-boy, and perverts the genteel deportment of a gentleman, into the idle buffoonery of a miserable tobacconist; his whole art is no other than a succession of frantic vociferation, such as I have heard in the cells of Bedlam, a slowness, hesitation, and oppression of speech, as if he was troubled with an asthma, convulsive startings, and a ductility of features, suited to the most extravagant transitions. In a word, he is blessed with a distinct voice, and a great share of vivacity; but in point of feeling, judgment, and grace, is, in my opinion, altogether defective. Not to mention his impropriety in dress, which is so absurd, that he acts the part of a youthful prince, in the habit of an undertaker. . . . I beg pardon for treating this darling of the English with so little ceremony; and to convince you of my candour, frankly confess, that notwithstanding all I have said, he is qualified to make a considerable figure in the low characters of humour, which are so relished by a London audience, if he could be prevailed upon to abate of that monstrous burlesque, which is an outrage against nature and common sense.[1]

[1] 1st ed., II, 138–139, quoted in H. S. Buck, *A Study in Smollett, Chiefly "Peregrine Pickle"*, pp. 154–155. For Garrick's stage business with the daggers (II. i, ii) see Sprague, *Shakespeare and the Actors*, pp. 238–239, 241–242. The allusion to the "miserable tobacconist" is to Garrick's famous role of Abel Drugger in Jonson's *Alchemist*. Francis Gentleman in *The Dramatic Censor*, 1770 (I, 107–108), praised in particular Garrick's conception of the dagger scene: "As Shakespeare rises above himself in many places, so does this his greatest and best commentator,

David Garrick and Mrs. Hannah Pritchard as Macbeth and Lady Macbeth

Smollett's irascible views about Garrick's naturalism were not shared by Robert Lewis in his excellent and very rare picaresque novel, *The Adventures of a Rake in the Character of a Public Orator* (1759). The hero makes up his mind to become a public orator, because he believes that "a well wrote Piece, justly pronounced, furnishes the most rational Entertainment the human Mind can be susceptible of."

The Drama has ever been regarded in this Light; for when the Skill of the Player is added to that of the Poet, and the one gives Utterance to the other's Conceptions, it is not the Actor or the Poet that we hear, 'tis the Character of the Drama that speaks to us, and rouses *our* Passions by the Expression of those *himself* feels. Do not our humid Eyes and sympathetic Breasts amply demonstrate this? Wherefore are our Immortal Poet's Plays, his *Macbeth* in particular, so much admired even by the Vulgar and the Illiterate? Is it because they understand him? Is it on Account of the Beauty of his Language? No, I will venture to affirm, that no one Person in an Hundred that attend theatrical Representations, can even fathom his Meaning. Wherefore then, I say, is it that they not only approve but *admire* him? a very essential Distinction of Mr. *Pope's,* though by him very absurdly applied. It is because Mr *Garrick,* proving now the Doctrine of the *Metempsychosis* beyond all Possibility of Doubt, shoots his Soul into the Characters he personates, and gives Life to inanimate Beings. *Shakespear's Macbeth* is scarcely intelligible to the Learned; Garrick's *Macbeth* lives, and is intelligible to the Vulgar. This proves to an evident Demonstration, that acting any Piece is preferable to reading it; and from what I have mentioned, we may lay down as an undoubted Truth, that as the most noble Principles and patriotic Sentiments, are inculcated in the Drama, which render it a School of Knowledge, and however it has been denied by some Writers, I will add, a School of Virtue; so those instructive Precepts which may be delivered by Orators, for forming the Manners and the Morals of Youth, will cause Oratory to be considered, if well applied, as a useful Assistant for this great End.[1]

Even after his experiences with a company of poor strollers the youth is not disillusioned about the power of oratory. Betterton could draw tears from soldiers with his forcible eloquence.

Is our Country widowed of these Lights?—Is she not still adorned, with those whose Action can master the Human Heart, and steal the Drops of

who not only presents his beautie[s] to the imagination, but brings them home feelingly to the heart: among a thousand other instances of almost necromantic merit; let us turn our recollection only to a few in the character of Macbeth; who ever saw the *immortal actor* start at, and trace the imaginary dagger previous to Duncan's murder, without embodying by sympathy, unsubstantial air into the alarming shape of such a weapon?" The dashing down of the drinking glass is a reference to one of the most continuous of all Shakespearean traditions. In the banquet scene (III. iv) Macbeth still drops his cup, and has always done so, and sometimes in the eighteenth century he did actually smash a glass. See Sprague, pp. 261–262, and Garrick's *Essay on Acting,* 1744, where the actor advises that the glass should not be dashed but gently dropped.

[1] II, 116–118. Bodleian.

Sorrow from the generous Eye? It were Ingratitude, O *Garrick,* not to say this Power is thine! [1]

Although Garrick is not mentioned, it is a safe assumption that it was he whom Ophelia Lenox saw when her sensibilities were aroused at a performance of *Macbeth* in Sarah Fielding's popular epistolary novel, *The History of Ophelia* (1760). Like Evelina, Ophelia, a virtuous orphan, leaves her retired cottage to be taught the ways of London society. Her friends Lord Dorchester and Lady Palestine accompany her on her first visit to the theater.

No one was admitted into the Box to us but Lord *Dorchester,* who excluded all others that I might not confine the Emotions so new a Sight would raise in me. My Lord had often read to me some of *Shakespear's* historical Plays, and it was to one of these he carried me, never chusing I should go to any others; and he gave me so poor a Character of the Performances of many of the other dramatic Poets, that I never felt a Desire of seeing them, tho' by the Play-Bills I found there was great Variety.

Had my Lord's only View been my Entertainment, in this he would have acted judiciously; I had been convinced by Observation, that Plays and Novels vitiate the Taste: I allow many of them to be extremely diverting, some very fine; but by the Multiplicity of Events, mixed with a good Deal of the Marvellous; they learn the Mind a Dissipation even in Reading. The simple Chain of Facts in History, appear ill to a Person used to Wonder; as moral Truths, and sound Reason, do, to one who has been accustomed to the Turns and Quibbles of false Wit, the enchanting Jingle of Rhime, or the pompous Sound of high-flown Metaphors. . . .

However, greatly as I had been entertained by the Plays I had heard, there was something so much more lively in the Representation of them on the Theatre as at first delighted me extremely. I had heard many of the Speeches much more to Advantage when my Lord read them; but in the Acting, the whole received such an Air of Truth, that I could scarcely disbelieve a Fact in it. This made my Agitation almost as strange as if I had been the Spectator of a real Tragedy. The Play was *Macbeth,* and Lord *Dorchester* and Lady *Palestine* were sufficiently taken up in observing the Passions imprest on my Countenance. They told me, I might more properly be said to act the Play, than some of the Persons on the Stage. Indeed, I believe I was more fatigued with my part of the Representation; for when it was over, I found my Mind quite weary with the Agitation it had been in. Anger was one of the Passions that had been excited, for I could not bear with Patience the Noises that were sometimes made; and was so intirely engaged that I could not utter a rational Sentence on any other Subject, even between the Acts: Nor did the Change of Scene change my Ideas: for after I went Home, they continued as much fixed on the Play, as during the Representation; and it was almost with Difficulty they at last gave place to Sleep.[2]

There are no fictional accounts of Garrick's Macbeth comparable

---

[1] II, 222.

[2] I, 159–162. For an analysis of this interesting novel see Foster, *History of the Pre-Romantic Novel in England,* pp. 76–77.

in excellence to Fielding's tribute to his Hamlet, but the power of his acting up to the time he resigned the role to Spranger Barry in 1768 appears in one of the most popular novels by the French adventurer, Pierre Henri Treyssac de Vergy, *The Mistakes of the Heart; or, Memoirs of Lady Carolina Pelham and Lady Victoria Nevil. In a Series of Letters* (1769–1771). Lady Carolina, already impressed with "the incomparable Garrick," whom she had seen in Hoadly's *Suspicious Husband* (1747), asks her brother: "Was not Garrick unusually great in Macbeth on Tuesday?" Her brother replies: "He was not, Carolina. Ever feeling, natural, and sublime, Garrick is immutably himself." [1]

Spranger Barry was considered in many roles to be almost Garrick's equal. Endowed in his prime with a voice which Francis Gentleman called "the pipe of love," and with eyes of "a languishing softness which set him above all competition in soft sensations," he prepossessed the female audience [2] and shone particularly as Romeo. He had acted Macbeth at Covent Garden when Garrick resigned the role to him at Drury Lane in 1768. High commendation of his performance appears in a curious *roman à clef* about the eccentric actress and singer Ann Catley, *Miss C—y's Cabinet of Curiosities; or, The Green-Room Broke Open. By Tristram Shandy, Gent.* (1765). The author of this short Shandean narrative holds no lofty opinion of actors and actresses, who are "Vagabonds, Spendthrifts, W's and R's":

They are incapable of doing a good Action, or entertaining a just Sentiment— Though they have the Works of Shakespear, and Dryden, and Otway, and Congreve, and Addison . . . by Heart; they are not so wise, or so witty, or so well-bred, as eminent Citizens who sell Raisins, and Oil, and Leather, and Bread, and Cheese, and Candles, and Soap, and Whiskey, and Coals, and Hats, and Wigs.[3]

In Miss C—y's cabinet there is found a paper attacking Barry:

It roundly asserted, that BARRY knew nothing of Acting—that his Attitudes were vile—his Pauses unnatural—his Elocution villainous—his Action distorted—that he had no Feeling—that he was a Parrot—in short, that he was a d—d bad Player— But that Mr. MOSSOP—ay, Mr. MOSSOP, in spight of his Arm-like Caudle-Cup, and his Adamantine Lungs, was a *Roman* Roscius, and an *English* Betterton, Booth, and Garrick united.[4]

[1] I, 110–111. For De Vergy see Foster, *Pre-Romantic Novel*, pp. 181–182, and Bruce Sutherland, "Pierre Henri Treyssac de Vergy," *MLQ*, IV (1943), 293–307. *The Mistakes of the Heart* is dedicated to J. J. Rousseau, Citizen of Geneva.
[2] *The Dramatic Censor*, 1770, II, 485.
[3] Pages 12–13. BM.
[4] Page 23. Henry Mossop was an actor of great merit, who wasted his life in struggling to be the head of the theater in Dublin. There is much information about him in William Cooke's *Memoirs of Charles Macklin*, 1804, pp. 240–267.

A Connaught squire supports the acting of his fellow Irishman, Henry Mossop, in the manner of Partridge's support of the King in *Hamlet* as the finest actor in the play:

He was . . . asked, if he had seen MOSSOP play?—He replied, Yes— He was next asked how he liked him?—"Why, by J—s," replied he, "he is the best Actor in the World, I believe; for he takes great Pains,—and throws himself into surprizing Postures,—and stands with his Arms a-Kimbow like a great Man,—and stalks majestically on the Stage,—and in the most common Scenes delivers himself with all the Strength of Lungs, and all the Force of Action, as you call it.—Oh, he is a great man!— But as to this BARRY here, at this What-d 'ye-call-'um House yonder, he is a very bad Actor—a monstrous bad One, by J—s. Why, he's no Actor at all, at all. He is not after taking any Pains—he does not put himself into hardly any Postures—he looks like a common Man—and walks like one—and doesn't speak with that Hemphasis and Power as the other Man does. Ah! I wish I could see *Him* do *Macbeth*— *Macbeth* would then be done something like— But as to BARRY, there is nothing in him but any Man may do—why, I could act myself like him; ay, and speak too; for if *Banquo's* Ghost was to appear to me at the Banquet, I should act and speak just as He does—and so I should in the other Scenes, where he does not seem to be a Player at all, at all, but the very Man himself whose Name he takes on him in the Play."

From this, may it please your Reverences, if the *Connaught* Gentleman is a Judge of Acting,—and that he is, I challenge all the dramatic and judicious People in the World to gainsay—it plainly appears, that the Dissecting Author is right in his Opinion—that Mr. MOSSOP is a much better Player than Mr. BARRY.[1]

On a less controversial level Harry Harper, hero of the attractive novel *The Prudential Lovers; or, The History of Harry Harper* (1773), makes his first appearance as an actor in the character of Macbeth at Edinburgh. Groomed by a sympathetic manager, who is no less a figure than Samuel Foote, Harry makes his trial flight in "a celebrated Scotch tragedy."

The pompous preface of Macbeth by a young Gentleman, being his first appearance on any Stage, had drawn a vast concourse of people to the Theatre, and though he was extremely perfect, had well studied the character, and flattered by many at different rehearsals; yet a je ne scai quoi prevailed over his senses, and his trembling heart in doleful thumps knocked ponderous at his ribs. In short, the audience were lavish of their

---

[1] Pages 27–28. Francis Gentleman observed in *The Dramatic Censor*, 1770, that Barry "even now, though overtaken by time, and impaired in his constitution, . . . has not the shadow of a competitor." The actor suffered from rheumatism, "yet true it is, that if he hobbled upon stilts, he would be better than any persons in his stile upon their best legs." Gentleman compared him to the time-worn ruins of Palmyra and Balbec (II, 203). For the contest between Barry and Mossop at the Dublin theaters see La Tourette Stockwell, *Dublin Theatres and Theatre Customs*, Kingsport, 1938, pp. 128–135.

praises, and Mr. Harper was flattered into vanity; between each Act he received the compliments of several Gentlemen, and at the end the Manager extolled him to the skies.[1]

With another amateur, Mr. Hilkirk, in Holcroft's *Alwyn* (1780), *Macbeth* was a favorite play. As a youth Hilkirk went to London to live with his patron Mr. Selden. There he fell in love with Selden's orphan niece, Julia Gowland, whom he marries at the melodramatic conclusion of the novel. But his love is temporarily competing with his passion for the theater and his constant attendance at a spouting club.

I joined the roarers, . . . whose tragic starts . . . operated strongly on my imagination. It came to my turn to exhibit, and I chose that scene in Macbeth, where the bloody dagger appears in the air. I was drest in a habit, made in imitation of Garrick's, with shaloon and tinsel. Banquo and Fleance had made their exit, and I was proceeding, with infinite applause, through the soliloquy: Just as I came to that place, where the hero says to the supposed dagger, "I see thee still," my astonished eye caught the terrible form of Mr. Selden; the effect this had upon me was evident from the audience; my knees knocked, my eyes went wild and rivetted, my voice faultered— I repeated,

> "I see thee still,
> And on thy blade and dudgeon gouts of blood,
> Which was not so before."

The picture of terror was so perfect, that the room echoed with plaudits.[2]

Selden commands the boy to give up spouting societies. Thinking his suit of Julia hopeless, Hilkirk joins the strollers.

The imagery of Macbeth's soliloquy on sleep was admired in the novel attributed to John Preston, teacher, *Genuine Letters from a Gentleman to a Young Lady His Pupil* (1772). The author, it will be recalled, held Hamlet's "To be or not to be" soliloquy in similar high regard. After a long coach journey, the teacher writes his pupil, Nancy Blisset, in a letter dated November 11, 1742, his reflections about the medicinal value of sleep:

To Children, and Persons advanced in Life, Sleep is a Medicine for many Ills; and surely the pleasantest of all Medicines. Did you ever read *Shakespeare's* Tragedy of *Macbeth?* if not get it, and send me your Opinion of it. I will transcribe his Passage on Sleep, which, for the luxuriant Variety of sweet and noble Images, is scarce to be equalled.

> *"The innocent Sleep,*
> *Sleep that knits up the ravell'd Sleeve of Care,*
> *The Death of each day's Life, sore Labour's Bath,*
> *Balm of hurt Minds, great Nature's second Course,*
> *Chief Nourisher in Life's Feast."*

[1] II, 84–85. BM.
[2] I, 21–22.

What a Group of beautiful Images are here! Nor has the great Bard assembled them merely to indulge his fine Fancy; no, they are of a Piece with the great Action of the Scene, and answer an important moral End; for by how much he endears to us the inestimable Blessing of Sleep, by so much he aggravates the atrocious Crime of Murder, from the Commission whereof *Macbeth* is but just returned. Observe too the first Epithet which he gives to Sleep, *innocent;* it is very copious. It not only implies that Sleep is innocent in itself, that while we sleep, we are free from Guilt, but that Sleep most naturally dwells with innocent and undisturbed Minds.

I have no doubt but I shall dream of you to-night for I have been dreaming of you all Day.[1]

8. *Antony and Cleopatra*

SHAKESPEARE'S magnificent tragedy of world empire, *Antony and Cleopatra,* was almost completely unknown to the eighteenth-century theater-goer, for it was supplanted for a century and a half by the finest of the "improvements," Dryden's *All for Love* (1678). From 1702 to 1776 Dryden's rewriting was acted no less than one hundred ten times, reaching the peak of its popularity during the first half of the century. During the period of Garrick's management of Drury Lane, *All for Love* was acted there only eleven times. It was pre-eminently a Covent Garden piece.

Garrick's devotion to Shakespeare's genuine texts persuaded him to an earnest but unsuccessful attempt to restore *Antony and Cleopatra* to the stage on January 3, 1759.[2] His friend, the Shakespearean

[1] I, 131–133. *Macbeth* was the only Shakespearean tragedy upon which a novel was based, but inasmuch as the novel was first published in English in 1708, is adopted from the French, and has no connection with *Macbeth* beyond the title, it has no importance for the present study. Written by Marie Catherine Jumelle de Bernville, Comtesse D'Aulnoy, who died in 1705, it was first printed in London as *The Secret History of Mack-beth, King of Scotland, Taken from a Very Ancient Original Manuscript,* in 1708. It was reprinted in 1741 in *The History of Hypolitus, Earl of Douglas. With the Secret History of Macbeth, King of Scotland* (pp. 213–294). Another edition appeared in 1768 as *A Key to the Drama; or, Memoirs, Intrigues, and Atchievements of Personages Who Have Been Chosen by the Most Celebrated Poets as the Fittest Characters for Theatrical Representations. . . . Vol. I. Containing the Life, Character, and Secret History of Macbeth. By a Gentleman, No Professed Author, but a Lover of History and of the Theatre.* See Jaggard, *Shakespeare Bibliography,* pp. 183, 278. The romance, which purports to be based on some private memoirs of a noble family (the Howards), tells of Macbeth's amorous young manhood; his erotic intrigue with Anabella, Lady Kyle; the weakness of the indolent King Duncan; Macbeth's desertion of Lady Kyle for Margaretta, daughter of the chieftain of Ross, and his ambition for the throne: "The active mind of *Macbeth* was ever soaring beyond the limits of his present condition; and he began to fancy, that by being so closely linked with the most powerful, as well as the most popular party, a passage would be open to him, through which he might gain even a prospect of the Crown" (*A Key to the Drama,* p. 68). Happily, no more "Keys" were published.

[2] See G. W. Stone, Jr., "Garrick's Presentation of *Antony and Cleopatra,*" RES, XIII (1937), 20–38.

editor Edward Capell, prepared the text, which was issued in 1758. He cut and rearranged scenes with considerable skill, concentrating on the tragedy of love and rendering action and characterization less complex. His version was shorter than Shakespeare's by a fifth, but Antony's character was not harmed, and Cleopatra's shining lines were scarcely touched. The splendid poetic passages and the grandeur of the original tragedy remained. Despite new costumes and scenery, the crowded audience manifested no great pleasure, and the revival lapsed after the sixth performance on May 18. Garrick's physical shortcomings as Antony, the inability of the company to support the other characters, and the great popularity of *All for Love* have been argued as reasons for the failure of this ambitious production.[1]

Although novelists occasionally had something to say about *All for Love,* they wrote almost nothing about *Antony and Cleopatra.* But Garrick's revival may have induced the author of *Love in High Life; or, The Amours of a Court* [?1760] to compare the barge scene as described by Shakespeare and Dryden.[2] The novel itself, which is little more than a *réchauffé* of classical love stories, includes a colorless paraphrase of North's brilliant prose description of the scene on the Cydnus. The author himself does not make a choice between the two poetical versions. Modern readers have not found it difficult to choose.

We apprehend that it will be an additional entertainment to our readers, to present them here with the poetical descriptions of this parade of Cleopatra's on the river Cydnus, as drawn by the two greatest poetic geniuses this kingdom has produced, to wit, Shakespear and Dryden.

It will also be a pleasure to observe the different points of light, in which those great men have considered it, and on what parts of the historical detail they have chosen to bestow their heightening strokes, and enliven with the strongest glow of colouring.

There is a greater strength, and a more energetic conciseness in the picture drawn by Shakespear. In that of Dryden, there is a milder, freer, and more elegant display of all the different parts that constitute the whole, which are perhaps too closely crowded together in Shakespear. He indeed presents his piece with an offhand, and unstudied magnificence; which Dryden being sensible of, strives to rival him, with a beautiful arrangement of several figures, and an unequalled harmony of expression.

For the reader's convenience both "Shakespear's picturesque description" and "Dryden's terse, florid and happy" lines are quoted.[3]

---

[1] Stone, pp. 34–36.

[2] Capell transposed the description of Cleopatra's barge to Act I, near the beginning of the play, giving the lines to Thyreus instead of to Enobarbus. "Thus Cleopatra in that marvellous description was made glorious and wonderful at the outset" (Stone, p. 28).

[3] *Antony and Cleopatra*, II. ii. 196–223; *All for Love*, III. i. 161–182.

It is apparent from reading the two pieces, one after the other, as they have been wrote, that Dryden was thoroughly sensible of the difficulty he laboured under, in being obliged to give Cleopatra's progress on the Cydnus in a poetical dress; it having been already executed in so strong a manner, by that foremost of dramatic writers, Shakespear.

Dryden, in order to compensate in some sort for the expressive vigour, infused into the description of England's proto-type for sublime diction, called into his assistance all the succour of tasteful and ingenious art, and has left it a disputed point among the connoisseurs of polite writing, which of the two pieces is the more masterly performance.[1]

The age was not yet prepared to express an outright preference for Shakespeare's genius unimproved by "art."

9. *The Tragedies Concluded*

OF THE remaining tragedies of Shakespeare, *Coriolanus* and *Timon of Athens,* there was complete disregard by writers of fiction. After the alterations of Tate and Dennis, *Coriolanus,* in a respectable version,[2] was revived for eight performances at Drury Lane in 1754 and 1755, with Mrs. Pritchard as Volumnia, but without Garrick. There were no other revivals at Drury Lane during Garrick's regime. *Timon of Athens,* in Shadwell's version of 1678, held the stage during the Cibber era, but the original tragedy has had an indifferent stage history. It was acted at Covent Garden in 1745 and 1746, but not again at either house during Garrick's time, although, without appearing in it himself, he produced Richard Cumberland's alteration, which failed, in 1771.

Finally, the patent houses and the strolling companies held no monopoly on Shakespeare's tragedies—or comedies. It delights us to read that, as with the Bertram children later at Mansfield Park, amateur theatricals were popular with young people. The colorful daughter of Colley Cibber, Mrs. Charlotte Charke, in *The History of Henry Dumont, Esq., and Miss Charlotte Evelyn* (1755) describes how her hero and heroine often attended dramatic performances in London, and how at the age of fifteen Henry persuaded his father to "let them have a compleat theatre built at the end of a green walk; where several young Ladies and Gentlemen formed a company of comedians, and exhibited many of Shakespeare's and Moliere's plays; nor was Terence excluded; whose Comedies were generally acted by the male part of their society, except sometimes Miss Evelyn, who was perfect mistress

[1] Pages 75–80. BM.
[2] Odell, *Shakespeare from Betterton to Irving,* I, 356.

of the Latin tongue, took an occasional part to fill up their number: between the acts she frequently entertain'd the nobility and gentry (who form'd their audience) with a song or a lesson on the harpsichord."[1]

Even in remote Wales, Shakespeare was not neglected by young folk. Mrs. Sarah Robinson Scott, sister of the bluestocking defender of Shakespeare, Mrs. Elizabeth Montagu, shows her own interest in Shakespeare in her rare novel, *The Test of Filial Duty. In a Series of Letters between Miss Emilia Leonard and Miss Charlotte Arlington* (1772). Her story teaches filial obedience in matrimonial affairs. When Emilia finds herself unable to obey her father's wish that she marry Lord Wilton, she goes into retirement in a secluded district in Wales. There the landlord of an inn describes Sir Owen ap Griffith and his fine family of five sons and three daughters. With three thousand a year Sir Owen maintains a spacious and hospitable home, with a well-filled library.

In winter, or wintry weather, the younger part of the company form little balls; while those of a less nimble age amuse themselves with being spectators of their mirth, or playing cards in the same room; and if by extraordinary chance, there happens to be any deficiency of numbers among the young, Sir Owen and his lady, and others by their example, will join in the dance, rather than their youthful guests and family should lose their entertainment. Sometimes they have little concerts, when their most musical friends are with them; at others the young people act Shakespear's tragedies, after the pieces have undergone from Sir Owen any necessary corrections, who can expunge whole scenes if he thinks proper, without fear of the critic's lash. These are the only plays they are permitted to act; and some persons who have been great frequenters of the best theatres have said, that although they had sometimes seen one or two characters in a play more exquisitely performed than by this little company, yet, on the whole, they never saw any representation so pleasing, as every part is well done.[2]

Even when there was no thought of an amateur production, solitude might always be diverted by a volume of Shakespeare's plays. Young ladies are advised to read the text of the play before seeing a representation. "This, to be sure, will lessen the pleasure of novelty and sur-

---

[1] 3rd ed., 1756, p. 28.

[2] II, 19–20. Folger. For Mrs. Scott as a novelist see Walter M. Crittenden, *The Life and Writings of Mrs. Sarah Scott*, Philadelphia, 1932; Foster, *History of the Pre-Romantic Novel*, pp. 40–41. There is a detailed account of the construction of a private theater, the reception of sixty actors from London, and the production of several non-Shakespearean plays at Mr. B——'s Lincolnshire estate, in the spurious continuation of *Pamela, Pamela in High Life; or, Virtue Rewarded*, 1741, pp. 4, 31, 36, 39, 75–76, 120–122, 139–140. Pamela is grieved that forty carpenters must work on the building on Sunday. The total charge of the actors was £326.

prize; but to compensate for that trifling loss, it will give you a more full and distinct view of the subject, and make you a more competent judge of the merit and abilities of the several actors." [1] So writes Portia to her daughter Sophia in an educational novel, concluding her admonitions with a charming picture of a young lady whom she had overheard reading in the country:

One evening as we were taking a walk along the banks of the river, which runs hard by the garden-wall, we espied, at a distance, a young lady, sitting in a kind of natural arbour, with a book in her hand, which she seemed to be reading, with great vehemence and emotion. We presently began to form conjectures what might be the subject of the book . . . but upon observing her air and manner more attentively, and even before we came within reach of the sound, we all agreed that it must be some play. As we approached nearer, and heard the tone of her voice, though without understanding the sense, we were still more confirmed in our former opinion. Miss was so deeply engaged, that we were almost close to her before she perceived us; which, however, when she did, she seemed to be a little surprised, put up her book, and rising, with a decent and modest blush, courtesy'd to the company. The countess, who was very well acquainted with the young lady (who happened to be the parson's daughter) begged her to tell us ingenuously what book it was she had been reading; upon which she pulled it out of her pocket, and shewed us that it was a volume of Shakespeare's plays.[2]

[1] Anon., *The Polite Lady; or, A Course of Female Education. In a Series of Letters, from a Mother, to Her Daughter,* 1760 (3rd ed., 1775, p. 140).

[2] Page 143.

CHAPTER FIVE

The Plays: The Romances

L IKE the dark or problem comedies, Shakespeare's final romances made little impression upon novelists. The plays themselves commonly reached the public in strange shapes. Of *Pericles* there were no productions during the Garrick era. *Cymbeline* underwent a number of transformations, the best of which, prepared by Garrick in 1761, has been called the most accurate of the eighteenth-century acting versions of Shakespeare.[1] Greatly curtailed, especially in the prolonged last act, but little altered otherwise, the play was offered ninety-eight times before Garrick left the stage.[2] For several seasons he was famous as Posthumus, but in 1763 he relinquished the role to William Powell, who was in turn succeeded by Samuel Reddish. Mrs. Yates and Mrs. Barry were the leading Imogens.

Textually, *Cymbeline* fared better than either *The Winter's Tale* or *The Tempest*. Drawing mainly from Shakespeare's last two acts, Garrick presented a three-act abridgment of *The Winter's Tale* in 1756, which he cast incomparably with all the finest performers at Drury Lane. Subsequently entitled *Florizel and Perdita*,[3] his version held the stage at Drury Lane for a decade and was revived at Covent Garden in 1774. Only during the season of 1771 at the same theater was there an attempt to produce Shakespeare's text,[4] which was dropped in

---

[1] *Cymbeline. A Tragedy. By Shakespear. With Alterations* [by David Garrick], 1762; reprinted in *The Dramatic Works of David Garrick, Esq.*, 1768, II, 83–164; and in Bell's *Shakespeare*, 2nd ed., 1774, II, 301–378. See Odell, *Shakespeare from Betterton to Irving*, I, 371–373.

[2] Dougald MacMillan, ed., *Drury Lane Calendar*, pp. 228–229.

[3] *Florizel and Perdita; or, The Winter's Tale. A Dramatic Pastoral*, 1758; reprinted in *The Dramatic Works of David Garrick*, II, 203–258. For the alteration see Odell, I, 360–361.

[4] The text is in Bell's *Shakespeare*, 2nd ed., 1774, V, 139–211.

favor of Garrick's. As for *The Tempest,* its history in the eighteenth century is a tale of distortion. The Davenant-Dryden version of 1667 persisted, despite revivals of the original play in 1746 and 1757 at Drury Lane. There was even a new operatic version by Garrick at Drury Lane in 1756,[1] in repentance for which, perhaps, he produced the original play in the next year in a revival which ran to eighteen performances. *The Tempest* was never acted at Covent Garden during Garrick's time, but in one form or another it was presented at his house during twenty-one seasons from 1747 to 1776.[2]

Cymbeline was performed by strollers in *Female Friendship; or, The Innocent Sufferer* (1770). Henry Melvill hires a servant, who relates the story of his life. Born two months after the marriage of a hostler father and a chambermaid mother, and educated at a charity school, the boy robs a henroost and determines to go to London. On the road, exhausted, he crawls into a barn inhabited by strollers. Their manager, Mr. Rantum, is a tyrant.

Supposing himself the best actor upon earth, he could not bear the least appearance of a slight; which occasioned him once, in the character of Alexander, to deprive Hephestion of a tooth for supposing he laughed at him; he was as selfish as proud, and took care, even when there was tolerable success, to glean so much, under pretence of stock-debt, that the company were very little above begging; which occasioned them to be very comical in tragedy, and sad in comedy.[3]

The youth, nevertheless, enlists with the company. After brief training as stage-sweeper, candle-snuffer, and mourner in Juliet's funeral procession, he is ready to perform.

[I]therefore pitch'd upon Jachimo, for my first attempt: Mr. Rantum said, that I knew Cymbeline to be a play for which they were not at all prepared; and which would inevitably put them to great inconveniences in the performance; but that having conceived a regard for me, he would oblige me, by having it represented; and, as an additional proof he would play Leonatus Posthumus.—The parts therefore were accordingly cast, and Mr. Rantum very kindly gave me some instructions, relative to my attitudes, voice, &c.
    In less than a fortnight we were all ready for the rehearsal: and the bills gave notice of "Cymbeline to be perform'd, the part of Jachimo by a young gentleman, being his first appearance on any stage."
    This of course filled the theatre, *alias* the barn, with all the neighbouring

[1] *The Tempest. An Opera. Taken from Shakespeare,* 1756. It should be noted that the text in Bell's *Shakespeare,* 2nd ed., 1774, III, 221–279, is almost entirely Shakespeare's.
[2] *Drury Lane Calendar,* pp. 331–333.
[3] I, 217–218.

families: and as the fatal hour drew nigh, when all my future fame was to be laid at stake, I felt myself in a situation not to be described.—The warning bell at length ringing,—I appear'd,—and the house re-ecchoed with applause: I went through the first act as well as could be expected; but when I stole an inestimable bracelet of black ribbons from Imogen's arm, who was reposed on a white sheet, laid over the skeleton box used in pantomime: the success I met with, was inexpressible, beyond my most sanguine expectations: her bed-chamber indeed, did not exactly answer that inimitable description given of it, by the immortal Shakespeare; the hangings were not silver'd silk, proud Cleopatra when she met her Roman, but the patch work of the wainscoat was concealed from enquiring eyes, by an old piece of tapestry, beautifully describing the history of Saint George and the Dragon; thus you see, we endeavoured to come as near the original as possible: and our audience being kind enough, to take the will for the deed, the whole went off with an uncommon eclat.

And give me leave to observe, that till within these two years, when the managers of Covent Garden, have very judiciously had one painted on purpose, I have frequently known a scene exhibited in this excellent play, which had no more resemblance to the description given of it, in the subsequent act, than that which our itinerant company was obliged to make use of: necessity indeed was plea sufficient for them; but surely at the theatres royal, it is so great an absurdity, and so glaring an affront offered to the understanding of the publick, as scarcely to be overlooked, or forgiven by any audience: for when we hear these beautiful lines,

> It was hang'd
> With tapestry of silver'd silk; the story
> Proud Cleopatra, when she met her Roman,
> And Cyndus [*sic*] swell'd above the banks, or for
> The press of boats, or pride, a piece of work
> So bravely done, so rich, that it did strive,
> In workmanship and value; which I wonder'd
> Could be so rarely, and exactly wrought,
> Since the true life on't was—
>
> > CYMBELINE

I say Sir, when we hear this glorious and animated description, we naturally refer our ideas, to the scene of which it is spoken; but which upon recollection, we shall find, was something ridiculously trifling, and foreign to the purpose;—but to proceed,—in the battle scene, I likewise gain'd great honour, when struck with the horrors of a guilty conscience; my nerveless arm refus'd its office, and obliged me to yield to Posthumus, his Romish weeds disguis'd by a carter's frock; but at the conclusion, I will not say I deserv'd, but I will venture to assure you, that I was loaded with vast applause; the men approv'd, and the women said I was quite a charming creature: which to do Mr. Rantum justice, I must attribute to his teaching.[1]

Ten years later, in *Masquerades; or, What You Will* (1780), a novel of manners which concentrates on such diversions of the nobility as amateur theatricals, masquerades, river parties, and *fêtes cham-*

---

[1] I, 219–223. The quoted passage is from *Cymbeline*, II. iv. 68–76.

pêtres, the heroine, Lady Julia Herbert, long in love with Lord Osmond, attends a masked ball at Lady Louisa Montague's. A partner has been provided for her, "as elegant a figure as my eyes ever beheld, in the habit of Jachimo," while Julia herself appears as a "young creature, who surpasses Shakespear's Imogen in beauty." Since "Jachimo" closely resembles Lord Osmond, nobody is astonished to find that the masked figure is indeed he, and all rejoice that this reunion of lovers ends at the altar.[1]

The Tempest was pilfered for an incidental entertainment in Thomas Amory's novel, *Memoirs of Several Ladies of Great Britain* (1755), in which the unnamed narrator of "The History of Mrs. Marinda Benlow" tells of meeting the "lively and rational" Miss Juliet West at Mrs. Benlow's home in 1741. This "for ever gay, ingenious and engaging" lady, passionately fond of reading from her infancy, "talks with freedom, grace and spirit, upon a vast variety of subjects."

Milton and *Shakespear* are her favorites. She has them in her hand night and morning. It is a fine entertainment, to hear her read, or repete those authors. . . . Nor is she less delightful in reading or repeting the tragedys of *Shakespear*. She has the gesture, the cadence, and the pause, in perfection. Not a syllable too long: not a syllable too slightly does she dwell on. She raises every effect of the passions which the poet intended.[2]

Miss West tells her friends a strange story of how she was kidnapped in 1738 and taken to the lavish estate of the rich and debauched Comus, who wanted to marry her. There Comus, who maintained a company of comedians for his amusement, served her a sumptuous meal, with music for violins:

When supper was ended, and the things were removed, a partition sunk at once, and a theatre appeared; representing a forest at a distance, and a beautiful valley stretching out towards it. Fields and orchards seemed in full bloom, the rivulets wandered along, and their banks were decked with woodbines and roses.

Here, Calista appeared asleep, and three shepherds came slowly forward; the music playing, and one of them singing.

Songs and pretty speeches between Thyrsis and Calista were followed by the nuptial masque originally composed to celebrate the contract of true love between Ferdinand and Miranda:

This scene of a comedie ballet was finely performed, and beautifully improved by the conclusion taken from Shakespear's Tempest; that is,

[1] IV, 200–210. Yale.
[2] Pages 97–99.

when the shepherds had done, then Juno, Iris, and Ceres appeared, descending in a machine of clouds, to bless this twain, and sung their blessings on them. Iris called the Naiads of the winding brooks, and by command of Juno, summoned the sun-burnt sickle-men to put their rye-straw hats on, and encounter those fresh nymphs in country-footing. The nymphs and reapers in a moment entered, properly habited, and concluded the scene with a graceful dance.[1]

It was the fate of *The Tempest* to be violated. As for Miss West, she was not. It is gratifying to know that the actress who impersonated Calista helped her to escape from Comus' clutches.

The account of the homage paid to Shakespeare by novelists known and anonymous in the few stories which have endured because they are classics, or in the more numerous ones which are now forgotten and difficult to trace because they did not rise above the level of popular circulating-library fiction, requires no formal summary. Sometimes serious, sometimes slight, sometimes exuding the spirit of comedy or burlesque so typical of the eighteenth century, the passages of criticism and the lively recreation of scenes from public, private, and provincial exhibitions of the plays add jewels to Shakespeare's diadem of praise. Even when paste, these gems are the contribution of a group of imaginative writers of the newest type of literature honoring the greatest imaginative writer of all. Their work, whether masterly or fumbling, provides additional datum points on the road to Shakespeare idolatry as the century moved onward towards the romantic criticism of Coleridge, Lamb, and Hazlitt.

[1] Pages 297–301. See *The Tempest*, IV. i. 60–139.

INDEX